SOCIETY
at the
CROSROADS

Choosing the right road
STEVEN CORD

Society at the Crossroads
Choosing the Right Road
by Steven B. Cord

© 2002 by Steven B. Cord
Aurora Press, 10528 Cross Fox Lane, Columbia MD 21044
aaurorapress@hotmail.com
(ph., fax) 1-410-997-1182

Cover and interior design and production © 2001 by
Pneuma Books: Complete Publisher's Services
www.pneumadesign.com/books/info.htm
Set in Dante 12 | 14

Printed in the United States of America
10 09 08 07 06 05 04 03 02 01   10 9 8 7 6 5 4 3 2 1

Publisher's Cataloging in Publication Data
(Provided by Quality Books, Inc.)

Cord, Steven B., 1928-
    Society at the Crossroads : Choosing the Right Road /
by Steven B. Cord. --1st ed.
    p. cm.
    Includes index
    LCCN 2001130787
    ISBN 0-9711742-4-5 (paperback)
    ISBN 0-9711742-3-7 (hardback)

    1. Ethical Relativism 2. Human rights 3. United
States--Social conditions.   I. Title.

BJ51.C67 2001   171'.7
                         QBI01-201306

To all those who realize that social problems have their origins in a false, unprovable ethical system, this book is dedicated.

ACKNOWLEDGMENTS

I have made a special effort to obtain the opinions of many people on social, cultural, and ethical issues; I am indebted to all of them. This book would have suffered without their input.

TABLE *of* CONTENTS

"Turning and turning in the widening gyre
The falcon cannot hear the falconer;
Things fall apart; the centre cannot hold;
Mere anarchy is loosed upon the world,
The blood-dimmed tide is loosed, and
    everywhere
The ceremony of innocence is drowned;
The best lack all conviction, while the worst
Are full of passionate intensity."

Wm. Butler Yeats

"I propose to beg no question, to shrink from no
conclusion but to follow truth wherever it may
lead. If the conclusions that we reach run count-
er to our prejudices, let us not flinch; if they chal-
lenge institutions that have long been deemed
wise and natural, let us not turn back."

Henry George

INTRODUCTION

LOOKING
FORWARD

This introduction offers a brief overview of this book's main ideas.

There existed in Persia and Syria in the twelfth century the much-feared Order of Assassins. It is commonly thought that this order was ensconced in an impregnable fortress whose leader, known as the Old Man of the Mountain, sent out his obedient minions throughout the world (but primarily in Islamic countries) to assassinate opponents. The order flourished for a century before being swept away by the Mongols, but many of its doctrines still hold sway in that area of the world.

New recruits were attracted to the order with hashish (the English word *assassin* is derived from the Arabic for one who smokes or chews hashish), a particularly strong form of marijuana. They progressed through various degrees of revealed knowledge after demonstrating their absolute obedience to the Order's ritual and to the commands of the Old Man until they reached the hallowed Inner Circle, the so-called Thirty-Second Degree of Ultimate Knowledge, at which time the One True Secret of the Universe was revealed. It was this: "All things are permitted."

"All things are permitted" – alas, the postmodern world is embracing that view with increasing fervor. Ever since the eighteenth century, philosophers and laypeople alike have steadily come to believe that there are no objective standards of good and evil. All ethical standards are increasingly regarded as matters of personal opinion only. It is thought that the individual, not reason, is the ultimate arbiter of correct ethics, and therefore it is not possible to prove any ethical standard to be true. Sociocultural dysfunctions are the inevitable result, as symbolized by the end-of-century massacre at Columbine High School.[1][†]

The basic cause of these sociocultural dysfunctions is the ethical theory asserting that all things are permitted. This postmodern ethical relativism is quite prevalent among the Western intelligentsia today, although most unusual in the world's history and even throughout the world. As *The Wall Street Journal* has asserted, "Welcome to morality in late 20th century America, where what's right and what's wrong is anyone's guess on any given day."[2]

We ought not to base ethics upon religion, if only because there are many conflicting religious beliefs and none are susceptible to empirical proof. As I point out at some length in a subsequent chapter, religion is not the correct determinant of prescriptive truth any more than it is the correct determinant of descriptive truth. The proof of ethical standards is no more a religious issue than is the proof of evolution. Nor, as we will see, can culture provide an ethical proof.

Follow the Truth wherever it may lead. Accept nothing that cannot be proven. But ignore at your peril and society's peril any ethical principle that can be proven.

If individuals are regarded as the ethical judge of their own behavior, then violence can be justified. No matter how much some ethical relativists might oppose violence, can't their subjectivist ethical philosophy justify it? If there are no provable limits to personal behavior, contradictory ethics can be justified (which by itself constitutes a disproof of ethical relativism). For instance, even apathy, an opposite of violence, can be justified, for if right or wrong are matters of personal opinion only, then why strive? Democracy becomes no more justifiable than despotism. Thieves can defend their stealing if they think it right. If we each live in our own ethical universe, there is no way to reason morally with one another and passion replaces persuasion and might determines right.

In our own time, do we not see a high level of violence, apathy, despotism, crime, and alienation? Our philosophies are not unhooked from our actions; we should not be surprised that cultural collapse follows the increasing ethical relativism of our time. If nothing moral can be *proven* true, then we will have moral chaos.

We may deplore the results of ethical relativism and admit that it has been the cause of our current social malaise, of the generation gap, of aimlessness in art and music, of our seemingly intractable economic problems, and so forth.[3] But if it is correct, then we have no choice but to put up with its bad social effects. If that's the way life is, we have no rational alternative. We must face the facts and treat things as they are, not as we might like them to be.

If this book is to go beyond the many fine books on cultural collapse, then it must present a *proof* that ethical relativism is false and that some particular ethical standard is true. Otherwise, it will have nothing new or valid to say, and there would remain no reasonable alternative to ethical relativism, bad as its consequences might be. If you are so completely welded to postmodern ethical preconceptions that you cannot consider an attempt at an ethical proof, you can't expect to get anything out of this book; don't ask for dry water. I hope, dear reader, you don't suffer from *neo-ideo-phobia* (fear of new ideas).

But what ethical standard can be proven true? At this late date in history, we are not likely to come up with anything ethically true or valid that has never been thought of before. This book is an attempt to prove the truth of the venerable ethical standard that *as an end in itself, individuals have a right to their own life, liberty, and property, limited only by the equal rights of others.* We will relate this standard to a provably true (though at this point unstated) ethical statement. You probably already choose, dear reader, to live by the equal-rights standard, but if it is only a personal opinion, it will not withstand the might-makes-right or die-for-your-religious-belief standards and will eventually be overcome. An airtight proof of its truth can prevent that, but you can search the philosophical literature for such a proof to no avail. This book will be of little use to you if it fails to prove the equal-rights doctrine to be true. Aren't you comforted to read a proof of the equal rights that you probably already believe in? Or do your prefer to don a moral hairshirt?

Believing that equal rights cannot be proven true is dangerously dysfunctional (not to mention wrong). When people believe that, they are in essence telling others to do whatever they want without limit. Sociocultural dysfunctions will inevitably follow.

Let us proceed as follows: First, we trace the rise of ethical relativism over the centuries. Then, we carefully document the current existence of cultural dysfunctions (e.g., crime, hard-drug use, illegitimacy, school decline) and show how these dysfunctions are caused by ethical relativism. Part II presents a proof of the equal-rights doctrine.

As you read, I ask you, dear reader, to face the facts, to treat things as they are, to be rigorously objective, and to hold this book up to the very highest standards of rational proof. You must be willing to discard ethical relativism, however deeply held, if it is disproved. Anything less on your part and you will be wasting your time in proceeding further. This book will have nothing to offer you.

John W. Gardner: "An excellent plumber is infinitely more admirable than an incompetent philosopher. The society that scorns excellence in plumbing because plumbing is a humble activity, and tolerates shoddiness in philosophy because philosophy is an exalted activity, will have nei-

ther good plumbing nor good philosophy. Neither
its pipes nor its theories will hold water."

We ought not to take equal rights for granted: History is writ in blood, in the twentieth century especially. More than two-fifths of current humanity live under dictatorship; the concept of individual rights is tenuously held by most Americans; for instance, the New Jersey legislature recently rejected the equal-rights philosophy on the grounds that it was anti-black, anti-women, and too pro-God;[4] property-rights-destroying taxation is growing everywhere.[5] Whenever we meet people who persist in believing that everyone accepts equal rights, we can be sure we have met people for whom logic and evidence are irrelevant.

Will a proof actually dispel cultural deterioration? It will help, but no doubt there are other relevant factors; the future is not for us to see. Although the actual moral applications of ethical principle are important, we here are primarily interested in what those correct ethical principles are, not in the moral applications to particular circumstances of reality.

This book makes a clear distinction between *ethical* and *moral*. Both words refer to how we should behave (not only sexually), but *moral* usually refers to how people *think* they should behave, or to the application of ethical principle to actual circumstances in reality, whereas *ethics*, with which we are more concerned, refers to how people *should* behave.[6†] Absolutely no one disputes that members of each culture and religion think they're right, but we want to find out what is rationally right. Even if everyone agreed on that, only popularity and not rightness would be established. Let us distinguish between morality and ethics.

We need a clear definition of *ethical relativism*. It is the belief that ethical principles are matters of personal subjective opinion *only* and cannot be proved true. By this standard, many people today are ethical relativists, no matter how strongly they hold to their ethical principles. Ethical relativists contradictorily accept the provability of mathematical principles, such as $a^2 + b^2 = c^2$ for flat right triangles, but they do not accept the provability of ethical principles (even though both mathematical and ethical principles are rational and are therefore equally subject to proof).

Ethical relativism is often incorrectly merged with equal rights, but the two concepts are entirely distinct. The equal rights doctrine is provable and claims there are correct limits to individual behavior; ethical relativism is unprovable and claims the individual is the ultimate arbiter of right and wrong. We should therefore separate these two concepts.

If a genuine rational proof of an ethical standard can be found, then this book has performed an important service. If it falls short of this elevated goal, then it is worthless, ready for the dung heap, merely one more encomium to equal rights – more eloquent ones abound. The sociocultural dysfunctions of our time will continue to go unexplained.

This book is written for the lay reader. It is free of sociological and philosophical jargon. But if it has anything new and true to say, then professionals can greatly benefit from it.

A word about endnotes: Let's take them seriously. Whenever a questionable fact or quotation is given, the source has generally been noted so that we can have sufficient information to judge the fact's validity. Generally, the source of each endnote (the so-called double endnote) is also given. In the few cases where full information did not exist, the sources are generally in the author's possession. For cultural history, popular magazines can be original sources of information and so have often been used; it is reassuring to know that many of them employ many competent researchers and fact-checkers.[7]† If an endnote is explanatory then its number will be followed by a †.

As we enter a new millennium, technological wonders as yet un-dreamed-of abound, but if ethical standards are unproven, disaster awaits. We must answer the compelling question: *What are the correct limits (if any) on our freedom?*

Now you, dear reader, are ready to read this book. Remember to apply to it the most rigorous standards of validation and proof.

INTRODUCTION

SOCIETY
at the
CROSSROADS

Whatever is true about nature or reality ("is") has no ethical significance ("ought") whatsoever. You simply cannot *logically* derive an "ought" from an "is." For instance, Locke said that because certain relations existed in the state of nature, they ought to be that way, but "ought" can't follow from "is." The "Is-Ought Barrier" can't be pierced.

PART ONE

Do the facts indicate that Ethical Relativism has been growing over time and that it has caused our society to become increasingly dysfunctional?

ETHICAL RELATIVISM: *Its* IMPACT *on Our* SOCIETY

CHAPTER ONE

The RISE *of* ETHICAL RELATIVISM *through the* CENTURIES

This chapter is not attempting here a detailed history of Western civilization but rather an interpretation based on commonly accepted facts. From the Middle Ages to the present, Western civilization has witnessed a constant progression from religious certitude, to respect for supposed rationality, to reliance on emotion and intuition, to deterministic scientism, to existential postmodern skepticism. In the beginning, everything had its place and explanation; now we know many facts but have little confidence. We have gone from ethical certitude to postmodern ethical relativism.

The Middle Ages (ca. 800–1650)[1]†

Religious faith was the dominant motif of the Middle Ages. The constant wars of that time were predominantly religious in character. Poor people built huge churches. Songs and culture dealt with matters religious. Religious doubters were few in number and harshly treated. During the Inquisition, people were tortured to death in the name of religion (proving that a false absolutism can be as corrosive as ethical relativism; one should be right for the right reason). In medieval times, few doubted that the ethical principles dictated by organized religion were absolutely correct, being decreed by God Almighty.

In the early Middle Ages in Europe, the Catholic church was universally dominant, dictating public and even individual thinking. The average person was more concerned about one's eternal life in the hereafter than in one's secular existence in this life.

Even in the latter part of the Middle Ages, during the time of exploration beyond Europe, religion was a prime motivating factor. Converting the natives or searching for religious freedom were the settlers' chief official motivation for embarking on their long overseas trips. When constitutions were set up, the existence of an Almighty God and an objective Ten Commandments-like ethical code were assumed to be true.

Religious motifs dominated medieval art and music. This was true even for the Renaissance (roughly 1200–1600) in the later Middle Ages, though secularity then was becoming more evident.

Once the king had been regarded as God and treated as such (old prayers demonstrate this fact), but during the Middle Ages the king came to be regarded as an ordinary person ruling by divine right, a comedown from his previous divine status but still religiously sanctioned. Eventually, John Locke and others, to their eternal credit, successfully substituted equal rights and other ethical doctrines in place of divine rights, however flawed their attempt at proof was.

Although we might be interested in what happened in medieval times, and there are many good books on that subject, we here are more interested in what can be technically called medieval meta-ethics – the basis for medieval ethical standards. Speaking generally, the Middle Agers clearly based their ethical principles four-square on religion. Few doubted that God had said, "Be good," and they were willing to let their church define good.

We cannot say that the people of the Middle Ages suffered from ethical relativism. They had little doubt as to what was right and wrong – their religion told them so – but this did not prevent violence (often religious in nature), if only because equal rights as an ethical standard was little known and certainly little practiced (for instance, the *Domesday Book* in 1086 listed 10 percent of England's people as slaves[2]). Misplaced ethical objectivism can do as much harm as ethical relativism.

Michael Schwartz, (President, Kent State University, in UCRA Measure, *8/9/92, p. 16): "Today, the notion of good and evil has blurred. Good and evil may still exist, but a person would have trouble defending that notion. A culturally divided society rejects the notion of common values. And sooner or later, if you say one thing is as good as another, depending on your perspective, then you are saying there are no common values."*

The Enlightenment (ca. 1650–1800)

Then came the Enlightenment, a term coined by its own not-so-modest philosophers. These philosophies emphasized reason – first logic and then fact-gathering empiricism (although both are surely needed). Reason began to supplant religion in social and individual thought. Education replaced prayer. God was regarded as being impersonal, a Clock-Maker who had created the universe and then stepped aside from His creation. Science was revered, so much so that in Paris, upper-class women dissected cadavers in their carriages on the way to the opera in a dedicated pursuit of knowledge. The philosopher Condorcet wrote a pæan to Reason even while in jail awaiting the guillotine.

Reason gradually became the accepted basis for ethical standards, at least for intellectuals. Although the Enlightenment philosophers asserted there was an objective code of ethical behavior for all people to follow, its reliance on secular reason for deriving ethics was a weaker reed to lean on than God's Revelation. Correct reason was not as obvious or as basic as God's revealed Word written down in the Bible and interpreted by the church.

John Locke (1632–1704) was the premier philosopher of the Enlightenment. He deserves eternal praise for having first clearly enunciated the doctrine of equal rights. It would be difficult to overestimate his influence upon his contemporaries, especially in the United States. The Declaration of Independence summarizes his views. Let us praise him for trying to ground ethical standards in reason, even if he did not succeed.

Motto of the University of Pennsylvania Law School: "Law without morals is in vain."

He asserted that individuals have an unlimited right to their life, liberty, and property when they exist alone in some hypothetical state of nature (never clearly defined).[3] In order to defend these rights, they enter society with these rights intact; they would hardly give them up since it was assumed that people joined society in order to better protect those rights. Upon entering society, people made a pact with society's government to have their rights protected. Although we can agree with Locke's conclusion that equal rights is true, we must reject his reasoning for the following reasons:

(1) *Reasonable people have differing definitions as to what natural rights are.* The Pope sincerely thinks birth control is unnatural; others think otherwise.

(2) *He egregiously violated the inviolable "Is-Ought Barrier" first formulated by David Hume.* We will see that Locke wasn't the first philosopher to attempt this logical futility. Whatever is true about nature or reality ("is") has no ethical significance ("ought") whatsoever. You simply cannot *logically* derive an "ought" from an "is." For instance, Locke said that because certain relations existed in the state of nature, they ought to be that way, but "ought" can't follow from "is." The "Is-Ought Barrier" can't be pierced. Ethics and reality inhabit different realms of thought. Might determines "is." Right determines "ought" or "should."

(3) *Were human beings rational in the state of nature (as Locke maintained) or irrational (as Hobbes maintained)?* No one can say; let's not get involved in that one.

(4) *Locke seems to have regarded our rights as being absolute,* but in fact they are limited by the equal rights of others. A subsequent chapter proves this to be so.

(5) *No one is really alone, unaffected by childhood or social influences.* No one is beyond the potential influence of society that can invade any state of nature. In fact, when Locke said that hermits join society to protect their rights from others who might invade their state of nature, he was asserting that no one stands alone in an inviolate state of nature, unaffected by society. [4†]

(6) *Rights are ethical claims that others should respect, but they can have no meaning in a state of nature where there are no others to respect or not to respect those claims.* We ought not to assume, as Locke did, that hermits brings rights into society. There are those who assert that when they join society, it is society that determines individual rights; Locke should at least have attempted to address this relevant (though misguided) assertion. It deserves an answer.

(7) *No one in fact ever signed such a pact as Locke describes, certainly no one living.* Even if people many millennia ago did agree to it (highly unlikely), it wouldn't bind us today. No one could sign for you or me. We inherit neither rights nor rightlessness. The "state of nature" is a hypothetical construct; it should still be proven (and not merely be assumed) to have application to reality and to ethics. Hypotheses can prove nothing.

(8) *Locke assumed that everyone would naturally choose to be rational.* He even called rationality an inalienable natural law, but this is belied by the fact that many people act irrationally. Anyway, in ethics, mere assumption cannot replace proof. There is no deterministic natural law in ethics.

(9) *According to Locke, God created reason, the state of nature, and individual rights.* But there's a problem with that: God's

will is inscrutable and no one has a provable insight into God's mind. Locke ought not to rest a proof on his personal concept of God.

(10) *His concept of landownership was unworkable even in his own time*. He stated that individuals should take as much land as they could use but leave as much good land for others, but how can that be accomplished? Who can figure that out? No wonder it has been ignored. A complete discussion of this important matter must await Chapters 8 and 9.

Because Enlightenment philosophers never offered an adequate proof of equal rights,[5†] their influence faded with the passing years. Their lack of ethical proof made people unreflectively think that ethical proof is rationally impossible and is only mere personal opinion.

Thomas Jefferson (1743–1826) was an able writer and Locke's great interpreter. He displayed much courage in signing the Declaration of Independence in the face of overwhelming enemy military power and the real possibility of being hanged as a traitor, but he erred badly by asserting that everyone had a right to "the pursuit of happiness" rather than a right to our property, the fruits of our labor. Why is happiness the greatest good? When criminals steal from their victims, their happiness may exceed the unhappiness of their victims, but rationally and ethically that is irrelevant. Happiness is a personal psychological matter, best left to the individual and not to society or government.[6†] Chapter 6 discusses happiness as an ethical standard in greater detail.

Jefferson committed another error by asserting that "we take these truths to be self-evident...." Alas! not so. Ethical truths are not self-evident; many people, especially nowadays, disagree; they require conclusive proof.[7†] A mere claim of self-evidence is no substitute for proof. One more thing: He should have added *as an end in itself* (since it is sometimes necessary to violate the rights of some individuals in order to protect the rights of others, as in a just war). Shouldn't he have pointed out the correct limitations on rights even at the risk of making his Declaration less popular? Nor in the Declaration did he distinguish between property claims to land and slaves

on the one hand, and to human-produced goods and services on the other.

To sum up: During the Enlightenment, reason was elevated as the ethical standard, but the proof for it was inadequate. Later generations therefore felt that no ethical standard had been proven true or could ever be proven true. The door was left open for a steady increase in ethical relativism.

The French Revolution embodied the Enlightenment and promised the rationalist's utopia. But it failed and ended in the dictatorship of Napoleon, thereby discrediting Reason. The Age of Romanticism followed.

R. B. Barrett:
"We live in times when it is rude
to have a moral certitude."

The Age of Romanticism (1789–1850)

There's the story about an Enlightenment philosopher who died and went to heaven. He came to a fork in the road that had two signs with arrows pointing in opposite directions, one reading, "This Way to Heaven," and the other reading, "This Way to a Discussion about Heaven." He chose the second pathway. Not so with the philosophers who followed in the next thought wave called Romanticism, a short but intense historical period with a great ensuing influence. Its philosophical advocates tended to be emotionally committed activists, but for them, emotion and intuition gradually came to overshadow revelation and reason as sources of truth.[8†] They began the move from ethical certainty toward ethical relativism.

As medieval revelation provided a stronger ethical guide than Enlightenment reason, so Enlightenment reason provided a stronger ethical guide than Romantic emotion and intuition. Reason is the same for all humans, Chinese and Frenchmen alike, whereas emotion and intuition are ephemeral and particular to every individual. Ethical proof was no longer regarded as likely; reason was being replaced by emotional affirmation. The Enlightenment hopes raised by the French Revolution died away, and contact with other cultures led to increasing doubts about one's own ethical standards.[9][†]

> George Horse Capture (Indian leader): "I had looked over the white mountain of success, saw the other side, and realized nothing [no proof] was there."

The Romantic emphasis on ephemeral emotion and intuition enhanced their literature, art, and music. The very word *romantic* comes from the Old French *romans*, a wandering troubadour's tale. Romantic poetry stressed exuberance, warmth, and flamboyance, like the anthem *La Marseillaise*, or the mystical and mysterious, as in Edgar Allen Poe's works. Passionate Romantic novels tended to be more moving than Enlightenment expositions and travelogues (compare Montesquieu's somewhat didactic *Persian Letters* with Swift's *Gulliver's Travels*) but they did not add to an understanding of ethical truth.

Romantic art stressed emotional scenes of nature, as in the Hudson River School of art or Delacroix's painting *Liberty Leading the People*. Romantic politics stressed nationalism and stormy revolt. Romantic music stressed the ephemeral, the suggestive, the sentimental. As the Enlightenment had emphasized the individual, Romanticism emphasized the nation, race, group, or society, presaging modern totalitarianism (most Romantics would have outright rejected it, but it was a logical conclusion). Individual equal rights as a doctrine was taken for granted; the Romantics were uninterested in proof.

The bottom line for us is this: By offering no proof of an ethical standard, Romanticism sent the Western world sliding toward ethical relativism.

> Stephen Barker: "The young no longer have any

moral barricades to storm."

The Age of Scientism (ca. 1850–1914)

Scientism, the next period in the history of Western social thought, further augmented the trend toward ethical relativism given initial impetus by Romanticism. The new plethora of consumer goods and leisure activities made materialistic philosophies seem plausible. The philosophers of the time began to think that matter was the fundamental and final reality, that the individual was a machine, and that the brain produced consciousness as the liver secreted bile. They questioned why nature was to be held up as the standard of behavior, thinking it should be dominated instead. If there was an ethical purpose to life, it was thought to be unknowable, like an unknown combination to a locked safe written on a slip of paper secreted in the safe itself.

Rationality itself was replaced by the somewhat different concept of scientism. Rationality came to be regarded as being irrelevant and limited by social or material influences. Positivists made a religion of science, thinking of scientists as revealers of God's plan for nature; in fact, God was often regarded as nothing more than a convenient social hypothesis. Scientists supposed themselves unencumbered by rationalistic illusions of any kind. They tended to regard all phenomena as being ultimately reducible to matter. (Of course, the *philosophy* that only matter is real, itself needs proof.) Darwin seemed to disprove the certainties of the Bible; Herbert Spencer applied Darwin's "survival of the fittest" hypothesis to society. (Analogists often make such unverifiable leaps of faith over the "Is-Ought Barrier.") Nineteenth-century scientism further opened the door to ethical relativism.

Walter Kaufman (in Psychology Today, *4/73, p.82): "The moral irrationalist implies that while it may be reasonable to keep your eyes open when you make relatively petty decisions, it makes no sense to keep them open and examine your impulsive preferences and significant alternatives when a choice is likely to mold your future. In other*

*words, be careful when you drive slowly, but when
you go over 50 miles an hour, shut your eyes!"*

Karl Marx was influenced by the scientistic philosophies that surrounded him. He was an economic determinist (though he could offer no proof for that assumption), believing that our economy determined – and not merely influenced – society and history. All our ideas about politics, ethics, law and religion, he thought, are by-products of our economic interests (but the existence of altruism would seem to disprove this doctrine).10† Marxism would be more impressive if its long-run predictions came true. He predicted, for instance, that the state would wither away, but neither in welfare-state Sweden or in Soviet communism did the state wither away (only individual rights did).

Positivists like Auguste Comte simplistically defined truth as correspondence to reality *only*. Comte deified science and defined ethics as being only subjective and emotive, but a definition is not a proof. (False beliefs are false, even if seemingly proved by definitions.)

Materialists felt science would somehow draw back more and more curtains of ignorance, revealing more and more truth about reality, with those truths made accessible by a growing material affluence. As for ethical proofs, they regarded them as unnecessary and even impossible.11†

*Charles Tart (an ardent critic of scientism; in a fit
of irony, he created this version of what he called
a Scientist's Creed): "I believe in the material universe as the only and ultimate reality, a universe
controlled by fixed physical laws and blind chance.
I affirm that the universe has no creator, no objective purpose and no objective meaning or destiny.
I believe that all judgments, values and moralities
are subjective, arising solely from biological drives
and chance. Free will is an illusion. Therefore, the
most rational values I can live by must be based on*

the knowledge that, for me, what pleases me is good; what pains me is bad."[12]

Ashcan realism dominated the literature of the time. It put forward minute descriptions of everyday life, not with the Romantic emphasis on the individual and his or her inner life but on the web of material circumstance that supposedly made each individual what he or she was; in other words, society determines or at least dominates individual actions and not merely influences them. The ash can and the backyard clothesline were thought to represent reality more than the front door or a building's elegant facade.[13†] The keepers of the received culture were upended when the new Ashcan-realist and impressionist writers and painters, more in tune with the spirit of the times, dissolved the ideological ground beneath their feet.[14†] The keepers of the received culture were unaware of what was happening to them and could not offer an adequate philosophical defense.

Sigmund Freud was one of the prominent thinkers of this time. He uncovered many useful psychological insights into human motivation, but his overall philosophy could be questioned. He likened rationality to the tip of the iceberg. To him, roiling emotions were beneath the mind's rational surface. These subconscious emotions determined rational thought so that at best we could only rationalize, not reason; that is, at best we only could project our subjective views on objective reality. He seemed to justify psychological determinism (despite determinism's unprovability); he limited the power of reason. Reason may indeed be limited, but it still applies to ethics.

Freud assumed that all judgments of aesthetic and ethical value were mere "attempts to prop up their illusions with arguments."[15] Freudianism, however, was weakened by disagreements among his followers and by their inability to predict human behavior; for instance, if they could predict which children would grow up morally straight and which would grow up to be criminals, the case for Freudianism would be much strengthened, but they couldn't do that. Wasn't Freud practicing "moral lobotomy"?

We should not overlook Charles Darwin, a great biological researcher who had a tremendous impact on his contemporaries, primarily because his views accorded with the zeitgeist of the time. He developed the theory of the evolution of species, but whatever one might think about evolution, it is completely irrelevant to ethical standards.[16†] That didn't stop many of his followers from drawing ethical conclusions from his biological researches, thereby attempting to cross the impassable Is-Ought Barrier.

Walter Lippmann (A Preface to Morals, p. 6): "We have come to see that Huxley was right when he said that 'a man's worst difficulties begin when he is able to do as he likes.' The evidences of these greater difficulties lie all about us...in the young men and women who are world-weary at twenty-two; in the multitude who drug themselves with pleasure...in the millions, at last free to think without fear of priest or policeman, who have made the moving pictures and the popular newspapers what they are."

Then there were physicists like Einstein and Planck. The great Albert Einstein developed the Theory of Relativity in a 1905 article, originally published in an obscure scientific journal.[17†] He showed how matter and energy are interchangeable and that weight, time, and shape depend on the speed of the object being studied. But all this hardly affects ethical principle. Einstein himself strongly objected to the tendency of nonscientists to apply physical relativity to ethical philosophy, and he opposed ethical relativism to the end of his life.

The same analysis applies equally as well to Max Planck's quantum theory of 1900. As David Hume said in the previous century, beware crossing the Great Divide between the world of "is" (facts) and the world of "ought" (logic). Nevertheless, physical relativity and Planck's quantum thesis popularized ethical relativism among superficial thinkers.

John Dewey (1859–1952), the famous pragmatic philosopher, located ethics not in reason but in ever-changing reality, thereby egregiously violating the Is-Ought Barrier. A later chapter will have more to say about his pragmatism; suffice it to say here that it led to the eclipse of reason by setting up subjective experience and a philosophically undefinable usefulness as the ethical goal instead.

Pragmatism (and utilitarianism, its philosophical cousin) denied that certainty in knowledge was achievable (except, contradictorily, for pragmatism or utilitarianism). Instead of consistency and accuracy, pragmatists stressed individual experience. (Utilitarians stressed happiness.) Realists regarded the statement that "Caesar crossed the Rubicon" as being true because competent observers reported that it corresponded to objective reality, according to the best evidence available, but pragmatists would hold it to be true because it is useful in understanding Roman history.

We should not underestimate the nineteenth-century importance of pragmatism. It became the reigning philosophy of the time. As the result of pragmatism's influence, the Social Gospel movement, emphasizing social service, grew in the United States and elsewhere. Pragmatism led Clarence Darrow, the renowned lawyer, to say that "laws should be like clothes. They should be made to fit the people they are meant to serve." This attitude led to a flexible interpretation of laws, as if written on rubber. Pragmatists tended to be strong advocates of democracy, not because they thought people have provable rights that the government should protect, but because democracy roused up many useful solutions; it was a means rather than an end in itself.

Since pragmatists were inculcated with strong ethical views in their youth, they tended to believe in nice goals as adults. But by maintaining that ethical rights are essentially matters of personal opinion only (experience and usefulness being subjective) they undermined the popular acceptance of provable rights; succeeding generations were left with a much more watered-down ethical inculcation than the pragmatists themselves had received. Pragmatism and utilitarianism were philosophical way-stations to existentialism. Add a mood of despair to pragmatism and we have existentialism, then postmodernism. Ordinary people who didn't know what pragmatism meant nevertheless looked at life pragmatically, unthinkingly merging ethical principle and moral application.

To Darwin, Marx, Freud, and Dewey, and to the nonscientific interpreters of Planck and Einstein, the physical world was not what it seemed, thereby undermining popular confidence in ethical certainty. But scientism itself failed to yield an emotionally satisfying outlook upon life. As the Age of Scientism wore on, the ability of human reason to answer the ultimate ethical questions was more and more called into question; there was an increasing disenchantment with reason. People drifted, unanchored by any sense of ethical purpose; the leading intellectual lights of the time didn't even attempt an ethical proof. The equal-rights doctrine was not disputed, but it came to be seen as rather irrelevant to life – in short, unprovable.

The scientistic period ended in the paralysis and nihilism of World War I. That war struck a death blow to an unfounded optimistic assumption of progress, but it also intensified ethical relativism. But the rise of such relativism had preceded that war. When 1914 came, no ethical standard had been proven true. The continuing undermining of reason proceeded unabated after the war and became a prominent cause of World War II.

Gertrude Stein (on her deathbed): "There ain't no answer. There ain't going to be any answer. There never has been an answer. That's the answer."

Daniel Bell (in Eli Ginzberg, ed., Technology and Social Change, *pp. 51, 59): "Twentieth century thought is characterized by the lack of confidence in the rational solution of social and cultural problems.... The whole breakdown of the rational cosmology is imminent and will ultimately create the most serious problems for society as a whole because of an alienation of the modes of perception about the world."*

Kenneth Clark (Civilization, p. 347): "We can destroy ourselves by cynicism and disillusion just as effectively as by bombs."

Page Smith (The Historian and History, p. 213): "We might say that he whom the gods would render impotent they must first convince of his impotence."

The Age of Relativism (1900–Present)

The twentieth century saw the rise of postmodern existentialism and a further move toward ethical relativism. Increasingly, truth was regarded as personal belief and nothing more. Before 1914, it was generally assumed that there was a solution to social problems; after 1918, people were much less sure, unaware of this subtle but definite shift. Although people are not puppets at the end of a string manipulated by the zeitgeist, it can be very compelling.

The new outlook, termed *existentialism*, held that each person defined him- or herself and there were no provable limits to our free will. Norman Mailer boasted that a movie he wrote was "an attack on the nature of reality."[18]† Many intellectuals followed the philosophy of Friedrich Nietszche (who died of syphilitic insanity; Nietszche had said God is dead, but as it happened God got the last word). Nietszche maintained that all philosophy is only personal confession; we experience only ourselves (nevertheless, reality is apt to break into our experiential shell).[19] Ethical relativism is an integral part of postmodern existentialism.

Jack Kerouac (On the Road, p. 238): "'Oh, man,' said Dean to me as we stood in front of a bar, 'dig the street of life, the Chinamen that cut by in

> Chicago. What a weird town…. Whee. Sal, we
> gotta go and never stop going till we get there.'
> "'Where we going, man?'
> "'I don't know but we gotta go.'"

World War II further eclipsed ethical rationality beyond what World War I had. Many intellectuals began to think it was fascist to suppose there was an ethical standard for everyone, though, contradictorily, they were often willing to punish criminals and fine miscreants. Denying an objective morality, they tended to embrace pacifism (peace at any price), thereby morally equating just and unjust causes.

During the Age of Scientism, ethical relativism had been assumed, but now it was preached. When I was managing editor of an intercollegiate literary magazine called *Pulse* in 1948 (our slogan: "No circulation, no *Pulse*"), I was consistently outvoted on editorial policy by the other more avant garde members of the staff who favored existentialist themes in the magazine (which at the time were unpopular not only with me but with our readers). But when I began college teaching in 1962, I was surprised to discover this existentialism was assumed to be true by most faculty and students. Out of habit and upbringing they generally chose to respect the equal rights of others, but they no more required proof of that view than proof of the existence of the nose on their faces or the heads on their shoulders.

The fall of communism, as epitomized by the fall of the Berlin Wall (1989), was another example of the effects of ethical relativism in the real world. Try as they might, the communist leaders could not keep out the doctrine; they couldn't maintain their communist views. Relativism seeped into their iron world, eventually overthrowing the communist establishment itself.

Subjectivism (the view that personal belief is the only true standard) was a central tenet of the new and increasingly dominant existentialism. The doctrine of equal rights was increasingly regarded as a convenient but unprovable ethical doctrine. The individual was regarded as the correct and final arbiter not only of right and wrong but often of truth and falsity as well. One prominent existentialist writer said that "a sense of truth was planted, as it were, in the marrow of my bones,"[20] and he then condoned nihilism and the pursuit of power as an end in itself as the only true alternative in life.[21] (He evidently thought with his bones.) The extreme subjectivism of solipsism – the belief that *only* oneself exists – characterized much social thought, although it was seldom applied to daily and vocational life. Even existentialists are likely to exit a room through an open door or treat customers the way they are; they tend to treat things as they are. Existentialists could not overlook objective reality in their everyday tasks, although in their philosophy they might slip into solipsism. Psychologists tell us that the only practicing solipsists are in insane asylums, but much formal modern existentialist and so-called postmodern philosophizing is quite solipsist.

Radical relativist Paul Feyerabend achieved some fame by claiming that scientific facts were mere social constructs (though he did not hesitate to seek medical attention upon learning he had cancer; it would seem he was afflicted with more than a social construct).[22]

Harold Loukes (Ethical Education, W/71, p. 8.): "*The middle class ethos, once thought to be 'right,' is now seen as an option…an option to be compared with a more vital, instinctive working-class morality…We are all taught not to look down on them [working class people] as moral inferiors, but to treat them as equals, and regard their behavior as justifiable.*"

Frank Goble (quoting an editor of one of our more distinguished women's magazines): "*The younger people on our editorial staff are now in control, and they are insisting that everything we publish, fiction or nonfiction alike, be 'permissive.' Anything that tries to hold up the standard of traditional morality, they regard not only as*

*having poor reader appeal but as a kind of evil in
its own right."*

Existentialists criticized the received ethical standards. They claimed they weren't proved but went even further by claiming they could never be proved (because their outlook was subjective). If it is generally believed that there is no ethical truth, then the quest begun by Odysseus and continued over more than two millennia has come to an end because there is nothing to seek. Existentialists were not affronted by this problem. Contemporary society became Nietzscheanized, existentialized; the Ten Commandments came to be regarded as the "Ten Highly Tentative Suggestions." When President Reagan condemned the Soviet government as "the evil empire," there was a loud outcry from the ethically relativized intelligentsia (how could evil exist?) even though such a strong condemnation was instrumental in bringing down the Soviet empire; more relevantly for us, the charge of evilness was objectively accurate.

Pure religious belief replaced a reasoned approach as the basis of religion. For example, fundamentalist Protestant churches gathered members to the detriment of mainline churches. In Judaism, its Reformed branch became more conservative and its emotional Chasidic movement achieved respect;[23] its Chabad movement infiltrated college campuses. Catholicism saw personal belief replacing traditions. The rise of religion itself was in keeping with the rise of subjectivism; America might even be said to be undergoing a fourth Great Awakening.

The dominant ethical relativism produced a general mood of despair, even for the average person who never thought about it. Thus, surveys of high-school seniors conducted by the University of Southern California found that of fourteen life goals, "finding purpose and meaning in life" decreased the most from 1976 to 1986. [24] But ethical relativism could also inspire conformity, since if all people are equally-valid fonts of ethical standards, then individuals should conform their views to that of the majority, because more people have them. Subjective relativism preached tolerance – but of what? Of evil? Of anything? A society's attitude toward ethical truth is basic.

Gil Orlovitz (*editor of* The Award Avant-Garde Reader, *ix*): *"Empirically all that is demonstrable [provable] is that we experience as creator or audience a series of perceptions. Now if we set forth that demonstration in the fictive [story] in such a fashion as to generate and sustain tension in the reader whether or not he is mystified by the significs [understandings], we have met the sole possible criterion."*

Ernest Hemingway: *"I only know that what is moral is what you feel good after and what is immoral is what you feel bad after."*

Cultural relativism and historicism reached its deepest and widest intensity in post-World War I Germany. There should be little wonder, then, that eventually irrationalism triumphed there most blatantly in the form of Nazism. (Although not an existentialist phenomenon, it was strongly relativistic.) Literature, ethics, and politics the world over became "Weimarized." This subjective existentialism resulted in the growing prominence of pessimistic and even despairing themes in art, literature, and culture. Aimlessness, aloneness, anomie, anxiety, and antiestablishmentarianism ensued. After all, if each individual is free to make up his or her own hierarchy of values and there is no provable ethical purpose to life, as postmodern existentialists maintain, then themes of pessimism and despair will surface.[25†] Utopias once had been the stuff of literature, but now there were dystopias. A recent decline in the birth rate throughout the West would seem to be a reflection of the growing mood of existentialist pessimism and despair. As Sartre said, "Man is *condemned* to freedom" (italics added). Translation:

People must choose although they have no provable standards of choice to guide them.

> *Anomie (dictionary definition): "a state of norm-lessness or lawlessness; a state of society in which normative standards of conduct and belief have weakened or disappeared; a similar condition in an individual commonly characterized by personal disorientation, anxiety and social isolation."*

> *Soren Kierkegaard (existentialist philosopher, quoted in* New Republic, *10/12/98, p. 27): "Depression is the most faithful mistress I have known."*

Existential postmodernism's impact on psychology has been deleterious. "The experience of a bounded moral community is missing," said Yale's Dr. Barbara Hargrove, a professor of divinity. "We ask these young people to ask questions, but we give them nothing to ask questions about: we give them no identity in the moral context."[26]

Sincerity became more important than objectivity; the distaste for being judgmental shrank the list of sins to just two: hypocrisy and smoking (tobacco, that is – marijuana was OK).[27†] Group loyalty became attenuated. No limits except social utility were imposed on criminality, divorce, illegitimacy, suicide, and euthanasia in art, music, and literature. Cultural collapse ensued, in the United States more than elsewhere. Throughout the Western world, existentialism made substantial inroads, although it was somewhat tempered in Europe by long and still-powerful tradition – when you are surrounded by the ruins of ancient Rome, tradition in everyday life seems more alive and harder to escape. All things had finally become permitted.

America enjoyed geographic isolation and a consensus arising from an inherited acceptance of the equal-rights heritage of

Thomas Jefferson and John Locke, but existentialist relativism was gradually dissipating this heritage, like acid eating away at metal. The outstanding characteristic of modern culture is that it enjoys an impressive degree of technical competence, it can do an enormous variety of things exceedingly well, but it lacks conviction as to whether any of these things are really worth doing. F. Scott Fitzgerald wrote that he felt like a little boy alone in a big house who now could do anything he wanted to do, but had suddenly discovered there was nothing he wanted to do.[28]

We cannot account for the increasing irrationalism and angst by reference to objective economic and scientific conditions, which in the twentieth century were better than ever; only an ethical-relativist philosophy could account for it. Only an ethical proof can provide a rational alternative to an existential ethical relativism, which leads inevitably to the view that nothing is intrinsically worthwhile, that life itself is meaningless, that the world is absurd, and that the only way to avoid an overwhelming pessimism and cynicism is to have an irrational leap of faith – but to prove irrationality, existentialists would have to use the criteria of rationality. I remember being belligerently told by a literature professor that he could live with contradictions; he later went on to become a college administrator in San Francisco.

Paul Roubiczek (in Existentialism, For & Against*): "Here we have to perform the act of faith; we need a constantly renewed willingness to accept what is beyond proof, we must risk the 'jump into the abyss' which can be justified, not by a preceding knowledge of its result, but only by the ensuing experience.…To discover the truth by which we live, we must start from personal experience and base our ideas on it, not vice versa. This is the central condition for all Existentialists, who never omit to emphasize that 'the personal is the real.'"*

> *Hazel Henderson: (Co-Director of the Princeton Center for Alternative Futures, in a Harper & Row filmstrip): "This of course sounds mystical and nonscientific, yet I think that when you have a society which is as complex as ours, as fast as ours, that the only way to understand it is with an intuitive flash of insight."*

> *Abraham Kaplan: "The new treason of the intellectuals is that we have shared and even contributed to the current loss of faith in the power of the human mind to cope with human problems, faith in the worth of reasoned discussion, faith even in the possibility of objective truth."*

In 1967, the prestigious *New York Review of Books* ran a cover illustrating how to make a Molotov cocktail and featuring an article in the same issue which asserted that "morality...starts at the barrel of a gun."[29] Well, why not, if no ethical limits to our freedom can be proved?

Harvard psychologist B. F. Skinner, in his best-selling book *Beyond Freedom and Dignity* (Knopf, 1971), contended that unchecked individualism guarantees overpopulation, pollution, hunger, and war. His answer? "Forget about freedom and dignity. Instead, develop a culture where environmental factors are manipulated and people are conditioned psychologically – the right behavior 're-enforced' with suitable rewards – to do the things that need to be done to preserve society, regardless of the price in lost freedom and dignity."[30] Many readers shared Skinner's chilling analysis.

If we can set any ethical goal for ourselves that we wish, apathy and violence are equally justifiable (their very contradictoriness would seem to disprove ethical relativism). If there is no objective ethical standard for rational people to appeal to, how can we communicate except by shouting at each other from our own little islands of belief? How can we persuade except by using force, as did Lenin, Hitler, and other twentieth-century dictators? Needed reforms might be accomplished without rational philosophy, but soon even do-gooders, if they feel there are no limits to their dedication, will become nihilistic terrorists and bomb-throwers.

World War II was partially funded by so-called Victory Bonds, supplanting World War I's similar Liberty Bonds, a name regarded in the 1940s as too moralistic; similarly the New Deal replaced the earlier Square Deal for the reform periods of the 1900s and 1930s. As an example of how popular culture has been affected by rising anti-rationalism and subjectivism, consider that ever since the 1960s when Chubby Checkers introduced the Twist, we have been dancing alone. Serious music composers no longer attempt to pursue objective beauty as did Mozart or Beethoven; rather they attempt to express their subjective feelings, like Cage.

The twentieth century saw a steady growth in ethical relativism. For instance, in 1997, the funeral of Princess Diana attracted more media attention than did the funeral, in the same week, of Mother Teresa. In America, an 1898 survey asked 1,440 twelve- to fourteen-year-olds, "What person of whom you have ever heard or read would you most like to resemble?" 40% chose either George Washington or Abraham Lincoln; Clara Barton, Annie Sullivan (Helen Keller's teacher), Julius Caesar and Christopher Columbus also received prominent mention. A similar poll conducted in 1948 with a comparable number of schoolchildren of similar age asked children, "Which one of all these persons that you know or have read about do you want most to be like 10 years from now?" This time, only a third of the respondents chose historical figures; sports figures accounted for 23%, entertainers for 14%; Joe Palooka, a comic-strip figure, was chosen more often than Jesus Christ. In 1986, nine of the ten figures most admired by American teenagers were entertainers (the exception being Ronald Reagan, but he was a former actor).[31] *Sic transit* ethical relativism.

Is not the Holocaust the inevitable result of an ethical relativism that asserts that there is no provable limitation on what we can do to each other? Deniers of the Holocaust take refuge in the prevailing view that truth is belief; they can convince impressionable young people that ovenizing fellow human beings is no worse than bad manners.[32][†]

The 1980s were alleged to have been a period characterized by narcissism, but isn't that a direct outgrowth of subjectivism, even though unintended? Wrote the famous pop-therapist Carl Rogers, "Doing what feels right proves to be a competent and trustworthy guide to behavior which is truly satisfying."[33] This subjectivist outlook continued into the next decade. For instance, the nine-year-old Anakin Skywalker is told to "feel, don't think!" in the movie *The Phantom Menace*. He is instructed to avoid the dangers of common sense and rational thought (which may be why he grows up to be Darth Vader).

John Chamberlain (Freeman, 1/74, p.52): "The parents were still living on the moral capital built up by their forebears who still held to the values of an individualism tempered by traditional Christianity. Underneath the correct behavior of the adult world the young sensed a complete lack of moral convictions."

In the existentialist climate of the twentieth century, pro-abortion sentiment grew from near-zero to full legality. Writes Robert Bork: "Since the Supreme Court's 1973 decision in *Roe v. Wade*, there have been perhaps over 30 million abortions in the United States. Three out of ten conceptions today end in the destruction of the fetus."[34] If people are regarded as not having rights, then neither do fetuses.

In parapsychology, we see the progression from the scientism of R. B. Rhine (who ran laboratory experiments using flash cards and dice rolls) to the reality-as-illusion emphasis on out-of-body experiences.

In industrial organizations, Walt Disney, Inc. replaced GM as the typical corporation.

> *Pablo Picasso: "I am only a public entertainer who has understood his time."*

> *Eric Hofer (in* The Temper of Our Time, *1967): "Even if we should banish poverty from the land, lift up the Negro to true equality, withdraw from Vietnam and give half the national income as foreign aid, the intellectual community will still see America as an air-conditioned nightmare unfit for them to live in."*

In art, impressionism dissolved the hard lines of objective reality. Then came cubism, abstract expressionism, pop art (a parody of art itself), and other artistic "isms"; we need not evaluate here the merits of these different artistic waves but clearly they represent a steady movement away from the objectively real toward subjective feelings.

We see the same trends in music and literature. They mirrored the new cultural outlook, which is no surprise. World War I accelerated but did not create this outlook; antirationalism preceded it. In the 1920s, the ideas and standards of the American past were subject to ferocious "debunking." F. Scott Fitzgerald explained that his generation had "grown up to find all gods dead, all wars fought, all faiths in man shaken." D. H. Lawrence thought the unconscious was the beacon light of civilization. "We are all responsible for an absence of values," wrote Albert Camus.[35] William Barrett, the existentialist writer, attacked rationalism as "technologism and bureaucratism and psychosis."[36] He also advocated the "suspension of the ethical" (Soren Kierkegaard's phrase) when crucial ethical decisions have to be made.[37] A recent rap song called for the killing of police officers and the sexual mutilation of women; our criminal justice system often displays an inability to punish adequately or convict the clearly guilty. The number of illegitimate births increased exponentially; our entertainment stresses sex and violence. The searing yet inexplicable economic depression of the 1930s further undermined general confidence in the real and the rational, as did the rise to prominence of a communist alternative.

History writing became fragmented into various sub-studies such as labor, ethnicity, and feminism.[38]† The historian's focus narrowed and the big picture of the past and present, both real and ethical, blurred. American history textbooks, which had characteristically ended on a high note of hope and promise, now tended toward pessimism; one such book concluded that "after 1963, America groped by starlight, lacking the beacon of agreed political purpose, and had the vision of statesmen who knew the night."[39] Non-American textbooks concluded similarly.

Psychology was also affected by existential subjectivism. Many psychologists believed with Marat-Sade that rationality is a barrier to understanding life and only the insane are rational and belong outside the bars; if anyone belonged behind bars, it was those who were rational.[40] One well-known psychiatrist, R. D. Laing, claimed that schizophrenia is not a mental breakdown but a mental breakthrough; it is a crucial voyage through "inner space" to a new life. He justified irrationality as being a reasonable reaction to the social irrationality around us. In a world gone mad, he believed, the uncertain line between sanity and madness is all but lost.[41]†

Improbable though it may seem, science and technology became increasingly under attack. On the stage and in avant-garde books, middle-class life was portrayed as oppressive and shot through with pathologies.

In accordance with the zeitgeist, irritability, irrationality, and incoherence reigned unchecked on college campuses (strikingly similar to what the Red Guards were doing in China at the time), thus leading inevitably to such cultural dysfunctions as the massacre at Columbine High School. Well-known invited speakers were heckled and classrooms disrupted; in the late 1960s rioters cowed the silent majority. (The latter's relativism drove them to apathy while the rioters' relativism drove them to irrational commitment.)[42]† For instance, Arthur Jensen, a University of California professor, was continually criticized in his campus newspaper and received several threatening telephone calls (frightening one of his research assistants into resignation) because of some black-white research he published; his critics, he said, "are not interested in what I'm saying."[43]

"Come mothers and fathers throughout the land/ don't criticize what you can't understand/Your sons and your daughters are beyond your command..."[44] ran the lyrics of a popular song. The police were regarded as guilty until proven innocent and criminals were victims to be sympathized with.[45]† Philosopher Herbert Marcuse advocated the withdrawal of toleration of speech and assembly from groups he disagreed with.[46] Political correctness (PC) was on the rise and was unsympathetic to such rational values as freedom, proof, individual achievement, and nongovernmental competitiveness and leaned toward political absolutism.[47]† It reserved particular disdain for the military. On campuses everywhere, reason was eclipsed. No people in history ever had it so good, yet no people ever felt so badly about it. A 1965 public opinion poll revealed that most people thought that others were dishonest and immoral.[48] After the campus upheavals of the 1960s, college students won much free speech but their relativism left them with little worth saying.

The New Left ("new" because it was existentialist) achieved some prominence in America and elsewhere, particularly among the committed young. It abhorred the bureaucratic and doctrinaire approach of the pro-socialist Old Left. Typical of the increasingly popular relativism, it had no vision or blueprint of what it wanted, being primarily antiestablishmentarian. When asked what the New Left proposed to do if it achieved power, Tom Hayden, a prominent New Left leader, replied: "First we'll make the revolution — then we'll find out what for." Tending toward personal affluence, New Leftists found they could riot and still eat; the college administrators, being themselves relativized, were disinclined to stop them.

Throughout the world, the economy was improving, impelled by new technological developments. Such prosperity, though, seemed to feed protest: History generally shows that protest is more intense when economic conditions are getting better than when conditions are harsh.

Even though a rationalistic elite had dominated Western thought for centuries, they were ethically bankrupt since they didn't prove their basic ethical philosophy; they could not withstand the nihilist onslaught of existentialism. Their dominance was eventually eclipsed. They were forced to give up control of the culture to the irrationalists, or often just quietly joined them. Perhaps now we can better understand Yeats' line from "The Second Coming": "Things fall apart; the centre cannot hold."

1968 was a watershed year. Some have called it America's suicide attempt but it was a worldwide phenomenon.[49] It certainly was not a watershed year politically: In the United States the conservative Nixon triumphed over the liberal Humphrey and the rebels of '68 failed politically elsewhere in the world. But they succeeded in affecting the culture. Even older people who had been objective realists and rationalists suddenly and unthinkingly flipped into subjectivism, assuming that's the way the world is and always had been. They took their new subjectivist outlook for granted; it never occurred to them to question it. They assumed it to be a fact of life. "If it feels good, do it" became the ethical norm. Hippie idealists rebelled from the directionlessness of straight society. In America from 1968 to 1975, the New Left may have been done in politically by its own excesses and the winding down of the Vietnam War, but then it took root in the media and academia.[50†] The 1990s saw the pursuit of profit and pleasure overshadowing ethical and philosophical certitude. It appropriately became known as the "whatever" decade since even intellectuals no longer cared to pursue the underlying meaning of life.

All of the earlier trends were intensified after 1968; subjectivist existentialism emerged as a dominant school of philosophy (particularly among literary people) and permeated all aspects of life and thought. Few people knew (or know now) what the word *existentialism* meant or accepted the label for themselves, but its tenets were widely adopted. People who in the 1930s had a logical positivist orientation now unconsciously adopted ethical relativism. This existentialism soon mutated into postmodernism. As David Gress has written: "With amazing speed, the language of liberation became the iron doctrine of multiculturalism and identity politics and spawned the mind-numbing language of political correctness."[51] Commenting on the greater affluence of the current generation of campus activists as compared with previous radical generations, sociologist Peter Berger observed that they were "not so much motivated by sympathy with black people in slums and yellow people in rice paddies as by boredom with Connecticut."[52]

Reason *magazine (5/99, quoting on an article 30 years previous): "The college president who sadly shakes his head and mumbles that he cannot understand what motivates [student] protesters is like that kind of parent who, after doing everything possible in the span of two decades to destroy his child's mind, laments to the world that the child refuses to think for himself. Well, what was expected?"*

In the words of Robert Bork, "Though not a single new fact about Columbus' life and exploits had been uncovered, the country's mood swung from one of uncritical adulation to one of loathing and condemnation, at least among the members of the 'intellectual' class."[53] "Do I want to?" and "Can I?" were on everyone's mind, especially the young, while the more important question "Should I?" was disregarded. "Just do it" (anything, whatever pleases) became the reigning doctrine. "Turn on, tune in, drop out," "Go with the flow."[54†] It is possible to believe, with Bork, "that American popular culture is in free fall, with the bottom not yet in sight."[55] But we can put too much emphasis on the doings of the year 1968. The intellectual softness was there before relativistic existentialism hit.

After 1968, existentialism gradually metamorphosed into postmodernism, which said, in incredibly dense and opaque prose, that truth does not exist and that all values and knowledge are socially constructed; they serve only the powerful. Language, it maintained, makes it impossible to know reality or truth. Sociologist

Bruno Latour purported to unmask the sadomasochistic desire for domination behind the formula $e = mc^2$ (!); other postmodernists term it a "sexed equation." (!!) Some postmodernists claimed that the direction of the research of male scientists was determined by their fear of menstrual fluids. (!!!)

Postmodern ethics was not unlike communist ethics: Both maintain that all ethics serve only the interests of a particular person or group. Both maintain that ethics is a naked pursuit of power. The dangers of nuclear proliferation may have abetted this irrationalism but it has been on the rise for some time. Postmodern ethical relativism has been inexorably developing for centuries. Of course, if equal rights can't be proven, ethical relativism is the only alternative.

As late as the 1940s, pragmatism reigned in America. It involved assuming equal rights (no proof was offered or thought necessary), but gradually its adherents, having no philosophical anchor, became postmodern existentialists, unbeknownst even to themselves. The same people who regarded themselves as hard-headed pragmatists in the 1940s became you-can't-prove-anything-philosophical existentialists and after 1968 they faded into postmodernism, unaware of their change. Not only did they come to assume that equal rights could never be proven (a most unusual view in history) but they even considered reality itself as subjective and unprovable. (Business and personal life, however, required a more realistic, less subjectivist outlook.) Many people nowadays favor equal rights and yet vociferously resist a proof of equal rights, even though they oppose murder, group discrimination, and robbery, thereby according rights to life, liberty, and property to other people. Many intellectuals nowadays would even banish the word *should* from the vocabulary.

Their allegiance to equal rights, bereft of the bedrock of an airtight proof, is a leftover from times past. Given the reigning ethical relativism, a second Constitutional Convention today in America would be a calamity: The Bill of Rights might be repealed.[56]

If people think there is no provable ethics, no ennobling purpose in life, then they'll live through their children, since they think rationality has nothing ethical to teach (although it used to be that rational adults were the model for right behavior, not children; don't adults learn anything in thirty years?). So people watch television, eat, drink, and try to be merry, and popular concern about screen celebrities replaces what is generally regarded as unprovable and therefore useless ethics.

Martin Luther is reported to have said, "I would plant a tree today even if I knew the world was going to end tomorrow."

Our point here is primarily to substantiate that postmodern existentialism and ethical relativism have been growing in dominance, especially in our time but steadily even before. Certainly, some of these changes have been beneficial: Racial and gender discrimination have been lessened, environmental concerns have been addressed, child labor has been outlawed in many countries, there is more concern for the handicapped and the elderly, and so on. These advances have occurred because there still is a residual belief in equal rights, which, even when proofless, can still motivate: The intervention in Kosovo is one of the few examples in history of a war pursued for moral ends only. But soon we had better underpin this belief in equal rights with a rational proof.

As this book is being written, the Age of Relativism is ongoing; it is a product of existentialism and postmodernism, in its somewhat more extreme form. But all the results are not yet in. Despite recent cultural trends, we may still be able to call it the Age of Ethical Rationalism. It might well be asked, What comes next? It's best not to ask; the future is not for us to see; what will be will be. We can only hope that a rational proof can turn the intellectual tide. Time alone will tell. We can only do our part before we leave this earth.

In our time, popular opinion has undergone a sea change about values cultural. We cannot expect existentialism or postmodernism to have no effect on our culture and that it would be just a plaything for philosophers or glitterati. Our changing ethical views affect politics and culture more than do transient superficial events;

it is with these views that this book is concerned. We stand poised at the edge of a magnificent future, provided we can contain the forces of misological irrationalism rising up all about us – and often within us.[57][†]

We have not tried here to document the chief historical periods in great detail. Rather we have chosen the generally accepted facts and themes of each social thought period and showed how Western civilization steadily moved from ethical certainty to ethical relativism, an important reason being that no valid ethical proof was ever successfully offered. Succeeding chapters show how culturally deleterious this has been and that it is demonstrably false, although fortunately there is an ethical standard that can be proven true. Without such a proof, existentialism or postmodernism, no matter how corrosive they may be, cannot successfully be refuted.

It does little good to rail against the collapse of culture. If we are really to understand what is happening all about us, we must go beyond conventional conservatism and liberalism and prove that ethical relativism is false and that an ethical rationalist alternative is true. Superficial arguments will lead to neither understanding nor a turning of the tide. We need a proof of an ethical standard. No matter how loud the railing, nothing else will do.

John Neary (in Life, *12/31/71, p. 76) felt existentially "like a man in a glass-bottomed boat, with no idea of the depths below, with only occasional glimpses of the creatures, with no control, really, over avoiding the rocky shore."*

Notice appearing on a bulletin board: "To Whom It May Concern: The world and all that's in it has been canceled due to lack of interest and an overabundance of nausea and disillusionment."

Here is a brief guide to the history of Western social thought:

Middle Ages = Reason and ethics are dominated by religious belief.

Enlightenment = Reason, inadequately argued for, determines ethical truth.

Romanticism = Reason and ethics are supplemented by intuition.

Scientism = Reason and ethics are supplanted by science and materialism.

Relativism = Reason and ethics are undermined by subjectivism.

References and footnoted material for this chapter begin on page 321 in the appendices.

CHAPTER TWO

The CURRENT RETREAT *from* REASON

This chapter puts our society and culture under the rigorously objective microscope and indicates to what extent rising ethical relativism has shaped them.

The Postmodern Undermining of Science

We live at a time when science has achieved more knowledge than ever before, and yet never has the theoretical basis of science been more under direct attack. Let us find out why.

First, let us see how science is being attacked; *undermined* is the better word. Scientific truth is being less and less regarded as something objective – "out there" – but rather as a belief reliant on the scientist's psychological frame of mind, gender, or position in society (an argument that used to be considered ad hominem). Reason is being replaced by linguistic analysis. Determinism is assumed to be true. Many theorists are saying we can only know ourselves or our perceptions, not what is "out there." Modern behaviorism denies the existence of consciousness. Modern psychology regards the conscious mind as being like the mere tip of the iceberg, controlled by forces from deep within us. Keynesian economics seems to regard wars and earthquakes as sources of prosperity because they lead to job creation (somewhat like ancient pyramid-building or digging unneeded holes and filling them up again). Science is increasingly regarded as only one of many ways to look at reality.[1†] "Truth = belief." Wrote Theodore Roszak in the *Atlantic Monthly* (5/72, p. 57): "Science, for so long regarded as our single valid picture of the world, now emerges as, also, a school: *a school of consciousness*, beside which alternative realities take their place." – in other words: postmodern ethical relativism.

An author in the Mensa Journal *(5/70, p. 7; Mensa is an organization for the upper 2% of the population in IQ): "What I agree with is sense; nonsense is anything I don't agree with. No one has the right to say more."*

The leading scientific doctrines of the twentieth century seem to lend support to this new "scientific" philosophy. I refer here to Einstein's Theory of Relativity (in which reality seems not to be directly knowable by the five senses), Heisenberg's Uncertainty Principle (we cannot know both the velocity and the position of atoms at any given moment), and Chaos Theory (randomness explains reality better than cause and effect). But in fact, these recent scientific theories do not contradict objective rationalism. There's nothing wrong or irrational about supplementing our direct sensory perceptions with tools such as the telescope, microscope, and computer; our direct sensory perceptions are surely limited and subject to revision, but objective truth exists nevertheless, and the velocity or position of atoms has nothing to do with ethical rationalism or ethical relativism. Randomness may explain some factual evidence, but ethical theories remain unaffected.

Some people wonder how in this age of great scientific achievement, the very precepts of science can be under serious attack, but they should consider the proceedings of a conference entitled "The Flight from Science and Reason," which took place in Spring 1995. Approximately 200 scientists, doctors, philosophers, educators, and thinkers were in attendance; they discussed "the contemporary flight from reason and its associated anti-science, its denial of even the hope of objectivism, and its relativist rejection of Enlightenment ideals."[2]

Wrote one evaluator of this conference: "The consensus of the presenters was that science-bashers come from all walks of academia. The usual culprits of anti-intellectualism, namely radical feminism (including notions of female science and male science), radical environmentalism (an unwillingness to look at opposing evidence), and social constructivism (knowledge considered as a product of the social, political, and historical pressures of the times rather than of objective truth), are joined by New Ageism and psychoanalysis in what is considered to be an attempt to debase rationality."[3]

To be sure, the most vituperative assault upon reason comes from the proponents of the Left activated by the cultural revolution of 1968, but since the proponents of the Right don't offer an airtight proof of reason, their defense of science and reason has been seriously deficient.[4†]

American students score badly in comparison with students from other lands, in part because American science education has been dumbed down; after all, if students, teachers, and publishers all have been relativized, then they will dumb down education and think nothing is worth learning in and of itself.

Relativism has affected all scientific specialties. For instance, a *New York Times* article reported that paleontologists who doubted the theory that a meteor's impact caused the extinction of dinosaurs were called militarists by their colleagues and felt their careers to be threatened because they seemed to support the use of nuclear weapons. Evidently these relativist critics felt that politics affected even such a scientific truth as dinosaur extinction.[5]

Paul Gross and Norman Levitt in their book *Higher Superstition: The Academic Left and Its Quarrels With Science* (Johns Hopkins Press, 1994) offer many examples of the anti-scientific outlook in American academia. Bruce Mazlish's comprehensive *Introduction to Contemporary History* or Rose-Marie Burke's expose of scientific relativism in France contain additional examples.

In 1994, Richard Herrnstein and Charles Murray, serious scholars both, were called racists when they came out with their detailed and documented study titled *The Bell Curve*, even though they clearly criticized racism. As careful research scientists, they tried to prove that there are inheritable differences in cognitive ability among the races – a legitimate scientific enterprise, one would think. But in so doing, they had violated relativist PC; ethical relativists made little attempt to deal with their scientific evidence.

Then there was the interesting hoax dreamed up by physicist Alan Sokal, a liberal. He wrote a tongue-in-cheek article titled "Transgressing the Boundaries: Toward a Transformative Hermeneutics of Quantum Gravity," which was accepted and published by the postmodern journal *Social Text* in a special issue on "Science Wars." Sokal took care to appeal to the editor's ideological preconceptions. Here is a typical excerpt from his article:

> Deep conceptual shifts within twentieth century science have undermined [the] Cartesian-Newtonian metaphysics...and, most recently, feminist and post-structuralist critiques have demystified the substantive content of mainstream Western scientific practice, revealing the ideology of domination concealed behind the facade of "objectivity".... It has thus become increasingly apparent that physical "reality" no less than social "reality" is at bottom a social and linguistic construct....[6]

When he revealed his hoax, Sokal said, "Anyone who believes that the laws of physics are mere social conventions is invited to try transgressing those conventions from the windows of my apartment (I live on the twenty-first floor)." He added that any competent undergraduate physics or math major could have spotted the article as a spoof that had no logical sequence of thought but relied upon strained analogies and bold assertions (and incomprehensible language).[7]

Mental compartmentalization is the main reason why scientific objectivity has come to be questioned at a time when it has achieved so many important breakthroughs. When it comes to everyday life or one's mode of making a living, relativists are likely to be rigorously scientific and objective (for instance, they agree that the easiest way to exit a room is to use the door), but when it comes to philosophizing, they feel free to speculate, even to the point of solipsism.

Many relativists feel that equality demands that each individual be the ultimate arbiter of ethical truth. Ethical relativists may feel that rationality should determine the means we use to pursue our goals, but they stoutly maintain that rationality has nothing to do with our choice of goals; they say each individual is the ultimate arbiter of that choice. They seem to be like motorists who are willing to exercise extreme care in following the curves in the road but don't know where they're going.

If the chief defenders of objectivity and science offer no ethical proof, ordinary people are likely to philosophize at will, without limit.

But the relativization of science has rippling effects on other disciplines. Take history as an example. Professional historians always thought of themselves as being rigorously scientific, basing their generalizations on original observations, but if they begin to assert that reason is mere unprovable opinion, then what is the use of their craft? Why should anyone read history? If the past is mere "construct," then aren't all opinions equally valid? Who would then need professional historians? If historians regard their subject as mere bunk, fables agreed upon, aren't they marginalizing their own subject? Aren't they shooting themselves in the foot?

"History is changing," say the ethical relativists – but that is one thing history does not do. It is our current views of history that might change.

Postmodern Ethical Relativism in Literature

It should come as no surprise that contemporary literary criticism is increasingly dominated by writers and critics who are ethical relativists. They embrace deconstruction, which asserts that words can refer only to other words and that we cannot know reality, only our reactions to it.[8] Deconstruction is a principal tool of postmodern ethical relativism. It maintains that at best, we can only put our view of reality into a social and cultural context. It arose in France in the mid-twentieth century. Its acerbic mood is an integral part of the theory: It is critical of current authority and past traditions (e.g., discrediting dead white males). The only truth, deconstructionists maintain, is the theory of deconstruction itself (for which no proof is offered). If all this sounds ethically relativist and existentialist, it's because it is.

Take, as an example, Saul Bellow's first collection of short fiction, *Mosby's Memoirs and Other Stories*. According to *Newsweek* (10/28/68, p. 122), it "presents a bleak vision of degeneration and decay: urban ghettoes in ruins, 'cities spilling their filth' into polluted rivers, skies filled with the specter of mushroom clouds. Weak doomed men and stronger doomed women grope through alien spiritual lands, faced with imminent death and unable to see any sign of rebirth or continuity." If writers are relativized, this is the vision they'll come up with. They are likely to regard all things as being permitted.

Other books have surveyed contemporary literature and the rootless hedonism of our times in greater detail than does this book,[9] but we can perform a useful service by looking for the causes of the social maladies they delineate so carefully.

Contemporary literature is strewn with sick novels and antiheroes (characters bereft of principle, purpose, order, or concern for equal rights, pursuing the basic animal instincts of sex, violence, and insanity). These antiheroes display mannerless, graceless exteriors below which we are sometimes led to believe there can lurk a heart of gold.

Many contemporary novels tend to be plotless and endless, filled with minute descriptions lacking a unifying theme, episodic without logical connection. Writers have become overwhelmed by weltschmerz. They no longer see bright hopeful utopias but science-fiction nightmares (e.g., *Jurassic Park*, *Brave New World*, and *1984*, where people are enthralled to machines, their rights submerged by a bleak totalitarian society. Science fiction is in vogue, but it looks at the future with a narrow antiutopian unease.

Schizophrenia is often regarded as just another view of reality, equally viable and equally nonprovable. The underlying philosophy of the popular British psychiatrist R. D. Laing is the often-quoted line from Shakespeare's *Macbeth*: Life is "a tale told by an idiot, full of sound and fury, signifying nothing."

Widely read modern-age novelist Norman Mailer asserts publicly that the cultural hero of the future might be a "philosophical psychopath."[10] He stated that Castro is "the first and greatest hero to appear in the world since the Second World War."[11] Mailer was a relativist not only about reality but about ethics also, in his life and utterances as well as in his writing. He typified many contemporary writers when he said there was an inner psychopath in us all.[12]

Homosexual playwrights expound critically and at length on family life to eager audiences. A deconstructionist author avers that "nothing in this book is true but it's the way things are" (?); nevertheless, he found a wide readership. Best-sellers urge "do your own thing" to the plaudits of intellectual magazines like the *Atlantic Monthly*. Intellectuals should be alienated, avers an article in *Harper's Monthly*. Good taste is out of fashion. Roseann becomes a contributing editor of the *New Yorker*. But before we cast stones at our novelists and editors, we must remember that the public buys their books and magazines; it is the real culprit. Only a proof of an ethical standard has a chance of turning this around. Optimism may not be in order, but we should do our duty.

Lest there be a reader with head in sand who still feels that contemporary literature could not possibly have taken this relativist turn, consider the much-admired Andre Gide, who wrote, "I arrange facts in such a way as to make them conform to truth more closely than they do in reality."[13] That was avant-garde in 1895 when

Gide said that, but not now. By mistaking "truth" for "belief," does not this reality relativism convert easily into ethical relativism?

The reputation of Thomas Mann, a cerebral novelist with a definite moral outlook, is now declining. Calvin Trilling asserts that "whenever in modern literature we find violence…and an insistence upon the sordid and disgusting and an insult offered to the prevailing morality or habit of life, we may assume that we are in the presence of the intention to destroy specious good"[14] (a term which he unfortunately made no attempt to define). As for Marcel Proust, reading him is like lying in someone else's dirty bath water. (Actually, Alexander Woolcott said that.[15]) Jean-Paul Sartre idealized Jean Genet, a self-confessed pervert and thief. Then there is Marshall McLuhan, who stated, "Most clear writing is a sign that there is no exploration going on. Clear prose indicates the absence of thought."[16] He practiced what he preached. Writing of Bunuel, the Spanish film director who specialized in portraying the sadomasochistic mentality, Henry Miller observed, "Either you are crazy, like the rest of humanity, or you are sane and healthy like Bunuel. And if you are sane and healthy you are an anarchist and throw bombs."[17]

It might be thought by some that this subjectivist-existentialist-deconstructionist-all-things-are-permitted nihilistic relativism typified the 1960s and 1970s more than the present, but no. Ethical relativism was newer then and hence more discussed, but now it is assumed to be true. For instance, *U.S. News & World Report* (12/30/96 – 1/6/97, p. 84) could comment that "the musical *Chicago* was deemed too relentlessly cynical for even a jaded New York audience when it opened, and flopped, in the summer of 1975. Now its revival is one of the hottest tickets on Broadway." (The plot revolves around two female murderers who use their momentary celebrity to get off the hook and become vaudeville stars.)

Penelope Leach has supplanted Dr. Benjamin Spock as the most widely read child-rearing expert. Spock was relativistic about child-rearing, but Leach has out-Spocked Spock. She argues that parents should not impose moral obligations on preschool children because it will bruise their self-esteem."[18] Spock never went that far.

Then there are the philosophers. According to Roger Kimball in the *Wall Street Journal* (2/15/94, A14), "Influential philosopher Richard Rorty speaks with contempt of 'metaphysical prigs,' i.e., those who still believe that philosophy has something to do with 'seeking the truth.' Presumably, Mr. Rorty's students are all thoroughly disabused of such 'priggishness.'"[19]

As for poetry, it has been thoroughly relativized. The exceptions are few. Lost in history are the three R's of poetry: rhyme, rhythm, and reason (meaning). Robert Frost says that the current love for dense free verse is like playing tennis with the net down; well, not quite – it's more like playing tennis without a ball (i.e., meaninglessness) and without baselines (i.e., without rationality).

Marya Mannes wrote, "Sensation now has priority over sense, reason has become the first casualty of revolution."[20] Novels now abound in which authors dissect their subconscious and take 300 pages to defecate on themselves. Asserts Columbia University literary critic Lionel Trilling in his book *Beyond Culture*: "The characteristic element of modern literature…is the bitter line of hostility to civilisation which runs through it."[21] But such negativism is inevitable if you believe that reason cannot provide a provably true ethical standard.

Irving Howe (a prominent critic for the New York Times Book Review *m 2/9/64, p. 1): "Above all else, the modernist outlook is committed to uncertainty: Where truth had once been seen as absolute, there now reigns the problematic. To many traditional critics and ordinary readers, the modernist writer often seems willfully inaccessible, obscure and even outrageous.*

"Poets like Eliot and Stevens, novelists like Joyce and Kafka, have been with us for some decades now; their work has been studied and overstudied; yet they remain the revolutionists of 20th-century literature, the true heroes of the avant-garde. And ordinary readers are quite right

when they find such writers difficult, though quite wrong if they conclude that the difficulty is not worth troubling over.

"The modernist writer can no longer accept the formal claims of society; he finds the traditional modes of expression worn out; he suspects the neatness and apparent coherence of the old literary forms, and in his search for freshness, is perfectly ready to risk exaggeration and fragmentariness. The usual morality seems to him stale, perhaps a mere hypocrisy. He wishes to arouse strong feelings in his audience, even if they are feelings of hostility; he wishes to shake men out of lethargy, middle-class comfort; the life shocking, the frightful, the weird and the sick.

Let us turn our attention now to drama. Not too long ago, the Theatre of the Absurd ruled unattenuated and supreme; its influence is still very extensive and its principles are now assumed. The historian of that genre, Martin Esslin, has written:

If a good play must have a cleverly constructed story, these have no story or plot to speak of; if a good play is judged by subtlety of characterization and motivation, these are often without recognizable characters and present the audience with almost mechanical puppets; if a good play has to have a fully explained theme, which is neatly exposed and finally solved, these often have neither a beginning nor an end; if a good play is to hold the mirror up to nature and portray the manners and mannerisms of the age in finely observed sketches, these seem often to be reflections of dramas and nightmares; if a good play relies on witty repartee and pointed dialogue, these often consist of incoherent babblings."[22]

But don't criticize Absurdist playwrights if you patronize their plays (more than once). An Absurdist outlook makes ethical proof difficult. Said Eugene Ionescu, one of the leading Absurdist playwrights: "Absurd is that which is devoid of purpose.... Cut off from his religious, metaphysical, and transcendental roots, man is lost; all his actions become senseless, absurd, useless."[23] In other words, all things are permitted. Ionescu and his fellow Absurdists do not make any attempt to regain those roots, but that has not affected their influence on the theater today.[24]†

Samuel Beckett, an influential postmodern ethical relativist and existentialist playwright, asserted that somehow he retained a terrible memory of life in his mother's womb. When asked by Alan Schneider to explain *Waiting for Godot*, his reply was, "If I knew I would have said so in my play."[25]

There may be a reader somewhere who doubts that absurdity characterizes the theater to this day, but consider *Rent*, a recent Pulitzer Prize-winning play. It celebrates a counterculture version of family values, as an odd assortment of unrelated people feed, clothe, and bury each other. At the play's end, the heroine sings, "There is no future/There is no past/Live each moment as my last.... No day but today."[26]

There is no need for us to dissect the theme of Luigi Pirandello's play, *Right You Are, If You Think You Are*. The title is self-explanatory. Yet it is highly regarded by the literati.

Modern playwrights – beat, angry, existentialist, Absurdist – relativists all – insult their audiences, who take it all good-naturedly. Many people today are willing to pay handsomely to be kicked in the groin, to have rationality derided, their achievements lambasted. The good people on stage are represented as being ineffectual goo-goos or hypocrites, the bad ones as being sincere, red-blooded, virile, Nietszchean superhumans unfettered by convention. Recent plays tend to the planless, deride logic, and feature antiheroes, masturbating lunatics, and cruelty for its own sake. It may be that nudity, obscenity, and degeneracy are part of life, but then so is diarrhea.[27]

But contemporary writers and playwrights are right to be relativist and existentialist if no ethical standard can be proven true. We leave the task of ethical proof to a subsequent chapter of this book.

Postmodern Ethical Relativism and Art

We might expect ethical relativism's impact on art would be the replacement of objective reality by the artist's personal vision – and that is exactly what is happening.

Impressionism first became popular in France in the 1880s and then eventually in America. Its popularity still continues today if we are to judge by what the sales-conscious furniture stores carry. Remember, it isn't important what we think is beautiful; beauty is whatever pleases individual emotions and so is purely subjective, even though many relativists seem to believe that it's beauty that is objective and it's ethics that is subjective. Whether we like an object or a painting is not what this book is all about; I may prefer *Mona Lisa* to *Whistler's Mother*, but I can't *prove* it is more beautiful. Rather we are concerned with the influence of ethical relativism on our culture and whether it can be proven true.

Impressionism blurred reality and replaced it with the subjective impression made upon the artist. Ethical relativism was working its way into the culture. Art may have become more expensive than it had been earlier, but it was no longer grand.

Impressionism was soon supplanted as the cutting edge of new art by cubism, Dadaism, surrealism, abstract expressionism, pop art, op art, and blank art. With each artistic wave, reality faded more and more, supplanted by personal visions, until today with-it intellectuals can show how cultural they are by objecting to a beer can on the highway but be willing to pay $5,000 for a painting of a soup can. A soup can painting is essentially meaningless, which is altogether consistent with the elevation of color and form over meaning by postmodern existentialism.

Matisse, Picasso, and others turned reality inside out. They generally did not attempt to communicate with their viewers, who being relativized also, admired them anyway. They tended to be primarily aesthetic, but today's cutting-edge artists are mainly transgressive; that is, they are primarily interested in violating established social taboos regarding sex, religion, race, and gender. Not surprisingly, much of their work is morally repugnant. Viewers have become accustomed to seeing and doing things they would previously have been horrified even to think about.

To what level has ethical relativism brought art? Well, the split carcasses of a cow and its calf floating in formaldehyde won the $30,000 Turner Prize, Britain's award for hip new art. The artist, Damien Hirst, edged out another strong contender whose art consisted of a twelve-minute videotape exploring her various body orifices[28]; at least we have an idea of what Hirst and his contender were depicting, which is more than can be said about much modern art today. A 1999 show at the Brooklyn Museum displayed a sympathetic portrait of a child murderer and a portrait of the Virgin Mary decorated with elephant feces and pornographic clippings.[29] None of this bodes well for the acceptance of ethical proof by our art intelligentsia.

The Establishment reaction to the first major showing of modern art in America, the Armory Exhibition of 1913, was negative and confused, but since the Establishment increasingly regarded descriptive and ethical truth as subjective, it was sure to lose out eventually. It could not defend itself. It was not even aware that its philosophical defense was dissolving, as if a rug were being pulled out from beneath it.

F.J.M. (Nation *magazine, which at that time represented Establishment opinion; 3/6/1913, pp. 241-3):* "On all hands I hear in the show the statement, 'At any rate, this new art is very living and interesting'.... Something like that might be one's feeling on first visiting a lunatic asylum.... Yet feeling as I do that Post-Impressionism is mostly ignorant splurge, and Cubism merely an occult and curious pedantry, I feel also that the Association has done a valuable service in bringing over a full representation of this latest eccentric work...."

> *"The platform of Post-Impressionism is a simple one with complete spontaneity independent of all images of outer nature. Swift, succinct, and powerful execution of symbolic color – these are the chief tenets of the movement....*
>
> *"On the whole, the case calls for cheerfulness. Either these new movements are aberrations and will promptly vanish, or else there is to be henceforth no art as the world has formerly understood the word and the thing. But this, I am assured by a friend of the new art, is highly desirable. In the future every man is to see nature and his own soul with the artist's eye."*

Robert Bork reports that he once asked a sculptor on the Yale University faculty what his sculpture, which looked like a half-melted tree stump, represented. The Yale sculptor replied, quite seriously: "Whatever you want it to be." Evidently, relativized Yale was willing to support a man whose idea of art was a three-dimensional Rorschach test;[30] it was clearly a manifestation of a barren subjectivist philosophy. Art that sneers at humanity is what the art establishment now lauds, whereas art that pursues beauty is looked down on as unsuitable.[31]

Ethical relativism has led to the "curious result that the photograph of a crucifix immersed in urine can be exhibited in a public school, but a crucifix not immersed in urine cannot be exhibited."[32]

Today, nonrealistic art dominates our high-art magazines. But not all our cultural observers take kindly to this nihilistic relativism. Gertrude Himmelfarb, for instance, in her book *On Looking Into the Abyss*, quotes Madame de Sevigne's famous remark that "no man is a hero to his valet." Today, she suggests, we live with a valet's view of the world: Everything is cut down to size – even below size: "It can no longer be taken for granted that Milton deserves to be more 'privileged' than Mickey Mouse, that high culture is higher...than popular culture."[33] Actually, these attacks on greatness say more about us than on the objects of our criticism. As Hegel observed, if no man is a hero to his valet, this is not because the man is not a hero but because the valet is a valet. We might share Ms. Himmelfarb's outlook, but note that she makes no attempt at ethical proof.

Architecture has also entered a postmodern relativist phase. For instance, Frank Gehry, a well-known postmodern architect, uses such materials as corrugated iron, chain-link fence, asbestos shingles, and raw plywood in his nonobjective sculptures; his formal interests lie with what he calls "a fascination with incoherent and illogical systems, a questioning of orderliness and functionality."[34]

The influence of ethical relativism upon contemporary art needs no further elaboration. Only Part II's proof of an ethical standard can alter this influence.

Postmodern Ethical-Relativism and Music

As with what has gone before, so with music. It is primarily emotional and therefore quite expressive of the mood of our time. It should come as no surprise that modern serious music (e.g., Stravinsky, Bartok, Schoenberg) reflects the relativistic postmodern zeitgeist of our time, which is to be compared with the stateliness, order, and beauty of Bach, Mozart, and Beethoven. That relativism is emerging in music is certainly clear.

The twentieth century has seen the annihilation of tonality in classical music. Tonality can be described as follows:

> that particular system of organizing tones which, after several centuries, was assumed to be the natural law of music. Tonality, as it evolved in the seventeenth century, is a system of seven-note scales in which one note is the focal point or tonic key. The function of each of the other notes in this scale is determined by its relationship to that key. This dynamic hierarchy dominated all Western music in the eighteenth and nineteenth centuries.... The trend toward atonality – music without a tonal center or key – accelerated in the late nineteenth century.[35]

Aleatory music is the latest manifestation of atonality. It is music in which anything goes, music by chance (aleatory) like the throw of the dice according to tables of random numbers. To the nonaleatorists (most of us) it sounds like noise and is painful, even harmful to the ears. Pitch is destroyed. It is totally disorganized music, with free improvisation, in keeping with subjective reality and ethics. It tends to sound like a conclave of car alarms or a magnified bathroom drip, and "captures the sounds of a surgery ward in the days before anesthesia."[36] It is hard to believe there was a time when music stressed harmony and melody. John Cage, a composer of aleatory music, featured long periods of silence (often three minutes!) and said, most relativistically and existentially, "Previously, my music had been based on the traditional idea that you had to say something. The charts [chance arrangements of notes] gave me my first indication of the possibility of saying nothing." Very relativist.

Aleatory music is similar to "chance dance," which explores the notion of chance or randomness in modern dance. It does not depict an idea, enact a story, or symbolize anything. It is movement in its most elemental and unadorned state; its sole aim is to direct our attention to unplanned interaction.

Serious contemporary music has thus seen the overshadowing of melody (symbolizing intellect) by rhythm (symbolizing emotion). It sounds like badly played classical music. Audiences, preferring music composed during the Enlightenment, detest atonal music and avoid it whenever possible (the cough level at atonal public recitals rises when it is played); classical music radio stations, which must cater to mass audiences, play Enlightenment music mostly. Young people detest atonal music,[37†] if only because for them music is primarily a form of revolt from adult moral standards and rock music does that better.

Before leaving our consideration of classical music, we must comment on its frightening decline in popularity, itself a relativist manifestation. One reason for this is that serious modern music features slips and slides, seeming shrieks, screams, squeaks, scrapes, stings, squeals, scratches, strugglings, and squawks, not to mention banging and clanging as well as groans and grumbles, or so it seems to general audiences to whose ears such music sounds discordant, disorganized, disjointed, discombobulated, deracinated, deleterious, distractive, decentralized, and deconstructive.[38]† It's the music of coming apart and might be considered fascistic in its irrationalism. Serious musicians are better than ever and are better paid than ever, but the classical audience is shrinking, shrinking. Classical compact discs and tapes simply do not sell well; over the years the classical music section at my local music store has shrunk to a small bookcase while the store itself has grown.[39] Unless we can offer an ethical proof as an alternative to ethical relativism, the future of classical music doesn't look bright. It will be done in by its relativized composers and musical directors. In a few years, if relativism continues to dominate, classical music will be supported by a few retirees listening to a few teenage wonders.[40]† In former days, only kings and aristocrats could listen to classical music. Now everyone can, but few do.

Brendan Koerner (U.S. News & World Report, 4/6/98, p. 57): "Less than 40 years ago, many cities boasted six to seven classical stations; now only 160 remain nationwide, and that number is dwindling. The core audience – wealthy, highly educated, serious about musicology – is graying considerably; one Maryland station found that, between 1987 and 1997, the average age of listeners jumped from 45 to 55."

Wolfgang Lewy (Israeli Philharmonic spokesman, on learning that a modern classical music concert was likely to lose money): "It will be worth it just to see how many people will turn out. Besides, the orchestra has an intellectual responsibility to play modern music, even if we do not always enjoy it."

We have not commented on New Age music. It's nice, good as background music, and conducive to amiable conversation. It essentially goes nowhere, and in that sense, it is ethically relativistic. It tends to justify what people want to do rather than what they should do.

Bert Kruse (Wall Street Journal, *10/20/95, A13*):
"What's music to a certain ear
Is to another clatter.
For all who dote on Liszt and Brahms,
Far more claim they don't matter."

Now let us consider popular music. It is characterized by its blaring beat, loosening the listener's mind from its moorings in objective space and time, erasing feelings of separation between self and surroundings. It is generally played so loud that rational thought becomes impossible. The difficult world of external objects becomes blurred and unreal; only the inner pulse feels real. Dream and dreamer seem to merge. It is entirely consistent with ethical relativism.

Take jazz as an example. It evokes a picture of the saxophone player standing out in the foreground and contorting from his instrument that piercing music, "endlessly sorrowful yet endlessly unsentimental, with no past, no memory, no future, no hope...."[41] In popular music, the twentieth century may have started off with rational, singable songs (e.g., "Sidewalks of New York," "The Bicycle Built for Two"), but it soon progressed to jazz and swing and then onto rock and roll, acid rock, hard rock, heavy-metal, punk, rap, gangsta rap, ska, alternative, and so on. The term *rock* has often been credited to Cleveland disc jockey Alan Freed in 1951 when he noticed white youth buying black rhythm-and-blues music (according to one source, it was a "ghetto euphemism for dancing and sex").[42†]

This new music rules the radio waves and sells well in supermarkets. It should come as no surprise that violence, and even death, accompany many rock and heavy-metal concerts,[43] and why not, if it is felt that no ethical standard can be proven? In short, it is the music of irrationality, of total limitless, anticonventional, personal freedom. Of postmodern relativism.

> *Jane Gunther* (Readers Digest, *6/73, p. 98):* *"Three things distinguish rock – the relentless beat, the freedom of conception and the overpowering volume. This is physical, powerful music. Amplifiers at rock concerts produce a sound intensity which sometimes reaches 120 decibels (a new jet, on takeoff, must not exceed 108)."*

Rap (and the musical fads that followed) expresses a particular rage against the police ("off the pigs!") and women in general; it celebrates the unconstrained self and savages those who would constrain. It uses language that would make a sailor blush. It favors rebellion without a cause, sex rather than love. Rap and its successors simply do not express tenderness or gentleness. But if each person is regarded as the ultimate arbiter of right and wrong, then there is nothing left for the individual but carnal appetite.

Today's pop musicians don't bother to hide their relativist and existentialist attitudes. Wrote *Newsweek* (6/20/77, p. 80): "Punkist Patti Smith, for instance, came on tough, spat at the audience and recited her mystical poetry over a primitive musical backup. Richard Hell, whose recent single 'We're the Blank Generation' has become a punk anthem, during performances wore a T shirt that read 'Please Kill Me.'"

> *Daniel Greene (quoted in Duncan Williams,* Trousered Apes, *p. 103): "Places long known for high-brow or Hollywood-slick entertainment now vibrate to the cacophony of 'psychedelic' and acid-rock; the trenchant strains of folk-and-protest rock; the sensual effusion of 'soul'; the raucous incongruity of a new and harsh 'music' made from an activity as old as mankind: destruction – instruments are smashed or blown up."*

Martha Bayles says that "only a fool would argue that music – especially music combined with gut-wrenching spectacle – has no impact on audiences."[44] But however vulgar, nihilistic or grating to the ear (or to the soul) that pop music may be, the point for us is that it has been clearly influenced by postmodern existentialism or ethical relativism.

I would say that rock and roll tends toward the raunchy, rude, ribald, rusty, runty, rambunctious, raspy, raw, and raucous (certainly not the rational, more the relativistic), but my personal musical taste is irrelevant to the main thesis of this book, which is the deleterious impact of ethical relativism on our culture and its unprovability.

The words of today's pop songs are often difficult to discern, but they accurately reflect the contemporary mood. For instance, here is a publishable stanza from the popular "Sounds of Silence:"

> And in the naked light I saw
> Ten thousand people, maybe more.
> People talking without speaking,
> People hearing without listening,
> People writing songs that voices never shared....
> And the sign said,
> The words of the prophets are written on the
> subway walls,
> and tenement halls
> And whispered in the sound of silence.[45†]

It could be said that the melody and not the words made this song popular, but what's important for us is that these words delineate the themes of aloneness, anti-establishmentarianism, despair, and subjectivism that characterize ethical relativism and existentialism.

Tom Leland (Atlanta psychiatrist, commenting on the Beatles, in Readers Digest, *12/67, p. 232): They "are speaking in an existential way about the meaninglessness of actuality."*

60

John Lennon (in 1971, quoted in U.S. News & World Report, 10/25/93, p. 232): "I don't believe in Kennedy. I don't believe in Beatles. I just believe in me."

Bob Dylan became a well-known pop singer even though he didn't have a good voice, but that undoubtedly helped him come across as sincere since it was assumed that his half-articulateness was prima facie proof of sincerity (logic and rhetorical skill being prima facie proof of hypocrisy, the mark of the manipulator). "The sincere man was therefore supposed to be confused and half articulate and anguished in his self-revelation."[46†]

Then there is the Elvis Presley phenomenon. After he died in 1977, a veritable cult about him enveloped the world. He was amazingly successful in his own time,[47†] even after his death. He embodied arrogance, self-righteousness, and sex. He was the classic "rebel without a cause." He unthinkingly epitomized postmodern existentialist themes.

It should come as no surprise that many rock and pop-music heroes have died from drug overdoses. It fit their lifestyle and philosophy of life.[48†]

On the Broadway musical stage, the cleverness of Oscar Hammerstein was replaced by the incomprehensible lyrics and unsingable music of his protégé Stephen Sondheim. Popular dancing shows the same relativist progression as classical dance. It has gone from the waltz to the tango to the lindy hop to the cha-cha to who-knows-what, from set sequences to improvisation to throwing your partner around to not touching your partner (frequently not even exchanging glances or words). The decorous and elegant round dances of the sixteenth century have metamorphosed into the wild and jerky "don't touch me" dances of today. Contemporary dances bespeak of personal isolation, in-your-face aggression, and revolt against order and discipline. Very existential, very postmodern, very relativist.

Postmodernism in Entertainment and Everyday Culture

If our thesis is correct – that ethical relativism is becoming increasingly dominant and deleterious – then we should not be surprised that it pervades popular entertainment and everyday culture. The evidence points in that direction.

Let us first look at everyday culture and start off with the movies. Remember, we are not trying to separate what we like from what we do not like. Aesthetic taste is purely subjective and not what primarily concerns us here. We are more interested in the influence of ethical relativism and that is an objective question, either true or false. If ethical bounds are down, then the primal instincts – sex and violence – will logically take over. And that is exactly what we find.

(1) We can start with *Bonnie and Clyde*: Audiences chuckled when strangers were murdered but were shocked when the sympathetically-portrayed young killers were themselves shot.

(2) This film was soon followed by Stanley Kubrick's pop-nihilist *A Clockwork Orange*, which made a big hit in the 1970s with audiences as well as with the critics. *Newsweek* and *Saturday Review* featured it in cover stories, and the New York Film Critics gave the film its annual 1971 best film award. Alex, its hero and narrator, is a jocular young sadist, an aesthete of violence who beats, robs, rapes and finally murders for pleasure. Society surrounds itself with objects of ugliness and unspirituality that the young regard as cool. (They feel liberated from the aspirations of the adults about them.) Nothing has any transcendent meaning. Meaninglessness is like a drug, putting one in a state where there is no reason even to try to sort things out morally or aesthetically.

(3) *American Graffiti*, *Grease!*, *Midnight Cowboy*, and *Easy Rider* were all acclaimed by the critics and at the box office. They all shared existentialist relativism. Movies have tended more and more toward the plotless and no-brainers.

(4) Actor James Dean became famous when he made *Rebel*

Without a Cause (emphasis added), but he grew up straight in a midwestern small town.

(5) The lines at movie box offices around the country ratify fables of cynicism, futility and despair. As Paul Zimmerman said in *Newsweek* (11/18/74, p.19): "These films supply images of a world going to hell physically to a public convinced things are going to hell morally.... The public votes with its dollars, selecting from a variety of visions those which confirm its own angers and aspirations.... Those who shake their heads at the lack of affirmative action and effective heroes in our films are like the aging *grande dame* who accuses her mirror of lying."

(6) Wrote Vincent Canby, in his day an influential movie critic: "The problem with 'They Call Me Mister Tibbs!' is that...it's inhibited by [Sidney] Poitier's own good taste and sense of mission."[49] No comment.

(7) *The Thief Who Came to Dinner*, a typical well-known 1973 movie, would have us believe that stealing jewels is a prankish, victimless crime. The lead character is a hero because he is an "honest thief" (i.e., untouched by hypocrisy). Traditional morality is turned upside down: The thief is a sympathetic guy, his victims are unsympathetic, the man trying to catch the thief is a jerk, and because we are all guilty, nobody is guilty. Present-day Hollywood standards dictate that there is nothing unethical about being a thief.

(8) In *Last Year at Marienbad*, it was impossible to tell who was doing what to whom, let alone why.

John W. Gardner (In New York Times Book Review, *1/26/64): "Once it was the skeptic, the critic of the status quo, who had to make a great effort. Today the skeptic is the status quo. The one who must make the effort is the man who seeks to create a new moral order."*

---

(9)   Then there are the violent blood-chilling computerized video-action games that teach kids to kill for thrill; one can only hope they will not learn.[50]

(10)   Wrote John Leo in *U.S. New & World Report* in 1992: "I knew I would not be going to see *Cape Fear* when a reviewer informed me that the [lead] DeNiro character bites into the cheek of a handcuffed woman and spits out a Dinty Moore Chunky Stew-sized piece of flesh. Over-the-top-of-hair-raising violence that would have been unthinkable in mainstream movies a decade or so ago now seems routine."

(11)   Then there's Madonna, the "Queen of Sleaze," whose immense popularity cannot be denied. Her lyrics urge the young to "do whatever feels good." She performs in her underwear while doing obscene dance steps. The criticism we might ascribe to her can also be directed to Hollywood moguls who employ her and to the audience that popularized her. We could compare Madonna and Demi Moore to Doris Day and even Jean Harlow, or Johnny Travolta to Clark Gable, to see the trend that movies have taken. There was no swearing in movies made before 1950; not so thereafter. To easily verify this, view old movies on late-night television.

Wrote Amy Holmes, columnist: "Not long ago, Madonna occupied the fringes of social trends. Now she seems almost normal – and that should trouble us all."[51]

Pauline Kael (film critic, in A.P. Dispatch, 5/4/74, p. 13): "The innocence of former years has been replaced by the bland acceptance of the inevitability of corruption and the contrived humor of the self-putdown."

Wall Street Journal (6/11/97, A22): "Read nearly any newspaper or magazine movie critic and

> *no matter how high the muck, you'll almost never*
> *encounter an explicit moral concern. Such judg-*
> *ments are, in a word, forbidden."*

---

(12) *Forrest Gump* gave the impression that morality may be okay for those with a low IQ (who are fortunate to be so); normal-intelligence people could see that morality is just a prop and a hoax.

(13) In Los Angeles, several local cinemas were showing a film titled *Devil's Angels* with the accompanying advertisement, "Violence is their God and they hunt in a pack like rabid dogs."[52] Meanwhile, a violent race riot was taking place in the city.

(14) Pessimism plagues our movies and therefore our minds, writes Michael Medved (without realizing that if ethical relativism can't be disproved, then there's nothing for an intellectually honest person to be optimistic about). To quote him:

> About a year ago I was on a panel with executives of three major film studios. After I criticized the irresponsible behavior of the movie industry, one panelist, furious, replied that while Hollywood is always blamed for the bad it does, it's never given credit for its positive impact. "You don't acknowledge that a movie like Lethal Weapon III saved thousands of lives," he said.
>
> I couldn't recall a life-giving message in this blood-spattered thriller. So I asked what he meant. "Well," he replied, "in that movie, right before the big chase scene, there was an intense, three-second close-up showing Mel Gibson and Danny Glover fastening their seat belts."
>
> He was suggesting that people would immediately imitate what they saw for three seconds,

but the rest of the movie's ultra-violent 118 minutes would have no influence at all. Isn't that
contradiction illogical and absurd? [53]

(15)   When we look at radio and television, the situation is no
different. Medved again:

> When an ad runs on TV, no one expects it will
> sell that product to everyone. If the commercial
> influences just one out of a thousand people,
> then it's considered a success. In the same way, if
> TV and movies provoke just one in a thousand
> to behave in the irresponsible, destructive way
> that is too often glorified in the media, then
> those images have made a profound impact on
> society.[54]

(16)   Still more Medved:

> About 350 characters appear each night on
> prime-time TV, but studies show an average of
> seven of these people are murdered every night.
> If this rate applied in reality, then in just 50 days
> everyone in the United States would be killed –
> and the last left could turn off the TV…. A
> Planned Parenthood survey found that every
> year on prime-time TV, there are 65,000 sexual
> references.

These broadcasting executives are like those tobacco executives
who denied any link between smoking and cancer. It may be hard
to believe, but there are people out there who worry about the effect of a Joe Camel billboard ad but who minimize the effects of
ethical relativism and violence in TV and movies. [55]

(17)   Here's more on television's dolorous influence: According to one source, American children, by age twelve, have

spent far more than double the time watching it than they have spent in the schoolroom. This source estimates that they will have watched 101,000 violent episodes, including an estimated 13,400 deaths.[56†] But this will not change so long as ethical relativism is regarded as true.

(18) On radio and television, we have gone from Bach to shock jocks, from the Brady Bunch to Roseann, from Beaver to Beavis, from Horatio Alger to Ernest Hemingway to Saul Bellows.[57†] Saturday morning cartoons are anti-establishmentarian and relativistic; parents would be affronted if they watched them. Television talk shows originally started out with serious subjects, but now they traffic in titillation. "Cultural pollution," William Bennett called them; "the revolt of the revolting," said Senator Joseph Lieberman. No doubt the term "junk TV" is apropos, but then we can also refer to "junk radio" (in almost every listening area, there are twenty pop music stations justifying the "junk" appellation).

(19) "On television, people hop into bed together but never go to church: They do drugs but not homework, and they kill one another."[58] No wonder that in a 1994 *U.S. News* survey, three out of five agreed that things were deteriorating rapidly in the United States[59]; ethical philosophy is not conducted in a vacuum. Yet it is difficult to blame the producers for violent plays and movies; they have much money at risk and feel compelled to give the audiences what they want (although it's a questionable way to make a living).

(20) It might be that television leads to the habit of "sound-bite thinking," the opposite of rational linear thinking (i.e., this causes that, which causes something else, which causes still something else, and so on). But the fault is more likely postmodern relativism. If television viewers wanted rational fare, they would get it. It would be profitable to give it to them. Without a *provable* ethical philosophy, they have no basis for resisting television.

(21) Jenny Jones, hostess of a violent talk show, was hit with a

$25 million verdict in a lawsuit (which she will appeal), but only if we can find an ethical proof will we solve the problem of violent talk shows. Violence is what relativized audiences want.

(22) A recent survey asserts that two out of three television shows include sexual content, compared with about half that in 1998.[60]

(23) Some years ago, the *Tonight Show* was beamed to Europe. In the promo, Jay Leno looks straight into the camera and wisecracked, "We're going to ruin your culture just like we ruined our own."[61] Postmodern relativism at work....
It can make you think this has become the land of Beavis and Butthead rather than of Jefferson and Lincoln.

The lowest common cultural denominator dominates television. This would not be a by-product of democracy if people were less consumed by subjectivism and its consequent voyeurism.

Wait – don't go away. There's still more. We haven't yet looked at everyday culture:

(1) Pleasures become hectic. (It is generally felt that the sure road to happiness is to pursue pleasure like a collar button rolled under a radiator.)

(2) We are witnessing the proletarianization of the dominant minority, which the late historian Arnold Toynbee asserted has always led to the prelude to the disintegration of civilizations.[62]

(3) Basketball star Latrell Sprewells nearly choked his coach and was banished for a year (attempting to kill one's coach – now that's going too far). Brashness is his style. But the CEO for the basketball-shoe company that hired him defended his company's action by saying that "players are not role models off the court." Yet later he enthused about how "kids still identify with ball players."[63]

(4) Birth rates are declining. (If anything goes, why have kids to tie you down?)

(5) The proliferation of video games offers players "the chance to engage in vicarious carnage of every sort.

These sources bring into homes depictions of graphic violence, often sexual in nature, never available to children and young people in the past."[64] Most young viewers do not become violent from this (most).

(6)   Schooling becomes overvocationalized. (If anything goes, what can a liberal education offer?)

(7)   It is now considered broad-minded to talk about values (beliefs) rather than virtues (good/evil). Hitler had scads of values; George Washington had virtues. Where we used to have heroes, we now have only role models.

(8)   Suburbanites become cloistered, segregated, and imprisoned; if anything goes, newcomers have no rights so let's pull up the drawbridge (via large-lot zoning and growth controls) to keep them out.

(9)   *Harper's* magazine advertises that its mission is "to make sense of a nonsensical world"[65] (If all ethical standards are equal, the world surely is nonsensical.)

(10)   Necrophiliac baseball cards sell big (if ethical relativism, why not necrophilia?).[66]

(11)   The animal-rights movement becomes popular. (If ethical relativism, why should humans have any more rights than animals?)

Thomas Mann: (novelist): "...his form is logic but his essence is confusion."

---

(12)   This book is not about abortion. Even pro-choice advocates are generally uncomfortable with abortion, yet it continues to spread, in part due to the broad acceptance of ethical relativism. After all, if people have no provable purpose, then neither do fetuses.

(13)   Underclass ethics has taken over. Writes Charles Murray disparagingly: "Take what you want. Respond violently to anyone who antagonizes you. Despise courtesy as weakness. Take pride in cheating (stealing, lying, exploiting) successfully."[67] Such a coarsening of American life is

no longer universally condemned but our media spews it forth with vigor. If you tell people they can do whatever they wish, they will. Of course, it would be useful if Murray and other social critics like him would attempt (or at least see the necessity for) an ethical proof.

(14) Filthy speech reveals an irritable mood in society, used when one feels "bitchy," which seems to be often. Filthy films and novels become popular because they appeal to the reigning mood of purposeless postmodern relativism. "Everybody I know is sarcastic all the time, in everything they say," according to Scott Dillers, an editor.[68] People nowadays tend toward the snarky, cynical, and hipper-than-thou. We have become the Wise Guy Nation.

(15) Human attention spans narrow to nanoseconds. (Television may have something to do with this, but so does ethical relativism, which says nothing is worth extended attention).

(16) The latest way to speak is to end sentences with a rising inflection, indicating uncertainty and the unknowingness of truth.

(17) The word *appropriate* often replaces the word *true*.

(18) In the Age of the Victim, nothing is considered anyone's fault (but nothing is, if ethical relativism is true).

(19) The decline of manners makes rational discourse difficult. The new birthday cards feature insults; in a cartoon, a birthday-card clerk says to a complaining customer, "Wait till you see next year's batch."

(20) Meaningful conversation becomes a lost art, which is to be expected if it is felt that there is little or nothing meaningful to talk about. Well, maybe it does not really matter: Few people may have anything important to say anymore, but then again no one's really listening.

(21) Debate – the meaningful exchange of different points of view to arrive at the objective truth – is no longer highly regarded. Just express your beliefs – that's regarded as being good enough.

(22) Tattoos, earrings, and body modifications are "in." They

are a repudiation of ethical norms. Random vandalism is also "in," for the same reason.

(23) Then there's punk rage: Grease-painted faces, torn jeans, green hairdos (if not orange or purple), filthy language, tank tops emblazoned with four-letter words, safety pins stuck through nostrils (or other body parts), idealization of Indians and primitives, swastika emblems, chains and manacles, and so on. And why not, if ethical relativism is true?

(24) Love is alien but sex is commonplace. The punks have out-hippied the hippies.

(25) Speech becomes fuzzy and ambiguous, full of "likes," "whatevers," and "you knows" (even when you don't); one critic called it "mallspeak." Adolescents rap, they do not converse, and their profanity is so pervasive it is not considered aberrant any more by mental health professionals.

(26) Punctuation becomes casual. (Relativism obscures precision and standards.)

(27) Short skirts are "like spitting in the eye, protesting against bourgeois values and the Establishment," says fashion photographer Irving Penn. (If the Establishment accepts ethical relativism, it can't logically defend itself and should expect to get spat at in the eye.)[69]

(28) Here's what's in: grungy dress (especially with the young), dress-down Fridays at the office (despite air-conditioning), tielessness, hatlessness, jeans, T-shirts or sweatshirts, jogging shoes, multicolored spiky haircuts, ground sitting (really sprawling), slacks instead of skirts for women, and unharmonious colors. Ethical relativism undercuts all standards. The one-time zoot-suiters have won out; in fact, they've been outdone.

(29) Skinheads and antigovernment white-supremacist militias defy equal rights. (If ethical relativism is true, aren't they entitled to their opinion?) Russia, in particular, is experiencing this phenomenon,[70] but so are other countries. If we are to consider only the welfare of our particular group and to hell with the country, then that is where we will go.

(30) "Now, three generations of an American family – children, parents and grandparents – can promenade the avenues of the world's great cities or spas similarly haberdashed and coutoured: Baggy shorts; T-shirts or sweat shirts with cartoons of woodpeckers or wart hogs or other images of popular-culture icons or asinine one-sentence philosophies; enormous ugly sneakers garishly decorated with various colors and stripes, zigzagged leather strips and mesh fabrics, looking like Buck Rogers spaceships straining to zoom away with the wearers' feet; ridiculous little "fanny packs" around their waists; and inevitably those ghastly caps [generally on backward]."[71] Re the ghastly caps: Some surviving Columbine students were willing to go on national television to talk about the massacre of fifteen classmates, "but by golly they're not going to take off those backward baseball caps to do it."[72] Ethical relativist attitudes even undercut dress codes.

> *Will Herberg* (Intercollegiate Review, *Fall 1986):* *"Children are shown no mercy; whatever their own gifts or predilections, they are dragooned very early into the 'have fun' and 'be a good fellow' competition of their elders."*

(31) Erect bearing, which once was considered a sign of moral rectitude, is out; the American Posture League is long defunct. "Cool stores like Crate & Barrel sell those massive stuffed armchairs that force you to lounge around casually like a sprawled-out cat."[73]

(32) Equality of results is idealized rather than equality of rights. (If nothing is worth anything then we're all equal and entitled to equal results.)

(33) Personal debt, excluding house mortgages and car loans, has risen steeply, especially among the young. Between 1990 and 1995, the average outstanding credit-card balance of households headed by those under 25 grew from $885 to

$1,721[74] (If ethical relativism is true, then why not stiff your creditors, and what is wrong with a little bankruptcy?)

(34)   A Stanford professor of psychology describes the freshman class of 1980 as having "a constricted expression of emotions, a low threshold of boredom, and an apparent absence of joy in anything that is not immediately consumable; hence the significance of music, drugs, alcohol, sex, and status-symbol possessions."[75] No comment.

May Sarton: (Readers Digest, 9/95, p. 191): "It is a very destructive system that worships youth the way we Americans do and gives young people no ideals of maturity to reach for, nothing to look forward to."

---

(35)   Graceless architecture dots our cities. (Relativism undercuts all standards, including aesthetic ones.)

(36)   Loyalty to a nation is diminishing. Patriotism is passè. Nations are busy fragmenting (e.g., Quebec from Canada, Wales and Scotland from the United Kingdom).

(37)   Let us not forget Woody Allen. In his art as in his life, he is the perfect exemplar of the do-whatever-makes-you-feel-good ethos.

(38)   Pornography pervades the Internet. (But only the eradication of ethical relativism can get rid of it; censorship can only tickle the surface of the problem while creating other problems.)

(39)   Parents of preteens: Listen to the music lyrics your kids are listening to – but prepare to be shocked. It's probably not what you had in mind when you were planning how to educate your children.

(40)   Rip-rapper Eminem (no hypocrite, he) won the 2001 Grammy Award.[76]

The artistic judgments expressed herein are purely subjective and unprovable; they express a personal point of view only and readers can feel free to reject them. But we can conclude that ethical relativism clearly dominates contemporary art, music, and literature, and that this is clearly deleterious, both socially and culturally. Ultimately, it can only be negated by an airtight proof of an ethical principle.

References and footnoted material for this chapter begin on page 330 in the appendices.

CHAPTER THREE

The CURRENT RETREAT *from* REASON, PART II

This chapter continues the discussion of Chapter 2.

Ethical Relativism and the Family

If ethical relativism is true, then we can expect the family to be put under stress. These things would occur:

(1) Excessive permissiveness in child-raising
(2) High divorce rate
(3) Excessive illegitimacy
(4) Much fatherlessness
(5) Much abortion
(6) Much teenage suicide

> *Citizens Commission on Human Rights:*
> *"There was a time when a moral individual was universally admired; now, many scorn him as a fool who clings to some outdated code that has no place in our modern*

> *world.... For most of this century, our moral*
> *structure has been under concerted and conscious*
> *assault. And, gradually but surely, we have been*
> *losing the battle.... Juvenile delinquency once con-*
> *sisted of smoking cigarettes. Today, kids kill each*
> *other in the most vicious ways in alarming num-*
> *bers on our city streets."*

Some critics see a "failure of moral nerve" in our time as the cause of weakening parental control. Well yes, but parents will be regarded as hypocrites if they profess high ethical standards and conformity to tradition and society. That may have sufficed in the old days when authority substituted for ethical proof, but clearly not now. With subjective ethical standards, children are left in an ethical vacuum. They're growing up in households quite different from the "Father-Knows-Best" or "Leave-It-to-Beaver" model of years gone by. Parents and children need the bolstering that ethical proof can offer.

Spanking is often equated with child abuse; it's out, but what's in? Who knows? For children, it's uncertainty. Teenage suicide rates[1] and runaways[2] are on the rise. Kids grow up old with drugs and sex.[3] They have always tended to decide issues primarily according to their morality, but what if they are given no provable ethical basis? The generation gap widens when the young assume a different ethical standard than their elders. We teach freedom to the young but not goals or limits; why should we be surprised when they act accordingly? Ethical permissiveness can be terrifying, like a trek through the vast Sahara desert.

Even worse off are those parents who doubt they have the right to determine a child's beliefs. "Adults are confused and at a loss," says psychiatrist Bernard Yudowitz. "They don't know what standards to set for their children or themselves. The bells that used to ring in your head to say no aren't ringing any more."[4] Into this moral vacuum springs television. By 1957, American kids were already watching an hour and a half of television per day,[5] and by now probably more. The family has been ethically relativized.

Since 1970, the social health of America's children has declined from 70 to 36 on a scale of 100. The low was in 1994 when it stood at 31; in 1997 (the last year for which complete statistics were available as of 8/99) the index registered 36, the third lowest in 28 years.[6]

There was a time when America elected a man who looked upon slavery as a moral issue and wanted to put it into the course of ultimate extinction by preventing its spread to the new western territories, but today's ethical relativism would undermine such "moral nerve."

Are economic stress, weakened sexual mores, misplaced government subsidies, lessened individual responsibility, and so on, causes of family pathology and disintegration? Of course, but not basically; they are the manifestations of family pathology and disintegration, not the basic causes. We still need to know why such manifestations exist.

Walter E. Williams (professor and columnist, in More Liberty Means Less Government, *1999, p. 41): "When Moynihan completed his report [on black family dissolution], according to Rowland Evans and Robert Novak [columnists], attempts were made to suppress its release. Professors Lee Rainwater and William Yancey suggested 'it would have been well to reduce the discussion of illegitimacy because of the inflammatory nature of the issue with its inevitable overtones of immorality.'"*

David Blankenhorn (family expert at the Institute for American Values, quoted in John Leo, Two Steps Ahead of the Though Police, *pp. 66-7): The social science data on the impact of "single parenting" is so clear yet so unacceptable to the intelligentsia "that it's the equivalent of having to argue over and over that the world is*

> *round. If it were just a matter of evidence, we*
> *wouldn't be having this debate. It would be over."*

Some labelers claim that it is right-wing to think our culture is dysfunctional, but either it is or it isn't. Left or right has nothing to do with the matter. Rationality should trump labels.

Family disintegration is unfortunately easy to document:

(1) In a relativized society, raising kids can be an uphill battle. Kids today are shaped by – kids today. Peer pressure. Parents are worried about an ever more powerful, ever more wayward and brazen youth culture (which parents cannot logically disparage if they themselves are ethical relativists).

(2) The marriage rate in the United States has plummeted to an all-time low, a 1999 Rutgers University study documented. This highly detailed study found that the national marriage rate dropped 43% over the previous four decades to its lowest point ever.[7†] The study found that the nationwide divorce rate grew after 1970, although it has plateau'd at a high level in recent years. The later age of marriage also indicates marriage decline.

(3) Families now have two breadwinners: "A scant 13 percent of the nation's families include a working father, stay-at-home mother and one or more children."[8] Professional child care is generally not an adequate alternative. Says *Newsweek* (5/10/99, 38): "Sixty-three percent of teenagers are in households where both parents work outside the home… [These teenagers often] are home by themselves in the afternoon. That unwelcome solitude can extend well into the evening; mealtime for this generation too often begins with a forlorn touch of the microwave." As it happens, ethical relativism leads to the two-breadwinner trend, as Chapters 8 and 9 make clear.

Then there's the increase in divorce. It hasn't been kind to the modern family:

(1) "In 1920, there were about 8 divorces per 1,000 married females; in 1985 the number reached 21.7."[9]

(2) "About 14% of white [American] women who married in the 1940s eventually divorced. But of those married in the late 1960s or early 1970s, about 50% have already been divorced."[10]

(3) Divorce rates doubled in the decade after the early 1960s.[11] Nearly one of seven 40-somethings is divorced, double the rate of 1975.[12]

(4) *The Wall Street Journal* (12/28/95), A6: "In 1960 there were four marriages for every divorce, while today there is one divorce for every marriage, and a 60% chance that a couple marrying today will end up divorced or permanently separated."

(5) The divorce rate was 2.8 per 1,000 population in 1948 and 4.3 per 1,000 in 1996.[13]

(6) *Reader's Digest* (6/71), p. 14: "That marriage needs perfecting can be seen from the latest federal statistics showing that the American divorce rate in 1970 was close to two-thirds higher than in 1960 – when it was already one of the highest in the world."

(7) The nationwide divorce rate has grown since 1970. A 7/1/99 Harvard study reports that nearly half of married couples in the United States eventually split up.[14]

Many social problems can be traced to divorce: "Among older, divorced women, there is a more pronounced record of ills – from migraines and high blood pressure to a sense, altogether, of a diminished standard of living and well-being."[15] Numerous examples of the problems posed by divorce can be found in the *Reader's Digest* (7/93, pp. 118-123, summarizing Barbara Defoe Whitehead's definitive article in the *Atlantic Monthly*, 4/93). Divorce is particularly bad for the young children involved.[16]

(8)   *Newsweek* (9/22/75, p. 48): "In an increasing number of divorce proceedings neither parent wants the children."

There should be no condemnation of those who divorce. Clearly, many marriages are not made in heaven. Marriage contracted by those in their twenties (or earlier) may not be viable many years later; marriage partners can start to think differently with the passing of years. Hard-drug users, illegitimate and otherwise dysfunctional parents are criticizable, but not those who divorce. Nevertheless, rising divorce rates are an indication that marriage is weakening and the family is under attack. It can be devastating for society and for the children involved. It reflects a relativist inability to share a common ethical outlook.[17†]

Maggie Gallagher: "...thirty years of the divorce culture have not yet undone the work of ages. [Marriage] is the only word that still speaks."

Enough is sufficient. It would be easy to quote more sources of divorce statistics, but the case has been fully substantiated.

There are some easy-to-apply divorce reforms. We could have a ten-day waiting period for a marriage license. A separation of a year should be one condition for granting a no-fault divorce (maybe longer if children are involved). Teenagers should have premarital counseling as a condition for obtaining a marriage license (the counselor having the legal right to defer marriage).

Illegitimacy is another important sign of a breakdown in the nuclear family. There is no shortage of statistics substantiating its prevalence:

(1)   Charles Murray has pointed out that "22 percent of the children born to white women in 1991 were born out of wedlock, a rate close to the 23.6 percent illegitimacy rate that prevailed among blacks when Daniel Patrick Moynihan drafted his famous 1965 report presaging the breakdown of the black family."[18]

(2)   In 1961, 20% of AFDC children were illegitimate. By 1993

the figure was almost 55%.[19] If we subsidize illegitimacy, we'll have more of it.

(3)   The illegitimacy birth rate in America was 3.5% in 1940, 12.5% in 1948, and 32.4% in 1996.[20] This increase occurred even though there was more condom distribution and birth control clinics in the later periods. The illegitimacy rate has declined recently but still is nowhere near 3.5% or 12.5%. As for AIDS, it generally shouldn't be idealized.

(4)   In 1993, a *Wall Street Journal* article said, "In the past three decades, the percentage of children born outside of marriage has risen fivefold, from 5% to 25%. This caused Senator Patrick Moynihan to comment that "today, a stunning 63% of black children are born out of wedlock..." but then in the same article he had to correct himself: "Alas, no longer. The newest ratios, just this moment arrived, are respectively 28% and 67%."[21]

(5)   *Investor's Business Daily* (6/22/95, A2): "30% of all babies born in 1993 were illegitimate, the government says, compared to just 8% in 1966 and fewer than 4% in 1950." Welfare seems only to exacerbate the problem: Two University of Washington researchers found that states that averaged $200 more a month in 1980 dollars in welfare benefits than the nationwide average were about 33% more likely to have illegitimate births among whites.[22] Maybe subsidizing illegitimacy is not the way to get rid of it.

(6)   The white illegitimacy birth rate doubled from 1980 to 1995 and was especially marked among post-teenage white women.[23] "This was not an increase in [middle-class] Murphy Browns, as some people might surmise. White illegitimacy is overwhelmingly a lower-income phenomenon."[24]

(7)   In 1990, the National Office of Education Statistics (U.S.) asked tenth-graders whether they would consider having a child without being married; only 53% said no.[25]

(8)   Senator Moynihan again: "In 1940, which is the first year for which we have reasonably hard numbers, one Ameri-

can child in twenty-five was born to an unmarried mother. Today the rate nationally is an unacceptable 1 in 3. In many of our major cities, it exceeds 1 in 2."[26] "A community that allows a large number of young men to grow up in broken homes, dominated by women, never acquiring any stable relationship to male authority, never acquiring any rational expectations about the future – that community asks for and gets chaos...crime, violence, unrest, unrestrained lashing out at the whole social structure – these are not only to be expected, they are virtually inevitable."[27]

(9) Illegitimacy appears to create a vicious cycle. Psychologist Kristin Moore says kids born out of wedlock are far more likely to go on welfare than kids born to married parents.[28] Shouldn't we be restigmatizing illegitimacy? We can redefine it as single parenting, but such "defining deviancy down," to use Senator Moynihan's phrase, doesn't alter the fact, or the impact.

(10) *U.S. News & World Report* (6/26/78, p. 59): "Figures released recently by the National Center for Health Statistics show that, for the first time in modern history, more than half of all black infants in the U.S. were born out of wedlock."

(11) "It used to be a shame to have children out of wedlock. That's not true any more," remarked Audrey Hale, director of Project Together, a nonprofit group in Benton Harbor, Michigan, where more than 80% of families are female-headed. But if there are no provable limits on individual freedom, as ethical relativism posits, then there will be more out-of-wedlocking; more than mere counter-ethical-relativist assertion is needed. The rising illegitimacy rate indicates a lack of personal responsibility and an increasingly popular sentiment that the rational limits to individual freedom are quite permeable.

(12) As recently as 1997, even amidst omnipresent prosperity, Robert Bork could say that illegitimacy was on the in-

crease.[29] In 1999, one out of five U.S. women gave birth by age 20.[30]

(13) A study of 18,000 students sponsored by the National Association of Elementary School Principals showed that youngsters from low-income two-parent families outperformed students from high-income single-parent homes.[31]

(14) Other countries, also relativized, are not exempt: "Whereas in 1901 only 4% of births in England and Wales were out of wedlock, by 1992 the figure was 32%,"[32] and about a quarter to two-thirds of babies in industrial countries (Japan excepted) were born out of wedlock.[33] Francis Fukuyama reports that "most Scandinavian countries today have illegitimacy rates nearly double those of the U.S."[34]

(15) According to the U.S. National Center for Health Statistics, illegitimacy was at an all-time high in 1998.[35]

Once again, enough is sufficient. More illegitimacy statistics than are quoted here can be given. The case is more than fully substantiated. An increase in illegitimacy reflects a deepening of the belief that personal freedom should not be limited, despite the restraining influence of AIDS awareness on teenage pregnancy and illegitimacy rates.

Given the rise in divorce and illegitimacy, there is naturally a rise in fatherlessness:

(1) "A generation ago, an American child could reasonably expect to grow up with his father or her father. Today, an American child can reasonably expect not to…. Tonight, about 40% of American children will go to sleep in homes in which their fathers do not live."[36]

(2) Single fathers raising children are becoming more common, with the percentage rising 25% in the past three years; the U.S. Census Bureau (1998) reported that single fathers totaled 2.1 million, up from 1.7 million in 1995 (although mothers still outnumbered fathers 5 to 1).[37]

(3) We should not be surprised that teenage fathers do not

provide good role models for their children. In fact, more than half have disappeared by the time their children have reached grade school.[38] According to the Congressional Budget Office, only 20% give formal child support.[39]

(4) *Reader's Digest* (2/97, p. 67): "Several studies found that the presence of the father is one of the determinants of girls' proficiency in mathematics. And one pioneering study showed that not merely paternal strictness but the amount of time fathers spent reading with their daughters was a strong predictor of their verbal ability. For sons, the results have been equally striking. Studies uncovered a strong relationship between the mathematical abilities of sons and their fathers' involvement. Other studies found a relationship between paternal nurturing and boys' verbal intelligence."

(5) Children not living with both biological parents were four times more likely to be suspended or expelled from school as children who lived with both parents, according to the journal *Family Planning Perspectives*.[40]

(6) Violent children are eleven times more likely not to live with their fathers, according to a study published in the *American Journal of Public Health*.[41]

(7) Said columnist William Raspberry: "My guess is that the greatest increase in child poverty in America is a direct result of the increase in the proportion of mothers-only households."[42]

Fatherlessness undoubtedly has bad social consequences, but we should be asking what causes it. Divorce and illegitimacy are clearly causes, but more basic is the view that no ethical standard can be proven, that all ethical standards are nothing more than mere personal preference or religious belief, in which case there are no limits to doing whatever one likes. More divorce, illegitimacy, and fatherlessness will inevitably follow. This book later has something to say about ethical prooflessness.

It is not easy to gather reliable statistics concerning abortion, but all observers agree that it has increased recently. However we debate the

86

right to life versus the right to choose, clearly an important underlying cause is permissive social attitudes. When only one out of five
teenage females is still a virgin by the age of twenty, an increase in
abortion will inevitably follow.[43] A higher abortion rate is exactly
what we would expect to result from a rise in ethical relativism.

(1)   Abortion became more widespread after the *Roe v. Wade*
       decision in 1973. Since that decision, writes Robert Bork
       (1997), "there have been perhaps over 30 million abortions
       in the United States. Three out of ten conceptions today
       end in the destruction of the fetus."[44] Another source
       claims that "in the mid-1990s, one of every four pregnan-
       cies terminated in abortion in the United States [still
       high]. The procedure ends more than 1.5 million embry-
       onic lives each year."[45] "I don't think that people realize
       that one in four pregnancies ends in abortion," avers
       Steven Levitt, abortion researcher and economist of the
       University of Chicago.[46]

(2)   Abortions out-number homicides by about fifty times.[47]

(3)   The Guttmacher Institute maintains that half of the na-
       tion's pregnancies are unintended, and at the current
       rates, 43% of American women will have at least one abor-
       tion before turning 45.[48]

---

*Irving Kristol on AIDS: "Why is Magic Johnson
regarded by our media as some kind of moral
hero, even a role model for the young? Mr.
Johnson, a basketball player of extraordinary talent, has tested HIV positive, as a result – he tells
us – of having been sexually promiscuous with
more than 200 women. One or some of these
women were infected with the HIV virus. As a
result, a brilliant career has been cut short, as has
a life. It is a sad story, to which compassion and
pity are appropriate responses. But it is also a sordid story of a man defeated by his unruly sexual
appetite. So why are we being asked to see him as*

> *an innocent victim, courageously coping with adversity?...Moreover, it is very probable that in the course of his promiscuous pursuits, he has infected others....*
>
> *"There are some innocent victims, to be sure. There are people who have been infected with the AIDS virus as a result of receiving a tainted blood transfusion. There are some who have contracted the disease from their bisexual husbands or lovers and then transmitted it to their children."*

(4) Since 1985, the number of unmarried opposite-sex couples living together in the U.S. has doubled. [49] Ethical relativism is the cause, abortion the result.

Concerning teenage runawaying and suicide, those who have been living under a rock for all these years should be apprised of the following:

(1) At least one million young Americans, most of them middle class, run away from home each year (1975 report).[50]

(2) The suicide rate for young people aged fifteen to twenty-four rose 300% from 1968 to 1983.[51]

(3) A September 1976 article in the *Columbia Teachers College Record* reported that according to statistics of the U.S. Department of Health, Education and Welfare (since renamed), the annual suicide rate for white males aged fifteen to nineteen shot up from 3.8 per 100,000 in 1951 to 10.3 per 100,000 in 1971; the suicide rate for white females aged fifteen to nineteen increased from 1.7 per 100,000 in 1951 to 3.0 in 1971. Ethical relativism seems to undermine happiness.

(4) 8.7% of teenagers attempted suicide in 1975[52]; researchers at the National Institute of Mental Health say that suicide attempts outnumber actual suicides by 50 to 1.[53] Dr. Cynthia Pfeffer, a Cornell University psychiatrist, found that 33% of adolescents have suicide impulses, up from about 10% in the 1960s.[54]

(5)   "Suicide is the second leading cause of death for young Americans between the ages of 15 and 24,"[55] said a 1995 report. A report issued four years later reported that one in ten college students and one in five high-schoolers seriously considered suicide in 1998, and during the Vietnam War more young men died of suicide than in battle.[56]

(6)   Teenage male suicide is up 30%, 1980 to 1998, according to Stephen R. Covey, a well-known sociologist.[57] Judging from this rising tide of suicide, children seem to be handicapped by their newly acquired postmodern self-direction.

(7)   The teenage incidence of anorexia (a form of attempted suicide) has recently risen precipitously.

(8)   Suicide is an adult problem as well as a teenage problem. There's a suicide attempt in the United States every 42 seconds (1998 report). In the United States, it's the eighth leading cause of death.[58] About 30,000 took their lives in 1997, a year that saw 19,000 homicides.[59] The suicide rate is 95% higher than it was twenty years ago.[60]

Suicide (as an end in itself) is ethically wrong, but an ethical relativist can't consistently maintain that.

Joseph Wood Krutch (New York Times columnist, quoted in Thomas Jefferson Research Center Newsletter, 3/76, p. 1): "Without standards, society lapses into anarchy and the individual becomes aware of an intolerable disharmony between himself and the universe."

Ethical Relativism and Hard Drugs

Drugs alter one's concept of reality, making it impossible to treat things as they are (or to prove an ethical standard). Addicts, to the extent of their addiction, are not free to understand reality or treat it as it is. They feel they are choosing their own reality, their own ethical standard; relativism completely undermines them.

Affluence is seen by some as a cause of drug addiction, but the nonaffluent are affected more by drug addiction. Affluence merely makes it all the more necessary to escape vacuity and find purpose in life, but postmodern ethical relativism makes this more difficult.

Without a doubt, some people are genetically predisposed to alcoholism and drug abuse, but they can more easily fight their predisposition if they haven't been relativized; rationality can reduce alcoholism and drug abuse. Not all of those afflicted are genetically predisposed.

Broken families have also been pointed to as a cause of increasing drug use. True enough, but only to a limited extent; not all addicts come from broken families, not all children of broken families are addicts, and then we need to know what causes broken families.

Drugs were used in the old pre-ethical-relativist days – they have always been available – but the philosophy then was antagonistic to their general use. Modern chemicals have certainly increased the number of hard drugs available, but hashish, the forerunner of marijuana, and cocaine were always available (where do you think the name "*Coca*-Cola" comes from?) and note that English peasants in the Middle Ages got high from LSD made from moldy rye bread. [61]† New technology is not the cause of increased drug use; ethical relativism is.

Free methadone clinics are not the answer. Methadone can be addictive and merely enables most addicts to stave off the inevitable depression that follows even methadone use. [62]

Chapter 1 shows that postmodern ethical relativism is on the rise. We could then expect statistics to show a rise in hard-drug use, and that's exactly what we see:

(1) In 1997, "at least 2.4 million young Americans will use drugs. In a recent survey by University of Michigan research scientists, more than half of high-school seniors admitted to using illicit substances at some point in their lives." [63]

(2) 11.3% of eighth-graders and 20.4% of tenth-graders said they had used marijuana within the last 30 days, according to a U.S. government drug survey. [64]

(3) A U.S. president in the 1990s says he once tried marijuana but did not inhale.

(4)   Joseph Califano Jr.: "A child who uses marijuana before age 12 is 42 times more likely to use cocaine, heroin or other drugs than one who first smokes pot after age 16."[65]

Pittsburgh Post-Gazette (Newspaper headline for Neil Peirce's column, 1/21/83, p. 7): "Drugs and Alcohol are Destroying our Nation's Young People."

---

(5)   "Drug use has increased threefold among young teens in the past five years. They think they are immune and can limit their involvement to soft drugs. That is a delusion – like trying to be a little bit pregnant."[66]

(6)   "Children who smoke pot are 85 times more likely to use cocaine," said the head of Columbia University's Center on Addiction and Substance Abuse."[67]

(7)   University of Michigan researcher Lloyd Johnston has been monitoring adolescent drug use since the mid-1970s and reports that "10% to 30% of people who try heroin get addicted. It's like skydiving with a 10% to 30% chance your parachute isn't going to work."[68]

(8)   "Inhalant abuse among youngsters is rising. A study of 50,000 students in the eighth, tenth and twelfth grades, conducted by the University of Michigan and sponsored by the National Institute on Drug Abuse, revealed that among 18,000 eighth-graders surveyed nationwide, 21.6% admitted having tried inhalants at least once."[69]

Dr. Laura Schlessinger: "Don't marinate in your weaknesses or self-indulgence." [Don't marinate others, either.]

---

(9)   "Today's daughters [in 1996] are 15 times more likely to begin using illegal drugs by the age of 15 than their mothers were."[70]

(10) "Heroin, and to a lesser extent cocaine, ecstasy and

cannabis, are generating big money in a country [Ireland] where excess was once measured in barrels of Guinness."[71] In the United States, ecstasy is rapidly becoming the teenage drug of choice.

(11) An article in *Allure* magazine (7/96) recounted that fashion model Zoe Fleischauer flipped through the British magazine *mag-ID*: "In one shot, the model's head was tilted back in stoned oblivion. Zoe could see the girl's eyes were half open, her pupils rolled back into her head. Then it hit her: The pictures were of her. She hadn't even remembered them being taken."[72]

(12) "Heroin-related deaths in the United States have risen from 1,918 in 1960 to 3,976 in 1995, a 107% increase.[73] Many rock stars have died of drug overdoses: Janis Joplin, Jerry Garcia, Jonathan Melvoin, Kurt Cobain, Shannon Hune, members of the bands Skinny Puppy and Hole. There are many other rockers who overdosed but did not die.[74]

(13) The U.S. Drug Enforcement Administration seized about 93 tons of cocaine in 1989, but only one ton in 1979.[75] Among other reasons was the precipitous rise in ethical relativism. Even with the best of law-enforcement efforts, it is impossible to seize enough drugs to significantly reduce supply or drive up prices for long. Says Drug Enforcement Administration chief Thomas Constantine, "You can do it forever and have a minimal effect on the market. The best control you can have is trying to get American citizens to cease using drugs."[76]

(14) Seventy-eight percent of teens say that illegal drugs are used and sold on school grounds. Substance abuse costs corporate America over $100 billion each year.[77]

(15) In 1999, the U.S. Department of Health & Human Services reported an increase in the use of heroine, methamphetamine ("speed"), and alcohol.[78]

Enough is sufficient. Although many things must be done to counter hard-drug use, they will all ultimately fail if we cannot prove an ethical principle to be true.

Alcohol is a drug and its abuse is clearly on the rise:

(1)   "Around a quarter of the sample in Gallup's 1994 poll, 27% acknowledged alcohol as a 'cause of trouble' in their families.... When Gallup first asked the question in 1950, only 14% identified alcohol as a problem."[79] The rise of postmodern ethical relativism was the basic cause.

(2)   Pollyannas, look the other way: Now we get to binge drinking on college campuses. I will spare the reader the many instances in my files by citing a Harvard University survey that showed that 44% of all undergraduates in the United States engaged in binge drinking.[80] This same study said that 39% drank "to get drunk" in 1993, but 52% had the same objective in 1997.[81] A later Harvard study (dated 7/1/99) found that as many as 490,000 of U.S. college students said they own guns, and those with alcohol problems were twice as likely to have them.[82] College authorities have taken severe repressive measures to reduce the severity of this problem, but if life is meaningless, bingeing on alcohol naturally follows. Postmodern ethical relativism seems to encourage an anything-goes atmosphere.

(3)   Fifty percent of U.S. kids try alcohol by the *fourth* grade. This percentage has tripled, from 1986 to 1996, according to New York State's Research Institute on Addictions.[83]

John R. (rehabbing teen): "My choice music is rap, and all they really rap about is sex, guns, money and drugs."

Ethical Relativism and Crime

If ethical relativism increasingly dominates the thinking of both society and criminals, we could expect an increase in crime. After all, if ethical rights are regarded as no more than convenient social conventions, then why not kill, kidnap, and rob if you think you can get away with it? Why not be envious of richer people and then act upon that envy? If society disarms itself by regarding limits on per-

SOCIETY AT THE CRO§ROADS

sonal freedom as mere opinion only, criminals will have less restraint. They have opinions, too, and have little regard for the opinions of others. Fear of being caught hardly deters them since characteristically they are optimistic about that (and they are often correct). "If it feels good, then it's morally OK," says society. Criminals listen and agree.

When the highly educated believe that criminals are victims of social conditions, that welfare recipients are primarily victims of economic injustice and racism, that hard-drug crimes are victimless, that single parenthood is merely a lifestyle choice, postmodern ethical relativism is at work, and it would be surprising if crime rates were unaffected.

> *John C. Gleeson (captain of San Francisco's Traffic Division) sees a real change in drivers' attitudes towards pedestrians: "There's no civility, no respect. Drivers seem to think, 'If I can save two seconds and run you over, I'll do it.'"*

If people hold to ethical relativism, why shouldn't society impose soft and rubbery sentences? Won't hardened criminals be released to circulate among their future victims? Many intellectuals rail against judgmentalism (unaware they are thereby making a judgment) and express more sympathy for the criminal than for the victim. With ethical rationalism unproved, the language of morality will not be considered sophisticated and a concern for individual rights will be considered naive. Jurors will more likely be intimidated to act like social workers. Criminals will more easily find those in society to excuse them on the grounds that they are not responsible for their acts since they are victims of social conditions ("society made me do it" as in the "sugar-made-me-kill" Twinkie defense). It's pleasant to live in crime-free cities, and we still can if we reform our ethical philosophy. It may be true that disproving ethical relativism will not reform many criminals, but it would help some (Christians have had some success with a moral approach in prison[84]); certainly an ethical proof would change the climate of opinion in which criminals operate.

Postmodern ethical relativism is the moral philosophy of criminal youth gangs, which should give ethical relativists cause to pause. It should come as no surprise that crime has either increased or plateau'd at a high level, but let us examine the factual record in some detail:

(1)   Between 1950 and 1992, according to U.S. Justice Department statistics, the number of serious crimes per 100 people rose from 1.2 to 5.9.[85] Homicides have increased nearly fivefold between 1900 and 1999.[86]

> *James Q. Wilson (prominent Harvard sociologist): "If you are tempted to take the criminal route to the easy life, you may go farther along that route if everywhere you turn you hear educated people saying – indeed, 'proving' – that life is meaningless and moral standards arbitrary."*

---

(2)   More than half of American companies have experienced at least one incident of workplace violence in the past three years, according to a national survey of the Society for Human Resource Management.[87]

(3)   Dennis Prager: "Since 1964, the United States has lost more people to American murderers than it lost in all of its wars against foreign armies put together."[88] That does not count pre-1964 murders. A 1974 study by three mathematicians at the Massachusetts Institute of Technology concluded that "an urban American boy born in 1974 is more likely to die by murder than an American soldier in World War II was to die in combat."[89]

(4)   Insurance fraud has increased with ethical relativism: In 1998, 36% of people surveyed by the Insurance Research Council said it's now considered acceptable to pad claims to make up for past premiums. That's up from 19% in 1993. And 40% would overstate claims to avoid paying a colli-

sion deductible, up from 22% in 1993. The Council says insurance fraud costs firms up to $30 billion a year.[90†]

(5) Computer hackers are often regarded as heroes even though they cost companies (and thus consumers) millions of dollars, maybe billions.[91] They may be smart, but they're criminals nevertheless.

Harrison Rainie (in U.S. News & World Report*):* "The newest terrorists...betray a special kind of madness. The bomb-planter at Centennial Olympic Park [Atlanta, 1996] and, perhaps, the evildoers who brought down TWA Flight 800, seem merely to want to create anarchy and get their jollies from the ensuing commotion. Whatever wrongs they seek to avenge, whatever leviathan they are trying to slay, whatever utopia they envision remains a mystery. Theirs are the ultimate modern crimes – perpetrated largely for the publicity and for the harm they cause. Conscienceless, nihilistic, deadly and done almost for sport, they have no purpose but the insane enjoyment of their performers."

---

(6) The murder rate in 1900 (as measured in ten states and the District of Columbia) was 1.2 per 100,000, but the national murder rate in 1993 was 9.5 per 100,000. (Murder is a reliable crime indicator because it is generally reported.)[92] But it can be worse overseas: In 1993, Colombia was reported to have 70 murders per 100,000 population.[93] In Australia, assaults rose 16% between 1996 and 1998, armed robberies jumped a startling 73%, and unlawful entries went up 8%.[94] As for Mexico, crime is out of control.[95]

(7) John J. DiIulio, Jr., a respected criminologist at Princeton University, reported that between 1977 and 1993 some 350,000 Americans were murdered.[96] In 1998 he estimated

that 500,000 persons who have committed some type of homicide are living free in the community.[97]

(8) Someone is murdered in the United States every 27 minutes on the average. But in the interval between the killings, 70 cars will be stolen, 125 homes will be burglarized, and 405 items will be swiped from someone's office or backyard, at an annual loss, conservatively estimated, of at least $15 billion.[98]

(9) The U.S. property-crime rate in 1998 was about five times greater than it was in the 1950s. (Crime has leveled off recently, but at a high level.)

(10) As reported in 1994, fully 35% of all those arrested for violent crimes were on probation, parole or pretrial release.[99]

(11) "Every year, 43 million Americans [or more than 17% of the total population] are the victims of violent or property crimes."[100]

(12) About 80% of state prisoners are recidivists, the majority being violent.[101] In other words, most future criminals are now in jail.

(13) "Today, in large American cities, fully 40% of young black men between the ages of seventeen and thirty-five are in prison, on probation, or on the lam...."[102]

(14) In 1960, the number of violent crimes in the U.S. "was just under 1,900 per 100,000 people; the number doubled within ten years, and more than tripled to almost 6,000 by 1980. After a brief decline, the crime rate began rising again and had reached almost 5,700 by 1992."[103]

(15) Chicago had a police force in the 1930s about a tenth of the size of the 1990s police force, but the streets were much safer in the 1930s; ethical relativism was less popular then. At night, criminals roam the streets while law-abiding citizens are imprisoned in their homes, afraid to venture out.[104]

John Leo: "Inner-city kids are routinely gunned down by stray bullets while walking to school or sitting in their apartments. Sounds of gunfire are not unusual in schools and upscale neighborhoods. A New York judge, Edwin Torres, says that 'the slaughter of the innocent marches unabated: subway riders, bodega owners, cabdrivers, babies; in laundromats, at cash machines, on elevators, in hallways.' In a letter to [Senator] Moynihan, he talked of 'the numbness, this near narcoleptic state' of a public that no longer expects anything better. People have adjusted to it as a new reality. As Moynihan says, 'The crime level has been normalized.'"

(17)   Car thefts occur in America every 20 seconds at an annual cost of over $7 billion.[105†]

(18)   Do not blame the high rate of incarceration on hard-drug possession. According to Rufus King, a lawyer and specialist in criminal justice, only about 8% (probably less) of the inmates in jail are there for that reason.[106]

(19)   Other countries surpass America in some crimes; relativist attitudes affect many overseas cultures also. Writes Morgan O. Reynolds: "The burglary rate in Australia is 40% higher than that in the U.S., in Canada 12% higher and in England and Wales 30% higher. Sweden and the Netherlands, despite their reputations as nearly crime-free, have burglary rates 35% and 84% greater than the United States. Only a few nations, including France and Switzerland, have lower burglary rates than the United States. The picture is much the same for auto theft.... The English assault rate was slightly higher than America's in 1981, but more than double by 1995."[107†] South Africa has one of the highest crime rates in the world, the per-capita murder rate being about four times that of the United States.[108] In New Zealand the total number of violent offenses increased 615%, from 2,937 in 1960 to 20,987 in 1990; Australia's crime rate paralleled other countries; the num-

ber of serious assaults, for example, rose 391% between 1973 and 1974 and 1991 and 1992 and the robbery rate increased 190%.[109] In Canada, there was a 340% greater incidence of violent crime over its 1965 figure.[110] England's property-crime rate is higher than in crime-ridden United States. Sweden has just as many assaults, robberies, and sex crimes as does the United States.[111] Ethical relativism has risen everywhere.

Sam Ewing (in Wall Street Journal, *4/17/96, A21): "These days you have to move quickly when opportunity knocks. By the time you turn off the alarm system, take off the guard chain and unlock the dead bolt, opportunity may be long gone."*

The rise in teenage lawlessness, almost unheard of a century ago, parallels the rise in ethical relativism. This rise can be an accurate predictor of the future level of crime.

(1) Lately we have been bedeviled by mass shootings perpetrated by hate-filled schizophrenic teenage loners, as at Columbine high school.

(2) The number of juvenile murderers tripled between 1984 and 1994, even though the teenage population remained stable in size.[112†]

(3) Juvenile crime leans toward violent predation. Juvenile homicide was twice as common in 1999 as it was in the mid-1980s.[113] An assistant warden at the Indiana State Penitentiary told Charles Colson that his biggest demand from older inmates was to be protected from the nineteen- and twenty-year-old kids.[114]

(4) In 1991, the FBI warned that violent juvenile crime was growing not only among minority youth in urban areas but among all races, all social classes, and lifestyles.[115†]

(5) The FBI reported that between 1983 and 1992, juvenile arrest rates for violent crime jumped 128% for murder and non-negligent manslaughter (versus 9% for adults); 95%

for aggravated assault (versus 69%); and 25% for rape (versus 14%).

(6) *U.S. News & World Report* (3/25/96, p. 29): "A series of tragedies – many involving young victims – put a human face on the statistics. A pregnant 15-year-old was shot to death on a St. Louis school bus. Two 16-year-old boys were charged in the murder of a Dutch woman tourist who mistakenly ended up in a rough Miami neighborhood. A young mother fell to her death under a New York subway car when a 15-year-old boy allegedly tried to steal her $60 earrings."[116†] Teenagers are more likely than even adults, who are set in their ways, to be affected by ethical relativism.

(7) *U.S. News & World Report* (4/8/91, p. 28): "A 1989 Chicago school survey showed that 39% of the children had seen a shooting."

(8) *TJRC Newsletter* (1-2/84): "Young people between the ages of 13 and 17 represent only 11% of the nation's population, yet account for 40% of all felony arrests."

(9) Between 1933 and 1980, the rates of arrests for persons aged eighteen to twenty-four increased 1,850% and the rates for persons under 18 increased 9,300%.[117]

(10) A 1996 study of the Josephson Institute reported that some 42% of teen boys and 31% of teen girls admitted stealing something during the previous year.[118]

Myron Magnet (Manhattan Institute fellow, The Dream and the Nightmare*): The beliefs and values transmitted to the underclass are "all the wrong ones, retarding rather than promoting self-development: you've been marred by victimization, you can't succeed without special treatment, your success or failure is really not in your own hands...your own self-destructive behavior is a legitimate expression of your history and your oppression."*

If there are no provable moral limits to individual behavior, criminals are no more morally sanctionable than the rest of us, and so sentencing will be light or nonexistent:

(1)   In Virginia, a female doctor, arrested on suspicion of drunk driving, screamed obscenities, tried to kick a state trooper in the groin, up-ended the breathalyzer table, failed the sobriety test, but was found innocent due to Post-Partum Syndrome.[119]

(2)   *Reader's Digest* (3/95, 169): "In Cambridge, Mass., after a 15-year-old was arraigned for murder, his friends cried not for the victim but for the high bail the judge had set. Students told reporters they didn't understand 'what the big deal was all about' and that 'people die every day.'"

(3)   *Reader's Digest* (8/98, 111): "Avon Park, Fla. – A 21-year-old ex-convict who got out of prison on early release was charged a month later with kidnapping and murdering a 78-year-old woman." By preventing adequate punishment, postmodern ethical relativism endangers the lives of innocents.

(4)   *Wall Street Journal* (12/15/97, editorial page): "It took a Swat team risking their lives to get John Edward Armstrong off the street forever. Taking two young children hostage in an Orlando home last Tuesday, after crashing his car and running from the police in another drug-related murder, Armstrong finally wrote the last chapter in his 12-page criminal record."

(5)   "Nationwide, suspects convicted of violence serve less than half their terms in prison."[120]

(6)   Alfred Blumstein of Carnegie Mellon University estimated that about one in 500 burglaries leads to the burglar's imprisonment.[121] But a relativist society is not likely to hound burglars into prison.

Despite the light sentencing, the imprisonment of criminals has escalated. It has gotten out of hand, but ethical relativism offers society no viable alternative.

(1)　One out of 167 Americans was in prison or jail at the end of 1995 (not counting parolees and probationers); state and federal prison populations far exceeded capacity.[122] As a result, many criminals escape long sentences because there is no room for them in prison.[123]

(2)　As of June 1996, 1.7 million Americans were incarcerated – a number roughly equivalent to the population of Utah.[124]

(3)　At the end of 1998, America's state and federal prisons were overstuffed with more than 1.3 million inmates (in local jails there were more), up from 774,000 in 1990.[125]

(4)　According to a 1998 article in the *Washington Monthly*, probationers are roughly three times jailees (together making a grand total of nearly 2% of the population).[126]

(5)　According to the U.S. Bureau of Justice Statistics (1998), if recent incarceration rates remain unchanged, 5% of Americans will serve time in jail at some time in their lives, and an estimated 28% of blacks will spend time in a federal or state prison.[127] We might ignore ethical relativism, but it will not ignore us; if we undermine behavior limits, then criminality and imprisonment will grow and neither retribution, rehabilitation, nor deterrence will work.

Let us turn now to shoplifting:

(1)　Fifteen Giant Tiger Stores of Cleveland reported they lost 3% of their sales to shoplifting (honest shoppers paid the passed-on cost). Store detectives reported that 85% of the nation's shoplifting was done by housewives and they figured that one of every sixty customers tried to steal something.[128] We are all constantly subject to temptation; crooks are not some kind of breed apart. But temptation is furthered by you-are-your-own-ethical-judge postmodern ethical relativism.

(2)　In *1982*, the *Ladies Home Journal* (1 / 82, 100) reported that 140 million instances of pilfering occur each year, and the FBI reported that shoplifting was rising at an annual rate of 20%, "the fastest-growing form of larceny in the United States." The same publication (p. 102) also reported that a five-year study financed by the Federal Law Enforcement Assistance Administration found that shoplifting costs American consumers up to 5 cents on every dollar spent in stores.

(3)   According to the *Reader's Digest* (6/96, 97), retailers spent almost as much to prevent shoplifting as actual shoplifting cost them.

(4)   A Josephson Institute survey found that 33% of high-school students had shoplifted in the previous 12 months and 61% had cheated on an exam. Said one student, "Ethics in today's society? What a joke!"[129] What we have is ethically relativist nihilism.

Now we go to bankruptcies. They have precipitously risen, just like all the other outgrowths of ethics-is-personal-opinion-only relativism:

(1)   A record-shattering 1,350,118 households filed for bankruptcy in 1997, more than 40 times the 1950 figure.[130]

(2)   According to a study by WEFA, a highly regarded econometric research firm in Bala Cynwyd, Pennsylvania, the cost to the U.S. economy was $44 billion; since that cost was passed on, it represented a hidden tax of $400 per household.[131] This, even in good times.

(3)   Concerning bankruptcy, U.S. Rep. James P. Moran (D., Va.) stated: "What was once the option of last resort has become the preferred option."[132] But if ethics is considered a matter of personal opinion only, why not stiff your creditors?

(4)   All taxes on labor and capital are robbery: They undermine the morality of private property. The government sets a bad example for bankruptors and society. (A subsequent chapter explains how to fund a government without such taxes.)[133]†

Crime nowadays is costly, both in America and overseas. Consider the following:

(1)   Crime costs Americans some $105 billion each year in medical costs and lost earnings, but once the pain and suffering and reduced quality of life are included, the 1996 cost climbed to at least $451 billion each year.[134] That's roughly $1,800 for each man, woman, and child in the United States. That does not include the costs of the criminal justice system, private actions to cut crime such as hiring security guards, buying alarm systems, and other crime-defensive actions (e.g., J-bars on steering wheels, car alarms, kill switches, gas cap locks). But the crime rate evidently is no better in ethically relativized England – English clergy are buying "personal security crucifixes" that emit alarms to ward off criminal attackers at a cost of $300-$400.[135] The average home security alarm without fancy gadgetry was priced at about $1,200 in 1998, though systems can go as high as $100,000 and beyond. Monthly monitoring by a security firm costs roughly $25 a month,[136] probably much more.

(2)   The average annual cost per prison inmate in 1996 was $33,334.[137]

(3)   In 1977, the cost of crime fighting was reported to exceed the cost of national defense.[138]†

(4)   Counting all costs, the 1995 cost of crime in the U.S. has been estimated to be $1,376 per household, 2.3% of the GNP.[139] That's equivalent to a hefty tax.

No discussion of crime can be complete without reference to its recent decrease. That's good news, but it is still much higher than it used to be; for instance, 1991 murders in New York City were ten times what they had been in 1951.[140]† In 1999, the U.S. murder rate was five times higher than it was 100 years previously and the U.S. violent crime was three times higher than it was in 1961.[141] According to P. J. O'Rourke, crime has increased fourfold, 1950 to 1998,[142] and the FBI reported that serious crime was higher in 1999 than in 1991.[143]

Crime has been reduced more by the introduction of some new innovative crime-fighting methods than by changes in ethically relativist attitudes, such as the following:

(1) Our police are now using crime maps, computers, huge DNA banks, digital fingerprints, after-school programs, and iris-eye-scan databases. They're targeting high-crime areas, cracking down on small violations (which tend to lead to larger ones), imposing teenage gun-toting bans and curfews, their numbers have increased and more is being spent on policing.[144†] The police now work more closely with the community and with criminally inclined groups, and so on.[145]

(2) Security cameras on busy street corners have been installed.

(3) People are taking more anticrime precautions, like foregoing late-night strolls (thereby putting themselves behind bars in their domiciles while the criminals are free to roam – the inevitable result of false ethical beliefs in society). Videos, computers, and cable television are keeping potential victims home more. Home crime-alarm systems have multiplied; so have window bars, pepper sprays, and cellular phones reporting car crime. Neighborhood crime watches have succeeded. People do not carry much cash now; they use credit cards instead. These factors counter the effects of ethical relativism.

(4) Private security personnel have increased lately; they are now almost three times the number of public police.[146]

(5) Putting more criminals than ever in jail at least takes them off the streets.[147]

(6) Tighter laws on assault guns lessen crime somewhat.

(7) The population is getting older (soon to change) and thus less likely to commit crimes.

(8) The post-1996 prosperity might finally be reducing crime. (But if prosperity should disappear, what then?)

(9) Many communities are gated and stores are now using closed-circuit television to catch shoplifters.[148†] Residen-

tial and business developments are increasingly being designed with anticrime security in mind.

(10) Religious ministers have achieved success with faith-based morality campaigns in prisons.

(11) Many taxicab drivers have developed a siege mentality, imprisoning themselves behind a metal wall in their cabs and driving with welded cash-boxes openable only at the taxicab garage. In order to forestall robberies, bus riders must now offer exact fares.

(12) Some police departments have taken to fudging their crime statistics more than before in order to look more effective.[149†]

In short, these factors unrelated to ethical relativism have made it difficult to measure the impact of ethical relativism.

But there are clouds on the horizon. Don't start celebrating yet. Keep your door locked. The number of fifteen- to twenty-five-year-olds, the group that commits the most violent crimes, has declined significantly in recent years (which accounts in part for the recent decrease in crime) but over the next ten years, the teen population will expand by 17%. The number of children under age ten are more numerous now than they have been since the 1950s.[150] Like athletes, violent criminals operate at their peak between the ages of fifteen and thirty-five. In addition, teen crooks are more menacing than adults because they are liable to act without fully considering the consequences.[151] Says James Alan Fox, Dean of Criminal Justice at Northwestern University, teenagers "pull the trigger over a leather jacket, a pair of sneakers or a joke."[152] Teenagers are less likely to resist the ethical relativist zeitgeist.[153†]

James Alan Fox : "We are facing a bloodbath of teen violence in the years ahead that will make 1995 look like the good old days. This calm before the crime storm won't last much longer."

To conclude: Postmodern ethical relativism dissolves the respect for the life, liberty and property rights of others, demoting such respect from ethical dictate to mere opinion only, thereby promoting criminality, though there are certainly other causes of crime. We have amply seen how crime has increased over time, though not uniformly due to factors other than ethical relativism. Ethical philosophizing is not unhinged from the culture we live in. Teaching ethics is not enough; teaching *provability* could be.

Postmodern Ethical Relativism and the Schools

We have seen how ethical relativism has steadily grown, especially in recent times. Its growing influence has caused a downslide in schools; this has been unfortunately easy to document.

If ethical relativism is on the upswing, we could expect social promotion, bull sessions instead of teaching, a proliferation of self-evaluation or evaluation by beginners (i.e., students), a hodgepodge smorgasbord hip curriculum making pop culture and MTV serious subjects of study; new narrow-focus studies overshadow the old integrating ones and massacres threaten our schools. Textbooks will be dumbed down to reflect lower standards. Curriculum fuzziness will mirror philosophical fuzziness. If there are no standards for knowledge, PC intolerance and conformity will proliferate. (Why fight for what can't be proven?)[154]† Won't a sense of purpose in our schools evaporate, won't standards lower? Won't grade inflation predominate? If ethical standards cannot be proven, what is worth learning? Facts will become disconnected. We could expect teachers and students to exhibit a noticeable lack of motivation. To the fore will spring up multiculturalism (not in the sense that cultures are mixing, which is obviously true, but in the postmodern ethical relativist sense that no culture should be criticized, except for some reason the western European one).

Is the current generation of students enjoying the victories won by previous generations? Will they be able to maintain those victories?

If all ethical standards are equal because they are matters of personal choice only, then pass-fail courses will spread ("no one should fail"), compulsory attendance and courses will be passé, as will be tests, homework, grades, and supervision of teachers. Self-evaluation and cynicism will spread among teachers and students alike. As Montaigne said, "No wind blows in favor of the ship that has no port of destination."[155]

The list of expectations can be extended indefinitely so as to include deconstruction. (That is, all knowledge is a mere social construct; the Holocaust, for instance, may or may not have happened, it being a matter of personal opinion.) Deconstruction stresses the shortcomings of heroes and heroic acts. Knowledge for its own sake is eclipsed by the pursuit of vocational information. (Why not pursue money if life is meaningless and reason is ethically limited?) If ethics is regarded as being oppressive, then why should it be taught? Why should pupils be "value-ridden"? Why not stress self-esteem rather than achievement? If ethical relativism is accepted, won't self-expression trump self-control? Won't feelings trump facts?

Then there's sex. It's here to stay, say the relativized postmodern multiculturalists, so let's teach it and permit it; down with limits to personal freedom; let's distribute condoms in class. "Lifestyle" will replace ethical standards.

Ethical relativism undermines liberal education in our schools, particularly in the United States. If parents, teachers, and students regard education as personal opinion only, then vocationalism will replace liberal education. Mere deprecation of these relativistic trends suffices to a limited extent, but that is very limited if the deprecators fail to offer an ethical proof.

All this is what we could expect. Now let us see what has actually happened.

First, there is the rising tide of postmodern subjectivism in U.S. schools:

(1)   In 1997, among Americans in the 18-34 age group, 79% believe that there are no absolute standards of ethics.[156†]

(2)   Lifestyle replaces moral standards. Writes Princeton professor James Billington, an eminent historian: "The failure of the universities to transmit traditional values has left the field wide open to ideologies and methodologies –

those modern substitutes for religion…. Schools impart values under the guise of imparting none…. In the university's ostensibly value-free and tradition-free environment, there is nonetheless periodic recognition of the need to have some moral commitments. So there are demonstrations for some cause – investment in South Africa [regarding apartheid], American policy in Central America, etc. These involve important moral issues about which people should inform and express themselves. But these tend to be the only publicly shared moral enthusiasms on campus."157

Lewis S. Feuer (Atlantic Monthly, *9/66, p. 87*): *"The intellectual is as susceptible to fashions as any other part of the community, and intellectual fashions are insidious in a way others are not. To fall behind the vanguard is a kind of spiritual death for the intellectual. Thus the old men and the middle-aged men in Berkeley were curiously adrift, and failed to supply that balancing principle, that measure of experience, which was the duty of their years."*

---

(3) If the schools won't teach ethics to our kids, television and peers will.

(4) Writes one observer: "Rather than teaching basic values, educators have tended to focus on *symptoms* of lost values – drugs, teenage pregnancy, dropouts, crime, violence, and a host of others"158 (italics added).

(5) Postmodern Afrocentric scholars have accused Aristotle of stealing his ideas from the library at Alexandria, presumably founded by blacks; the only thing is, the library wasn't built until after Aristotle's death.159

(6) Education seems adrift, its top levels avoiding terms like "right" or "wrong." Notes David Scott, a former physicist and chancellor of the University of Massachusetts: "Mod-

ernism has directed exhaustive objective focus on the world as a database but excluded anything having to do with meaning. This causes wisdom to drop out of favor a goal of education."[160]

(7) From *Newsweek* (6/11/69, p. 64): "At Wellesley College, Sen. Edward W. Brooke ended his commencement speech last week with a list of advances the government has made against social ills. The number of poor families, Brooke told the 401 black-gowned girls and their families and friends, dropped from 22% of the population in 1959 to 13.3% in 1967. When he finished, Hillary Rodham, 21, a sprightly blonde from Park Ridge, Ill., went to the podium. She had been chosen by her graduating classmates as the first student in Wellesley's history to speak at commencement and began her scheduled remarks with a spirited extemporaneous rebuttal. Condemning Brooke's 'empty rhetoric,' Miss Rodham asked, 'What does it mean that 13.3% of Americans are poor? How about talking about the humans, not the statistics?' The graduates rewarded her with a louder and longer ovation than they had given the senator."

(8) Some thirty years later, Karen Lehrman toured women's studies classes at four colleges and found that "sometimes they consist of consciousness-raising psychobabble, with the students' feelings and experiences valued as much as anything professors or texts have to offer." Lehrman also reported "touchy-feely classes" stressing "subjectivity over objectivity, feelings over facts, instinct over logic."[161] But why not, if there is no ethical proof?

Camile Paglia (in Sex, Art, and American Culture): *"Lacan, Derrida and Foucault [postmodernist philosophers] are the perfect prophets for the weak, anxious academic personality, trapped in verbal formulas and perennially defeated by circumstance. They offer self-excul-*

> *pating cosmic explanation for the normal profes-*
> *sorial state of resentment, alienation, dithering*
> *passivity, and inaction."*

(9) Wrote Wendy Shalit on her mandatory freshmen orientation session: "...at a session on 'Race, Gender, Identity and Community,' all the students in my freshman class were herded into a darkened auditorium. There we were asked to keep our eyes closed while various slurs were hurled at us from all directions. This marked the conclusion of 'diversity sensitivity,' and rounded out our freshman orientation.'"[162] Should such ethically relativist diversity substitute for rationality?

(10) If people think that ethics is religion based, they will think that teaching ethics in schools violates separation of church and state.

(11) "While a majority of schools still select a single valedictorian, the trend across the country is to eliminate the honor or spread it around."[163] If ethics is not proven, then we will have equality of result.

(12) In 1918, the National Education Association issued a well-known report that displayed contempt for "mere information."[164] But if ethical relativism is true, why not?

(13) Peggy McIntosh of Wellesley College, one of the doyennes of the relativism-in-education movement, has written that the emphasis on right and wrong answers is culturally oppressive, unfair to minority children.[165]

(14) Observed television and radio personality Charles Osgood: "There are certain things you do because they are right, and certain things you don't do because they are wrong. Many kids are growing up without a sense of that."[166] Well yes, but an ethical proof would help.

(15) Scott Feldmann (intellectual property attorney): "As a student at U.C. Berkeley's Boalt Hall School of Law in the early '90s, I learned that because objective truth is an illusion, the rule of law is a farce."[167]

> *Joyce Maynard (a nineteen-year-old student, quoted in* Newsweek, *12/25/72, her picture displaying tired, dispirited, world-weary eyes): "The big line I remember from our school days was 'There is no one right answer. What's your opinion?'"*

(16) "All knowledge is tentative," reported the Social Studies Syllabus Review & Development Committee (New York State, 1991).[168]

(17) Wrote Max Rafferty, one-time head of California education: "To Dewey, knowledge equals experience. There are no self-evident truths, no universals, no absolutes of any kind. Anything that satisfies a want is good."[169] Well, unless Rafferty *proves* otherwise, why not?

(18) The American Civil Liberties Union complained about a nonsectarian Michigan exhortation to children to "seek truth."[170]

(19) "We must not teach morality," say many educationists. But that is teaching morality.

(20) "Let the parents teach morality, not us," say many educationists. But what if there are no parents, or they do not teach it or know how to?

(21) A professor of philosophy states that he is surrounded by a new crop of young professors who are total nihilists: "They don't believe in anything at all" – this in the philosophy department of a well-known Catholic college.[171]

> *Alexander Solzhenitsyn (quoted in* The Wall Street Journal, *3/15/93, p. A12): "The West…has been undergoing an erosion and obscuring of high morals and ethical ideals."*

(22) The widely accepted "Values Clarification" approach assumes ethical subjectivity (i.e., no proof is possible). The coauthor of a popular teaching textbook asserts that

"when operating with the value theory, it is entirely possible that children will choose not to develop values."[172] But this is uncriticizable if there is no ethical proof.

(23) Sidney Simon of the School of Education at the University of Massachusetts: "None of us has the 'right' set of values to pass on to other people's children."[173]

If we continue to teach about tolerance and diversity instead of about good and evil, we will end up with tolerance of evil. But first we must prove what is good and what is evil.

Let's talk now about ethical instruction. Since ethical subjectivism abounds, we can expect little ethical instruction and much do-whatever-you-want:

(1) John Leo (*U.S. News & World Report*, 6/16/97, 19): "Told by the schools to construct their own value systems, students are often led to challenge parental values or to dismiss almost any adult objections as illegitimate."

(2) "*Relativism* is the key word today," said William Cole of Harvard. "There's a general conception in the literary-academic world that holding things to high standards – like logic – is patriarchal, Eurocentric, and conservative. If you say, 'This paper is no good because you don't support your argument,' that's almost like being racist and sexist."[174] True, so why didn't Cole provide ethical proof?

(3) The feminist *Wellesley Report* disparaged analytical ("vertical") thinking.[175]

> *Yolanda Moses (president, City College of New York, quoted in U.S. New s& World Report, 8/15/94, p. 20): American universities "are products of Western society in which masculine values like an orientation toward achievement and objectivity are valued over cooperation, comnnectedness and subjectivity."*

(4) John Leo (1999) reported that a new resource guide issued

by the U.S. Department of Education maintained that "the use of any educational test which has a significant disparate impact on members of any particular race, national origin, or sex is discriminatory" unless the school using the test can prove otherwise (thus making all educational tests suspect).[176]

(5) One fourth-grade California textbook tells teachers: "Your job is...not to judge the rightness and wrongness of each student's answer. Let those determinations come from the class.... Avoid showing any verbal or nonverbal signs of approval and ask, 'Does everyone agree?'"[177] Fuzzy thinking.

Lewis Carroll (in Alice in Wonderland, *quoted by George F. Will in* Newsweek, *2/7/76, p. 84): A race-course was marked out "in a sort of circle...and then all the party were placed along the course, here and there. There was 'One, two, three, and away!' but they began running when they liked, and left off when they liked, so that it was not easy to know when the race was over. However, when they had been running half-an-hour or so...the Dodo suddenly called out, 'The race is over!' and they all crowded round it, panting and asking, 'But who has won?'...At last the Dodo said, "Everybody has won, and all must have prizes'."*

---

(6) Fritz Perls, the popular founder of Gestalt psychology, set the tone for ethical subjectivism by denouncing intellect as "a drag" and "a whore."[178]

(7) "Do it because I say so," say many teachers. That's inadequate and fascistic; an ethical proof is needed.

Alexis deTocqueville (1835): "America is great because she is good, but if America ever ceases to be good, America will cease to be great."

(8)   George Benson and Thomas Engeman provided impressive evidence in their book *Amoral America* that emphasis on ethical instruction has declined in our schools: "Until the First World War, ethics was a required course (in addition to chapel attendance) for undergraduates in private liberal arts colleges of denominational background. The texts for these courses can still be found in college libraries.... Although these books vary in their approach to the true ground for ethics – emphasizing first natural law, then passion, then reason [i.e., pragmatism] – they all share a common concern for improving the character of students."[179] But without an adequate anti-relativist proof, such an emphasis has vanished from our schools.

(9)   Good penmanship was once taught (in less relativist days) by asking pupils to copy beautifully written moral precepts, such as: "Wit should never wound," "A stitch in time saves nine," "Great men were good boys," "Justice is a common right," and "Zeal for justice is worthy of praise."

George Nicholaw (KNX, Los Angeles): "Children cannot heed a message they have not heard."

(10)   A fourth "R" is needed – Reading, writing, 'rithmetic – and reason.

(11)   Wrote Kathleen Kennedy Townsend, Lieutenant Governor of Maryland: "The consensus of the high school teachers and administrators participating in a curriculum workshop I ran last summer said it all: "Values – we can't get into that."[180] But the teachers and administrators are right, if no ethical principle can be proven true.

(12)   Kathleen Townsend again: "Education was influenced by the pragmatism of William James and John Dewey, which rejected metaphysical notions of human conduct."[181] Pragmatism is ethically relativist.

(13)   Kathleen Townsend again: "One teacher training text says, "There is no right or wrong answer to any question of value."[182] Ethical relativism assumes that all values are equal.

Although ethical instruction has declined in U.S. schools and elsewhere, it has nevertheless proven its worth:

(1)   In issue after issue, the *Thomas Jefferson Research Center Newsletter* (1148 N. Lake Ave., Pasadena, CA 91104) documented that its system of formal character education lowers classroom criminality and improves classroom behavior. For instance, a survey of 176 schools that adopted their values curriculum found that 77% reported a decrease in discipline problems, 68% boasted an increase in attendance, and 64% showed a decrease in vandalism.[183]

(2)   More proof that ethical instruction works in our schools: When it was used in Dade County (Miami), Florida, teachers asserted that student standards noticeably improved and school vandalism dropped 16%.[184†]

(3)   David Gergen says we should teach morality to our children,[185] but how can we successfully do so if all we can tell our children is that ethics is a matter of personal opinion only?

(4)   I was told at Teachers College, Columbia, that attitudes are caught, not taught.

Henry Steele Commager (eminent historian, quoted in Life *magazine, September 1999, p. 40): "Many of the failures we ascribe to contemporary education are in fact failure of a society as a whole."*

Let's talk now about self-esteem, which seems to have become a new morality:

(1)   U.S. Education Secretary Richard Riley backed an expensive "I Like Me" campaign for public schools.[186]

(2)   There is almost no research evidence that self-esteem programs work. For instance, a California task force praised self-esteem as the prime goal of education and used the book *The Social Importance of Self-Esteem* for research, even though it admitted, "One of the disappointing aspects of every chapter in this volume...is how low the associations between self-esteem and its consequences are in research to date."[187]

(3)   Self-esteem is deeply rooted in modern ethical subjectivism. In the words of a *New York Times Magazine* article of 8/28/77: "No one should be made to feel 'inferior' because of his way of speaking and writing." Some teachers emulate slum students in language, habits and dress. Nongraded schools, open classrooms, modular scheduling electives and mini-courses proliferate. "One high school in Connecticut had 125 electives for a student body of 1,000." Evidently, everything was regarded as being as good as everything else.

(4)   After an extensive review of education-school theory, Rita Kramer concluded: "Self-esteem has replaced understanding as the goal of education."[188] But, Ms. Kramer, understanding requires proof.

Self-esteem leads naturally to grade inflation (if educational standards are subjectivized, so will grades):

(1)   College grading goes up like price inflation but in conjunction with lower achievement scores on the SAT. It is one way for weak academic departments to attract students. The professor's power replaces standards of knowledge.

(2)   At Harvard University, the mean grade is better than a B+, up from B- twenty-five years ago. In 1992, 48% of William College's 520 seniors graduated with honors; in 1985, only 31% did.[189] Maybe students are getting brighter, but grade inflation is a more likely explanation.

(3)   *U.S. News & World Report* (2/7/00, 50)[190]†: "More and more students say they're tuning out during high school, yet a record number earn A's. Does this mean America is producing an unusually talented bunch of graduates who don't have to hit the books to make top marks?"

(4)   "Everybody's happy, including the emperor [who wore no clothes]," said Lehigh University education professor Zirkel, "just as long as no one presses the truth on the matter."[191] At best, effort should garner an "E."

(5)   At the University of Pittsburgh, where the average grade rose from C to B from 1969 to 1974, a dean remarked cheerfully that "we're getting away from the old concept that people shall be required to jump through hoops."[192] At Stanford, the chairman of an investigating committee passed the grade-inflation phenomenon off because "we just live in a nonjudgmental society."[193] Someone should inform him that he had just made a judgment.

(6)   According to a *New York Times* article, "studies of gang members and criminals show that their self-esteem is as high as that of overachievers. In fact, one influential study concluded that violence is often the work of people with unrealistically high self-esteem, attacking others who challenge their self-image. Another study disproved the familiar theory that welfare mothers become pregnant to boost their self-esteem.... Will someone please tell the schools?"[194] Yes, but someone should ask the *New York Times* to provide an ethical proof to substitute for self-esteem.

(7)   Though SAT scores are down, grade point averages were up.[195]

(8)   Arthur Levine, president of Columbia University's Teachers College, says his survey supports the contention that "A grades are going through the sky, and C grades are going through the floor."[196]

(9)   In 1972, 28.4% of those taking the SAT said they had A or B averages in high school. By 1993 it was 83%; meanwhile, SAT

scores were falling. Said one Harvard senior: "Since so many of us have A- averages, our grades are meaningless."[197] But the most apropos comment on grade inflation was made by Boston University Professor Edwin Delattre: "If everything is subjective and arbitrary, and you try to apply standards, you run afoul of the prevailing ethos of the time."[198] It's all reminiscent of Garrison Keilor's Lake Wobegon, where all the children are above average.

Cheating is extensive in our schools. It is indicative of the need to strengthen the accepted moral code with more than mere personal exhortation:

(1) According to a survey conducted by Rutgers University professor Donald McCabe, 70% of college students have cheated on a test at least once, 87% have cheated on some form of written work, and 52% have outright copied from someone. He also found that of 15,000 students surveyed at thirty-one mostly private, highly competitive universities, 87% of business majors and 67% of humanities majors cheated at least once during college.[199]

(2) A professor at another American university caught twenty-five business ethics students cheating on a multiple-choice test, but some of those caught blamed him for not administering the test more carefully.[200]

(3) University of Pennsylvania president Sheldon Hackney absolved the students who destroyed an entire run of a campus newspaper because they did not like the paper's editorial. (He said he saw both sides of a difficult question.)[201]

(4) *U.S. News & World Report* (11/22/99, p. 56) cites many studies showing that anywhere from three-quarters of students to an astonishing 98% cheat. So it should not surprise that over 90% of college students say politicians cheat often (Ibid, p. 64). Postmodern ethical relativism undermines society.

(5) In a survey of top high-school juniors and seniors conducted for *Who's Who Among High School Students*, 78%

said they had cheated and 89% said cheating was common at their schools.[202] Postmodern ethical relativism at work.

(6)   Unethical school behavior is not limited to the United States. Drugs, shoplifting, and alcohol have been rising in Japan,[203] though the problem there is not as bad as in the United States, which has been more affected by postmodern ethical relativism.

The equal right to life, liberty, and property can no longer be taken for granted on campuses these days. Consider the following:

(1)   There are massacres in our schools. (Columbine was only one of many.)

(2)   1968 marked a turning point in cultural history and saw assorted student protests break out not only in the United States but also in Belgium, Britain, Egypt, Indonesia, Italy, Mexico, Poland, Spain, France, and West Germany. In the United States, "out went the...tradition of universities policing adolescents in *loco parentis*."[204] There were numerous false fire alarms on college campuses, and law books were burned.[205] I was teaching at the time and remember taking home my papers for fear they would be destroyed overnight. Many on the faculty joined the rioters. A general atmosphere of hysteria prevailed.

(3)   Well-known speakers invited to speak at campuses were hooted down; there was a loss of the tolerance necessary for rational discourse.[206]† Linda Chavez, a former Reagan administration official, was invited to give the commencement address at the University of Northern Colorado, but then it was discovered that she opposed affirmative action and thought Hispanic immigrants should learn English as quickly as possible. Because of these politically incorrect views, she was disinvited by the university president.[207]

(4)   The May 16, 1970 issue (p. 1) of *Measure*, a newsletter, reported these events: Security guards at Columbia University were locked up, the Alma Mater statue was bombed, laboratories at Antioch College were padlocked with an

extortion note being sent to the college authorities, and twelve persons suffered gunshot wounds on the SUNY-Buffalo campus. Of course, if ethical principles are relative because we each create our own values, then terrorist militants will not be restrained. (They surely are sincerely committed to their own values.)

(5)   The schools are no longer havens of safety for our children. The trashing of school bathrooms reflects a much more fundamental problem than merely keeping them in good repair. CNN reported a precipitous rise in school crime, also increased drug use.[208] A 1997 issue of *Investor's Business Daily* reported that "at least three million crimes now occur on or near school grounds each year; a good many of these weren't minor offenses.[209] A 1998 issue of *Investor's Business Daily* reported that one in twelve high schoolers was threatened or injured by a weapon at school; fully 5% of high schoolers say they missed at least one day in the last month because they were afraid to go to school.[210] Sociologist Stephen R. Covey reports that the homicide rate for children aged fourteen to seventeen (in and out of school) has risen 172% since 1985.[211] Pollyannas take note: All of these reports occurred after 1996, when the problem plateaued at a high level. Our schools have literally become blackboard jungles, replete with guards, front-door locks, metal detectors, student identification badges, and so on. They threaten to become combat zones or penal institutions with the inmates in constant danger.[212]†

(6)   A recent poll of MBA students conducted by a pair of business professors found that 73% would hire a competitor's employee to obtain trade secrets. The same survey found that only 60% of *convicted criminals* would do so" (author's italics).[213]

(7)   Fifty-seven percent of public schools reported moderate to serious discipline problems in the 1996-97 school year.[214] Why be good if goodness is only opinion?

(8) In 1940, public school teachers identified these top problems: talking out of turn, chewing gum, making noise, running in halls, cutting in line, dress code infraction, littering. In the more relativist 1990, the top problems were: Drug abuse, alcohol abuse, pregnancy, suicide, rape, robbery, assault.[215]

(9) In 1999, the well-known sociologist Stephen R. Covey reported that one-fourth of all adolescents contracted a sexually transmitted disease before they graduate from high school.[216]

(10) According to a Department of Education survey, more than one in ten public school teachers have been physically assaulted at some time by students.[217]

Michael Schwartz, president, Kent State University, quoted in UCRA Measure, *10/12, p. 8): "The current notion of equality of opportunity is in jeopardy of giving way to the notion of equality of outcome."*

U.S. teacher-education schools especially are beset by problems:

(1) Because of ethical relativism, attempts to shape the character of the young were viewed by the education school intelligentsia as indoctrination and promotion of conformity.

---

*Thomas Sowell (*Inside American education: The Decline, the Deception, the Dogmas, *1993): "Professors of education rank as low among college and university faculty members as education students do among other students.... In short, some of the least qualified students, taught by the least qualified professors in the lowest quality courses supply most American public school teachers."*

---

(2) In education-school theory, equity is out, replaced by equality with the dumbest kid in class. Some education professors proclaimed in *The Harvard Educational Review* that it simply was not fair to judge a program according to how well it taught children to read and calculate; they said the program might have other goals, such as developing a repertoire of abilities for building a broad and varied experiential base.[218]

(3) A study by the Public Agenda research group found that only 7% of education professors think teachers should be conveyers of knowledge. [219]

(4) A 1997 Public Agenda survey documented that disadvantaged children especially benefit from traditional "direct instruction" (i.e., the teacher transmits information directly to the pupils), but even for this group, education professors advocate that children "construct their own knowledge."[220]

(5) College students who earn education degrees have lower LSAT, GMAT and GRE scores than any other major, excepting only social-work majors.[221] When they become teachers, they are apt to preach the ethical relativism they have been taught.

(6) *Newsweek* (12/8/75, 60) reports that "many [high school English] teachers seem to believe that [grammar] rules stifle spontaneity." A Public Agenda poll in 1998 revealed that fewer than one in five education professors think teachers should stress grammar, spelling, and punctuation.[222] Concerning ebonics, read *The Wall Street Journal*, 1/22/97, A14.

(7) Fifty-nine percent of newly graduated teachers in Massachusetts failed a literacy exam given by the state in 1998.[223] Almost 20% of prospective teachers in California failed a statewide test in the years between 1983 and 1991. Ten percent of veteran teachers in Arkansas failed their basic skills exam in 1985, and 10% of Texas teachers could not pass

their state test in 1986. After 1985, Georgia had to fail a large percentage of veteran teachers renewing their licenses.[224]

(8) One-third of high-school math teachers and two-fifths of science teachers neither majored nor minored in their subjects while in college.[225] This may be educational malpractice, but it is the inevitable result of so-what ethical relativism.

(9) Glenda Lappan, a Michigan State math professor, remembers one summer school where teachers bypassed the academic courses and enrolled by the hundreds in a dress-for-success class.[226]

(10) College education departments emphasize feelings, subjectivity, and self-esteem at the expense of actual learning and thinking. But with ethical relativism, how could it be otherwise?

(11) Education schools have seen to it that in the teaching of mathematics, proof, and logic are out. Textbooks have become fat "coffee-table books." Constructivism dominates; constructivists say that students understand and remember only what they "construct" for themselves. Teachers are demoted to "facilitators," wandering from one "cooperative learning group" to another.

(12) Albert Einstein couldn't teach today in U.S. public schools.

If anything goes ethically, then fads will sweep through our schools:

(1) Curriculum diversity has been advocated by ethical relativists for whom objective truth has been replaced by race, gender, and class (the postmodernist trinity). Is this not the new Marxism?

(2) Here's a partial list of teacher-education courses at the University of Massachusetts – Amherst: "Social Diversity in Education" (four different courses), "Embracing Diversity," "Diversity and Change," "Oppression & Education," "Introduction to Multicultural Education," "Jewish Oppression," Lesbian/Gay/Bisexual Oppression," "Oppression of the Disabled," "Erroneous Beliefs." Maybe this ex-

plains why 59% of prospective teachers in Massachusetts flunked a basic literacy test. Comments John Leo, tongue-in-cheek: "But at least they are prepared to drill children in separatism, oppression, and erroneous beliefs."[227]

(3)   Postmodern ethical relativism has infected our colleges. They are unsure of their mission and offer such pop culture courses as "The Biology of *ER*" (Purdue), "Issues in Rock Music and Rock Culture" (Columbia), "The Physics, History and Technique of Juggling" (Duke), "Vampires: The Undead" (U/Penn.)[228] If college professors cannot prove what ought to be (any more than kindergarten teachers can) then they should not expect their students to prefer a liberal education.

(4)   U.S. colleges are dumping Shakespeare for Madonna and vegetarianism. Georgetown offers such courses as "Film Noir / Hardboiled Detective Fiction" and "Prison Literature." Oberlin offers "S-M Debates" and "ACT-UP."[229] (But our high schools are not far behind: An English magnet program for the best and brightest in the Los Angeles suburb of North Hollywood schedules a day each week for working in the school garden, but this course [Weed-pulling 101?] takes time away from a consideration of Shakespeare).[230] The teacher says this gives these bright students "a chance to fail."

(5)   Walter Williams again: "The National Association of Scholars put out a devastating report about the dumbing-down of college curriculum that includes courses for credit like 'queer theory,' the works of Pee Wee Herman, and watching Oprah or Montel Williams."[231] But he did not attempt to prove what should take their place.

(6)   More weird college courses: "How Tasty Were My French Sisters" (Stanford University) and "The African American Vampire" (Florida State University). Anything goes in a relativist world.[232]

(7)   A student was rejected by University of California at Los

Angeles as a tutor because it was felt he might not validate his tutee's feelings.

(8)   The whole math approach asserts that getting the right answer to a math problem can be much less important than having a good rationale for a wrong one. It can be called "fuzzy math." A standards commission chaired by a past president of the National Council of Teachers of Mathematics denounced the schools' "preoccupation with computation and other traditional skills." Students, the commission said, should use calculators so that they could become "active participants in creating knowledge."[233]

(9)   The Department of Defense introduced fuzzy whole math in its schools, holding that right or wrong answers are not as critical as showing thinking skills.[234] It didn't work.

(10)   Lynne Cheney (former chairperson of the National Endowment for the Humanities) noted that some in the U.S. math community have proposed a scoring system for a national math exam by which students could get full credit for wrong answers if accompanied by "appropriate strategies."[235]

(11)   Then there are the famous (or infamous) sex-education classes where elementary pupils learn how to stretch a condom over a banana.

(12)   Millions of dollars were spent on classroom computers and other technology, but a study showed they had no effect. [236]

(13)   A report by the American Association of University Women asserted that there was no evidence that "single sex education works."[237] With ethical relativism it certainly won't.

(14)   In affluent Clarkstown High School, the relativized teacher in a class titled "Sex Respect" informed the fifteen- and sixteen-year-olds that "within a year you will no longer be able to call them rubbers [condoms]. They're going to be made out of polyurethane. They'll be much thinner and more effective, like Saran Wrap." In the same

high school, a student said that society needs more values. The teacher replied, "It's not that simple. In a free society it's very difficult to say, This is right and this is not."[238] But unless a disproof of ethical relativism is offered, the teacher is correct.

(15) School uniforms can help because students might behave the way they are dressed (sloppy dressing leads to sloppy thinking) but given ethical relativism, school uniforms will not suffice.

(16) Is the open classroom (no doors, no walls) favored by postmodernists better termed a bullpen of babble?

We should not be surprised that primary and secondary students in U.S. schools ridden by ethical relativism are not doing well:

(1) What students do not know about their country's history would fill a book (and has). According to a 1994 survey of the National Assessment of Educational Progress, only one high school senior in five could say in which century Lincoln was president; only one in five knew anything about Reconstruction. [239] Maybe it's because many history textbooks, as compared with earlier works, are fraught with dumbed-down, multiculturalist, postmodern ethical relativism. Our smart bombs are smarter than our high school kids – at least they can find Kosovo.

(2) New York recently found that more than half its fourth graders flunked standard English.[240]

(3) High school students averaged 48% on a 1998-99 nationwide survey of basic economic principles conducted by the National Council on Economic Education (U.S.).[241]

(4) Benjamin J. Stein (Hollywood writer): "I have not yet found one single student in Los Angeles...who could tell me the years when World War II was fought.... A few have known how many U.S. senators California has, but none has known how many Nevada or Oregon has. ('Really? Even though they're so small?')"[242]

National Assessment of Educational Progress:
"Between 1970 and 1980, both 13- and 17-year-olds became less likely to try to interpret what they read and more likely to simply make unexplained value judgments about it. One way of character-izing the change during the '70s is to say that 17-year-olds' papers became somewhat more like 13-year-olds' papers. The end result is an emphasis on shallow and superficial opinions at the expense of reasoned and disciplined thought...."

---

(5) According to a survey of *Who's Who Among American High Schools*, more than half of the teens surveyed said they spend only an hour a day or less on homework. Some 57% of teachers say students are less studious now than they were when the teachers started their careers.[243]

(6) U.S. Department of Education researchers found that American textbooks are "a mile wide and an inch deep."[244] Ethical relativism = standardlessness.

(7) Walter Williams: "On a recent test, one-third of high school seniors couldn't identify Abraham Lincoln or the countries we fought during World War II."[245]

(8) A U.S. Department of Education report found that only 11% of twelfth-grade students tested at the proficient level in history; in eighth grade, 14% tested at that level; in fourth grade, 17%.[246]†

(9) About one-third of job applicants tested by the American Management Association in 1998 lacked the literacy or math skills for the positions they sought.[247] Maybe our schools spend too much time teaching students how to put condoms on bananas.

(10) The public school curriculum is filling up on nonacademic subjects. A report (1994) of the National Educational Commission on Time & Learning found that high schools require students to spend barely 41% of classroom time

on academic subjects. [248] Don't think that philosophy has no impact on real life.

(11) In 1940, a sixth-grade reader was assumed to have a knowledge of 100,000 words; in 1990, 25,000.[249] Language skills will deteriorate if nothing is regarded as worth learning.

(12) A member of the New York State's Regents Committee was reported as saying, "We don't need text books on World War II. We only need to ask one question: Why was the bomb dropped?"[250]

(13) A friend of mine, Esko Newhill, told me that the publishers of his high school textbook on sociology had asked him to dumb down a revision of his textbook. (He refused.)

(14) American history students in grades five through eight should study ancient Mali's grandiose Mansa Musa, according to a multicultural study funded by the U.S. National Endowment for the Humanities.[251] This study also asked students to know the exploits of Ebenezer McIntosh (a brawling street lout of the 1760s who whipped up anti-British mobs to sack the homes of various colonial officials).[252] Doesn't studying Mansa Musa and Ebenezer McIntosh divert attention from George Washington, Benjamin Franklin, and the like? This would seem to be the fruit of ethically relativist multiculturalism.

(15) The guide to a widely used elementary-level reading series advises: "To help students begin to develop cultural awareness and understanding, they first need to learn who they are – their ethnicity, gender, and social class – and how they are viewed by society.... Both students and teachers have participated in relationships of domination, submission, oppression, and privilege which have helped to shape who they are and how they see the world."[253] – *sic transit* postmodern ethical relativism.

(16) John Leo: "Our high school students don't seem able to find China on the map. In one survey, 45% of high school juniors didn't realize that nine is 9% of one hundred, and in another, 95% of seniors couldn't figure out a bus sched-

ule. American business is said to spend as much money each year teaching basics to high school grads as the public schools spend on high school education (mis-education?)."[254]

(17)   Two professors at Indiana University of Pennsylvania actually urged teachers to encourage intentional errors in English as "the only way to end its oppression of linguistic minorities and learning writers." (They later won an award from the National Council of Teachers of English.)[255]

(18)   Union rules often require that teaching perks go to senior teachers, not to the junior teachers that need them most. Also, schools tend to get bigger budgets if they *fail*.

(19)   WNBC's *Today Show* (2/17/99, 8:08 a.m.): One in five teachers feel unprepared.

(20)   A 1999 study by the U.S. Education Department revealed that a majority of 60,000 students lack grade-level writing skills.[256] If students cannot write well, they are unlikely to think well. But if anything goes –?

(21)   In 1966, 64% of high school seniors reported doing less than one hour of homework per night.[257] Why do homework if what you know is as good as what you have been taught?

(22)   In 1995, nearly 30% of first-time college freshmen enrolled in at least one remedial course, and 80% of all public four-year universities offered remedial courses.[258] Why learn if you embrace ethical relativism?

(23)   A U.S. Department of Education study found that only one in four high school seniors is well informed about constitutional government, how the nation's laws work, and the ideals and values of democracy. [259]

(24)   According to U.S. manufacturers, 40% of all seventeen-year-olds do not have the math skills and 60% lack the reading skills to hold down a production job at a manufacturing company.[260] No comment.

(25)   The 1996 national English standards stressed word-identification strategies and "writing process elements."[261] Meanwhile, the language skills of U.S. students continue

to deteriorate. If ethical relativism predominates, then so will fuzzy language.

(26) U.S. fourth-grade students did fairly well in international math and science comparisons but less well in the eighth grade and were at the bottom in the twelfth grade.[262] It takes time for ethical relativism to maul math, science, truth, and reason.

(27) The U.S. federal government says it will spend $12 billion over seven years to hire 100,000 new teachers for grades one through three in order to reduce class size from twenty-two to a hoped-for eighteen.[263] But this small reduction is unlikely to make a big difference, says Robert Slavin, a researcher at Johns Hopkins University and head of a successful reading program.[264] Anyway, as of this writing these teachers have not yet been hired, and they are almost certain, if ever hired, to be inexperienced. Keep in mind that the average South Korean class size is forty-three.[265] It would be more effective to combat the view that there is really nothing worth learning.

(28) Some Texas high school football teams have twelve coaches and electric cleat cleaners.[266] Well, why not stress football if all real and ethical knowledge is personal opinion only? Football players already have opinions.

(29) *U.S. News & World Report* (4/1/96, 58): "Seventy-two percent of students can't meet suggested standards [in reading & writing]. Just 1 in 3 can write a well-developed review of a school performance, and only 8 percent are able to write a persuasive essay on a subject like: Why random drug searches should (or should not) be allowed in school." Three in four cannot meet suggested standards in mathematics, nor can 86% meet history standards.

(30) Illinois tested four elementary grades; 40% of the pupils flunked. In New York, more than half of all fourth graders failed the English test. In Virginia, tests found that 93% of public schools were failing to teach students to state standards. 43% of Massachusetts teachers failed performance

tests.[267] Isn't this consistent with the predominance of ethical relativism?

(31) The SATs have been "recentered" (i.e., dumbed down) and yet, year after year, our students do poorly on them.[268]†

(32) A special twenty-one-member panel headed by former Secretary of Labor William Wirtz concluded that "there is clearly observable evidence of diminished seriousness of purpose and attention to mastery of skills and knowledge."[269] The reason is to be found in the dominant ethical philosophy.

(33) Despite the more than six dozen illiteracy programs, literacy among young people has precipitously declined.[270] Less than half of one percent of World War II Army recruits read below a fourth-grade level, but today, that proportion is ten times higher.[271]

(34) Sandra Stotsky, Harvard researcher and author of *Losing Our Language*, a study of elementary-reading textbooks, found that a strong theme of the new readers is the value of emotive responses over analytical reasoning. Wrote one reviewer: "It's not hard to picture angry eleven-year-old boys working out their 'feelings' about volatile subjects – like black-white conflict – with their fists at recess."[272] An ethical proof is needed.

(35) According to Walter Williams, the parents of a sixth-grade girl in East Stroudsburg, Pennsylvania, are suing the school district because she was subject to a body-cavity search. The school physician claimed it was necessary to "retract the labia."[273] Better she should have spent her time proving ethicality.

(36) The mandatory New York State eleventh grade American history curriculum (1987 edition) listed the Iroquois tribal government along with the Enlightenment as one of two major influences on the American Constitution; gone were references to Ben Franklin, James Madison, Andrew Jackson, Louisiana Purchase, the conduct of the Civil

War, and the Gettysburg Address.[274] "Don't know much about history," goes the old song lyric….

(37) Sandra Stotsky examined state educational standards and found that fewer than half demanded "competence in using standard English orally and in writing."[275] And why not, if Stotsky et al. provide no ethical proof?

(38) The National Commission on Education has concluded that "for the first time in history, the educational skills of one generation will not surpass, will not equal, will not even approach those of their parents….[276]

(39) There is a 50% attrition rate of teachers in their first five years of teaching[277] – but if teachers are called "facilitators" or "co-learners," why teach? What is to be taught?

I had to leave out some really good statistics showing how badly our schools are doing and therefore how much an ethical proof is needed to counter ethical relativism. But I didn't want to unbalance the book. Just remember – our schools are the mirror of our society.

American students have not done well in international comparisons, hindered as they've been by ethical relativism:

(1) Among the twenty-one nations in a recent highly publicized study, relativized American high school seniors came in sixteenth in general science knowledge, nineteenth in general math skills, and last in physics. The U.S. performance was actually worse than it looked, because Asian nations, which do particularly well in these comparisons, were not involved in this study.[278] If these Asian nations had participated, the United States might have been fighting for thirty-ninth or fortieth place in a forty-one-nation field.[279] The only antidote for the United States: Get rid of ethical relativism.

John Updike (quoted in The Wall Street Journal, *3/15/93, p. A12): "The fact that, compared to the inhabitants of Africa and Russia, we still live*

> *well cannot ease the pain of feeling we no longer*
> *live nobly."*

(2)   It may be thought that international comparisons fail because the U.S. educates a larger percentage of its children than do foreign countries, but this explanation cannot excuse a comparison, invidious for the United States, between its *advanced* students and foreign *advanced* students. These Americans came in fifteenth among sixteen nations in math and sixteenth (dead last) in science.[280] Another source reports that when 14% of American seniors qualified for an international math test they came out second worst out of forty-one countries.[281] But not to worry: New immigrants, not yet fully relativized by American culture, might yet save the country.

(3)   A U.S. Department of Education study (1991) found that U.S. thirteen-year-olds scored below twelve other countries in both math and science achievement.[282] But a *U.S. News & World Report* article (8/1/94, 15) reported they were next to last. (They edged out Jordanians.)

(4)   Writes Walter Williams: "Kids from poor countries like Ireland and Slovenia beat the daylights out of our kids in math. On international surveys, French kids come in second in reading ability while our kids come in sixth. Might money explain the difference? The answer is a big fat no. We spend more money per pupil on education than any other country – $6,000 on the average while the French spend $4,600."[283] A more likely reason for this disparity is that U.S. kids are more affected by ethical relativism than non-U.S. kids. But that's all right: American students scored highest on self-esteem.

(5)   It would be hard to think of a more monocultural, insular and self-complacent nation than Japan, yet its students far outshine American students in international competitions, indicating that multiculturalism will not improve education. Only an ethical proof will.

(6) U.S. primary schools spend 25% more than the international average, yet our students compare badly.[284] Don't blame television: The American students aren't watching significantly more television than their peers overseas.[285]

(7) "In the U.S., we call our best students nerd or dweeb," says Educational Testing Service president Gregory Anrig. "As a nation, I think we have conflicting feelings about people who are smart, and as parents, we send conflicting messages to our children about being smart."[286] But such "conflicting feelings" follow from ethical relativism.

National Commission on Excellence in Education (1983, quoted in Investors' Business Daily, *4/3/96, p. A2): "If an unfriendly foreign power had attempted to impose on America the mediocre educational performance that exists today, we might well have viewed it as an act of war."*

If U.S. primary and secondary students aren't measuring up to standards, we cannot be optimistic about U.S. college students. Consider the following:

(1) In 1995, 22% of freshmen enrolled in public four-year institutions and 41% of those in two-year colleges had to take remedial classes.[287] Seventy-six percent of professors teaching college freshmen and almost two-thirds of employers believe a high school diploma isn't a guarantee that a student has learned the basics.[288] Albert Shanker, past AFT president, reported that 89% of four-year colleges offer remediation.[289] The California State University system found that 54% of the 1994 class needed basic instruction.[290] Again, *sic semper* ethical relativism.

(2) The U.S. government's National Assessment of Educational Progress reported that student papers in 1974 showed a trend toward very short words, a simple vocabu-

lary and incoherent paragraphs as compared with student papers written in 1969.[291]

(3)   According to the National Endowment for the Humanities, large numbers of college seniors believed that Karl Marx's dictum, "from each according to his ability, to each according to his need," is in the U.S. Constitution. Nor do they have any idea when Columbus discovered America.

(4)   One survey found that only about 20% of eligible voters in the 18-25 age group cast ballots in the 1996 presidential election.[292] In national surveys 58% of college freshmen in 1966 said they considered it important to keep abreast of political affairs; by 1996 only 29% felt that way.[293]

(5)   Walter Williams: "A recent U.S. Department of Education report said that 53% of college graduates could not figure out how much change they should get back after putting down $3 to pay for a 60-cent bowl of soup and a $1.95 sandwich." [294]

(6)   A study by UCLA and the American Council of Education compared the attitudes of nine million freshmen, 1967 to 1997. The study found that interest in such philosophical questions as "What is life all about?" and "Who is God?" is down, while interest in being very well off financially was up.[295] This is what postmodern ethical relativism has wrought.

(7)   A 1996 study by the National Association of Scholars of 50 top American colleges reported that the average class length fell by 6% from 1964 to 1993, while the number of class days a year dropped by nearly a fifth in that same time.[296]

(8)   A 1998 report found that 62% of CCNY graduates (my alma mater – I attended 1944-48) did not pass the state's certification test although 80% of them ended up teaching in New York City schools.[297]

(9)   Commented philosopher Christina Hoff Sommers (Clark University): "The half-baked relativism of the college student tends to undermine his common sense. In a term

paper that is far from atypical, one of my students wrote
that Jonathan Swift's 'modest proposal' for solving the
problem of hunger in Ireland by harvesting Irish babies
for food was "good for Swift's society, but not for ours."[298]
Ms. Sommers, what is "whole-baked relativism"?

It has been reported that some college students think that Latin
Americans speak Latin, but I have not been able to substantiate that.

U.S. education doesn't suffer from having too little money
spent on it:

(1)　In 1960, for every U.S. public school teacher there were approximately twenty-six students enrolled; in 1995, there
were seventeen.[299] A study by Eric Hanushek, a University
of Rochester educational researcher, found that between
1970 and 1990, American schools reduced the average
pupil-teacher ratio to 17.2 from 22.3; he concluded after ex-
amining nearly 200 studies that "extensive evidence that
teacher salaries, per-pupil expenditures and class size were
unrelated to academic performance.[300] A study by the National Assessment of Educational Progress concurred.[301]
If knowledge is regarded as mere personal opinion, mone-
tary efforts will be mere fingers in a leaking dam.

(2)　Since 1960, pupil-teacher ratios in the public schools have
fallen by a third, teachers have better credentials, and per-
student spending has tripled, yet student performance
has declined.[302] Attitudinal change can better account for
this slide.

(3)　The average salary of U.S. public school teachers rose 45%
in real dollars from 1960 to 1995.[303] The basic way to improve education: Prove ethics. It doesn't cost anything.

(4)　Writes Thomas Sowell: "In mathematics…the average
class size in Japan is 43, compared to 20 in the U.S. Within
the United States, the ratio of pupils to teachers declined
throughout the entire era from the 1960s to the 1980s,
when test scores were also declining."[304]

(5)   Real per pupil spending more than tripled between 1960 and 1996.[305] The United States is near the top in education spending but close to last in achievement. If U.S. schools were businesses, they would be headed for bankruptcy.

(6)   John Chubb, formerly a senior fellow with the Brookings Institution, and Terry Moe of Stanford University, examined characteristics of more than 500 public and private high schools. They found that neither total spending, teacher salaries, nor student-teacher ratios had any significant effect upon student performance.[306]

(7)   New York City spent $68 million to reduce its student dropout rate, only to see it rise by 5%.[307] Better it should have provided an ethical proof – that would've been cheaper.

(8)   Only 55% of the District of Columbia's ninth-graders in 1985[308] graduated high school in 1989, a much lower percentage than the national average even though D.C. expenditures were 30% higher than the national average.[309]

(9)   Maybe private-school vouchers will save our public schools despite ethical relativism. Well, probably vouchers are a good idea: Give parents and children a choice and do not penalize parents with both taxes and tuition if they choose private or home-schooling for their children. Schools run by racists can make us nervous, but certainly private voucher-supported schools can be tried out here and there rather than everywhere at once. (This may require national tests to make sure voucher schools are up to standard.) If voucher students (many of whom are poor) do better than public-school students, perhaps it is because they are not facing such tough competition. But voucher schools would be more effective without ethical relativism.[310†]

Lest you think that ethical relativism is only burdening U.S. schools, you should know that an English observer, Dr. Theodore Dalrymple, reports many examples of educational dumbing down in his country. He concludes that "English schools give you Alzheimer's."[311]

To conclude: We are a nation that perhaps for the first time in the history of mankind, fears its young. What's gone wrong? Education now tops the list of the most important public issues[312] and it accurately reflects the surrounding society. Although I had to leave out 700 good sources on educational dissolution, it must be said that in some ways our schools are better than ever – they are less racist and sexist than they have ever been – but in many important ways they are seriously deficient, primarily because they, like society at large, rest on the shifting sands of ethical relativism. If nothing can be proven worthy of time and effort, then our schools and our society cannot avoid failure. Schools reflect society and if the schools are defective, so is society.

> *Robert Hutchins (President, University of Chicago): "Relativism, scientism, skepticism and anti-intellectualism, the Four Horsemen of the philosophical Apocalypse, have produced that chaos in education which will end in the disintegration of the West."*

References and footnoted material for this chapter begin on page 334 in the appendices.

CHAPTER FOUR

Why
CULTURAL
COLLAPSE?

*This chapter examines the reasons often given
for the cultural collapse described in the previous two chapters.*

Today, we stand at the very pinnacle of accomplishment in
the world's history. We are daily flooded with technological
advances. Our medical researchers have expanded life expectancy far beyond what people a mere century ago could
have expected. Child labor, race and sex discrimination, unsafe working conditions, and so on have been greatly alleviat-
ed. Income per capita is higher than ever. Yet the quality of literature, art, music, entertainment, and everyday life
constantly lowers. Crime, hard-drug use, illegitimacy, and
suicide are rising. Our families and schools are disintegrating.
Scientific reasoning is under attack. The silent majority
seems unable to defend itself. A crisis of confidence exists.
We can legitimately ask how this can be. At the very moment
when our material accomplishments are at their apex, our so-

cial philosophy is at its nadir. Here are some frequent explanations, with accompanying analysis:

(1) *Violent television, radio, movies, video games, dumbed-down schooling, rock lyrics, etc. are the prime causes of our cultural collapse.* This is a commonly offered explanation,[1†] but it cannot suffice because these are the details, the manifestations, of cultural collapse. We still want to know what caused these things to happen. They are the evidence rather than the explanation of our cultural collapse. We should not ascribe the cause of rain, for instance, to the falling of a barometric reading. To be sure, violence breeds violence, but what breeds violence initially? Let us not be satisfied with superficial social analysis.

Many social commentators have nevertheless tried to explain cultural dysfunction in this fashion. Robert Bork, for example, ascribes the cause of cultural collapse to radical individualism and equalitarianism.[2] Well yes, if you realize what he means by these terms: He does not oppose what is ordinarily defined as individualism and equalitarianism, but when he calls these qualities "radical," he refers to the subjectivication of individual ethical values which results in *excessive* (i.e., limitless) individualism and equalitarianism – here called ethical relativism. When he refers to radical or subjective equalitarianism, he means equality of result. OK, such equality is wrong, we should want equality of rights instead, but this needs proof. However, Bork does not prove any ethical standard to be true, nor does he attempt to do so; he just busily delineates the cultural collapse, which is useful as far as it goes.

(2) *Peering below the surface of events, some say that the increasing affluence we have enjoyed has loosened the individual from the necessity of being rational; people now have the money to indulge in hard drugs and free sex.* But:

　　(a) Many of the affluent reject ethical relativism. The two are unrelated.

　　(b) The affluent engage in cultural dysfunctions (e.g.,

crime, hard-drug use) less than the nonaffluent. General affluence merely makes an antidote to ethical relativism all the more desirable.

(c) This explanation can hardly account for the rise in ethical irrationalism among the nonaffluent.

(d) Nor can it account for the rise in ethical irrationalism in nonaffluent countries.

(3) *Some social analysts say that poverty has caused the increase in crime, hard-drug use, violent entertainment, and so on.* (this is the exact reverse of the "affluent" explanation). But:

(a) We had less crime, teenage pregnancy, hard-drug use, etc. in poorer times (all the past, especially on the American frontier and during the 1930s).

(b) Poverty has lessened in the United States, but not all sociocultural dysfunctions have. For instance, a recent U.S. Census Bureau report found that the poverty line had dropped to 12.7% in 1998; virtually every type of household saw big gains and the unemployment rate was markedly lower than in the 1970s.[3†] Also, the poor today in America have more household conveniences than typical middle-class Americans of a generation ago: In 1971 about 83% of all American homes had a refrigerator; in 1994, nearly 98% of poor households owned one.[4]

(c) Increased expenditures for welfare and education have not reduced sociocultural dysfunctions.

(d) Poorer countries have fewer of these dysfunctions.

(e) The proportion of American blacks below the poverty line, well above 30% as of 1990, has decreased recently (27% in 1999) and black unemployment in America has dropped to 9% in 1999 from 15% in 1985[5] – so we should not ascribe heightened black crime, teenage illegitimacy, etc., to increasing poverty. Blacks were poorer in slavery times and yet teenage illegitimacy and crime among blacks is higher now. Ethical relativism holds blacks back more than does slavery and Jim Crow.

(f) Crime causes poverty more than poverty causes crime: It weakens the trust upon which free enterprise rests, it impoverishes the victim and generally does not enrich the criminal. Although there was considerable looting during the July 1977 blackout in New York City, a city study showed that income among the 2,706 adult accused perpetrators averaged about the same as New York's population in general.[6] If poverty was the cause of crime, how is it that the great majority of poor New Yorkers refrained from looting? It was low ethical standards and not poverty that motivated the looters. Modern criminals do not steal bread for their starving children; rather they steal televisions and camcorders.[7]†

(g) Most young people brought up in poverty-stricken neighborhoods grow up straight. A distinguished team of Harvard criminologists, Drs. Sheldon and Eleanor Glueck, studied the lives of more than 2,000 young delinquents over a period of many years and found that only a small proportion, perhaps 5 to 15 percent, of boys reared in underprivileged areas became delinquents.[8] They found that moral upbringing was much more important than poverty as a crime breeder. Their study has been frequently replicated.[9]†

(h) The "poverty-breeds-crime" advocates do not seem to realize how discriminatory their analysis is; in effect, they are saying that rich people are morally superior to poor people. That is unsupportable.

(i) Some social analysts feel that there has been an increasing disparity in income between rich and poor which increases envy and therefore sociocultural dysfunctions, but ethical rationalism can dispel such envy, and it would seem that the disparity is actually decreasing. A recent study of more than 50,000 Americans from all socioeconomic backgrounds, covering more than twenty years, showed that the bottom fifth of income earners in 1975 increased their 1991 income by four times more than the top fifth.[10] Furthermore, a study by Charles Baird (economics professor, California State University at Hayward) reported that 29% of the families in the lowest quintile in 1975 had moved to the top quintile in 1991; only 5.1% of those in the lowest quintile in 1975 remained there in 1991.[11]

(j) A widening disparity of income could not possibly account for the cultural dysfunctions of upper-incomers.[12]† But postmodern misology can.[13]

(4) *Some say the Vietnam War accounts for these dysfunctions.* But they seem to ignore the following:

    (a) Only a minority of Americans (noisy they were, to be sure) opposed the war.

    (b) The comparable Korean War (the "Forgotten War") did not create these pathologies. Wars do not necessarily do that; they seem only to accelerate preexisting sociocultural trends.

    (c) The people of nations uninvolved in Vietnam also exhibited a rise in ethical relativism and its consequent sociocultural pathologies.

(5) *Some social analysts ascribe these sociocultural dysfunctions to a younger population.* But consider the following:

    (a) These deficiencies did not exist as much in times previous when the nation's population was even younger.

(b) Ethical relativism has nothing to do with age. The elderly, more than before, are also afflicted by it.

(6) *Other analysts ascribe these cultural dysfunctions to an abandoning of religion,* but consider this:

    (a) Rather than being abandoned, religion has been on the rise recently.

    (b) Religion is not the *correct* source of ethicality, as we will soon see.

(7) *Still other social analysts ascribe these deficiencies to urbanization; they think cities are impersonal.* But think of the following:

    (a) City dwellers can resist these pathologies – most do.

    (b) Large cities have more crime, hard-drug use, and so on than previously in less-relativistic days.

    (c) Many of our cities (especially those most beset by sociocultural dysfunctions) have declined in population while ethical relativism has increased.

    (d) These deficiencies are prevalent in smaller cities and in rural areas also.

(8) *Maybe there are psychological causes for sociocultural dysfunctions.* However, there is no evidence that psychological effectiveness has declined recently. Some psychological analysts say that criminals have not received enough love as children – what, less than yesterday's criminals? How could that be substantiated? Are today's mothers more unloving than yesterday's mothers were? The psychological causes for these dysfunctions stand in need of empirical substantiation.

Dennis Prager (rabbi and radio talk-show host, quoted in The Wall Street Journal, *5/7/98, p. A22): "One day when my older son was two years old and playing in a park, a five-year-old boy walked over to him and threw him onto the concrete. The boy's mother, seeing what her son had done, ran over to him and cried, 'Honey, what's troubling you?' I knew nothing about this woman, but I was certain that she was highly educated. One must learn to respond the way she did. The average mother a generation ago [in less relativistic times] would have severely reprimanded any child of hers who threw down a toddler."*

(9) *Some believe an increasing rate of technological change undercuts ethical standards.* But they cannot explain the following:

   (a) What is there about technological change that necessarily undercuts ethical standards and produces cultural dysfunction? It does not seem logical to stop or hinder technological improvement in order to respect the equal rights of others. Rather technological change magnifies the impact of both ethical rationality and relativism.

   (b) There are many people who are immersed in technological change yet maintain high cultural standards; all could do so.

   (c) Although it is true that chemical hard drugs like LSD and speed, products of high technology, are now available, nonchemical hard drugs such as marijuana, heroin, cocaine, opium, and so on were always available. The greater variety today is irrelevant. When guns were necessary for hunting, there were more guns per capita than now, yet there was less sociocultural dysfunction. Cars were available to crooks in the 1950s, but there was less sociocultural dysfunction then – also less ethical relativism. Neither guns nor cars are the primary causes for the increase in crime today.

Technological improvements become a problem only if it is generally felt that there are no provable limits to individual behavior. If people have definite and provable ethical standards, technology will present no problem. It would seem wiser to seek attitudinal causes for attitudinal changes.

The rise of ethical relativism (or "lack of structure," as some put it) can provide a direct satisfactory explanation for cultural dysfunction. If a society says that the right to life is a matter of personal opinion only, murders are likely to increase (because murderers will believe their potential victims have no provable right to life). With such a relativistic view, we can expect an increase in suicides (because life is regarded as being pointless). If it is generally thought that the right to property is a matter of personal opinion *only*, won't burglars be less restrained? Won't they say that in their opinion (as well as that of everybody in society) none of their victims have provable property rights? Aren't hard-drug users living in their own drug-made morally relativist world? If ethics is a matter of personal opinion *only*, ethical standards will not be convincingly taught in our schools; students will be left standardless and will do whatever they wish or can get away with. If parents and teachers think there are no provable standards, children will think likewise. No wonder our high schools have become veritable jungles. What should society expect if it believes *all is permitted*?

If there are no recognized limits to personal behavior, why not risk illegitimacy? Is not the view that there is no ethical truth responsible in large part for the rise in social pathologies? After all, why not do whatever you want to do and chase fun if you think there is no provable right, no provable wrong?

It is a copout to say the matter of cultural dysfunction is complicated. An airtight thoroughly-rational disproof of ethical relativism can be simple and can counter cultural decline. Obviously, a proof of an ethical standard has more power than personal opinions. Merely to show that ethical relativism has deleterious sociocultural consequences is not good enough, because if ethical relativism is true, then we will have to put up with the deleteriousness, because that is how the world would be; after all, we should treat things as they are. But in order to disprove ethical relativism, we will have to prove the truth of some ethical standard (we do this in Part II).

> *Burdette Backus: "For all [reason's] limitations it serves us well, and those who advocate its abandonment are simply telling a man who is groping his way through the dark by the light of a candle to blow out the light."*

Before this chapter ends, we must discuss the very recent decline in some of these social pathologies. If ethical relativism is their main cause, yet its influence has not declined in the past five years and these pathologies have, could it be that maybe ethical relativism has little or no social impact at all? Could it only be a theoretical plaything for philosophers?

Well, no. Some of these sociocultural pathologies have declined in recent years, but many have not (and some of these declines are due to factors having nothing to do with our ethical outlook). Historian Gertrude Himmelfarb, writing in 1999, is worth quoting in this respect:

If the rate of divorce has fallen, the rate of cohabitation has almost doubled in the past decade alone [1990s], and couples living together without benefit of marriage can separate (and do so more frequently) without benefit of divorce. If the rate of out-of-wedlock births (relative to the number of unmarried women of child-bearing age) has decreased, the ratio of such births (relative to all births) has only leveled off, and at a very high level. One-third of all children, two-thirds of black children and three-fourths of the children of teenagers are born out of wedlock. If there are fewer abortions, it is partly because unmarried motherhood has become more respectable (and the number of single-parent households continues to increase). If older girls are less sexually active, younger ones (below the age of 15) are more so. If fewer children are dropping out of school, it is because more failing children are automatically promoted.[14]

We may have enjoyed a slight (but welcome) decline in crime in the past few years because of nonethical factors, but unfortunately the levels of crime and other social pathologies are still much higher now than twenty years ago, forty years ago, or a century ago. And so it is with most other sociocultural dysfunctions. In the case of abortion and illegitimacy, teenagers are embracing birth-control pills and injections to ward off pregnancy, thereby masking the impact of ethical relativism[15]; even still, there is more teenage abortion and illegitimacy now than ever. We should not expect the course of history to be perfectly smooth, with no short-term side-steps or back steps.

Maybe, as Senator Moynihan puts it, we have just become accustomed to cultural dysfunction. We normalize and legitimize it and are merely defining deviancy down.

References and footnoted material for this chapter begin on page 349 in the appendices.

CHAPTER FIVE

The
INADEQUACY
of
OTHER
PHILOSOPHIES

Existing philosophies do not provide us with a provable alternative to ethical relativism. They offer no valid or conclusive proof of the truth of a particular ethical standard and so cannot present any rational explanation of our cultural free fall.

Nature as the Source of Ethics

Nature is *not* the correct source of ethics. Natural law is descriptive of nature, yes, but prescriptive for humankind, no.

(1) *There certainly are some invariable sequences in nature but it begs the question to say that free-willing individuals should therefore follow nature.* Why so? Nothing is "self-evident"; everything ethical is disputed, especially these days.

(2) *Are earthquakes ethically right because they are natural? Are bacteria-caused diseases ethically right?* Anesthesia and vaccination are not natural, being

human-made, but they are not unethical. Nature is not always benign.

(3) *Nature is red in tooth and claw – is that what we should follow?* The natural law of the jungle consigns many animals to horrible deaths – ripped apart, eaten by their predators – what has that got to do with equal rights for free-willing humans?

(4) *Nature has many different aspects – which should we follow?* For instance, even the simple act of walking uphill contravenes the natural law of gravity, but it should be done if we are to follow still other laws of nature, such as those that make us hunt for our evening meal.

(5) *Above all, using natural law as a source for ethics attempts to contravene the uncontravenable Is-Ought Barrier.* Whatever is natural is an "is," but we cannot logically go from "is" to "ought." The *ought* is in correct tho*ught*, not out there in nature or reality as Locke and other Enlightenment philosophers believed. Later, we discuss the Is-Ought Barrier more fully.

Kantian Duty

Immanuel Kant (1724-1804) was a leading philosopher of immense learning. He lived and taught in Koenigsberg, East Prussia. He typified Romanticism and might have improved on the ethical philosophy of John Locke, but he failed to do so; his attempts at ethical proof were no more successful than those of Locke's. Professional philosophers have derived much pleasure in presenting exceptions that disprove Kant's categorical imperatives:

(1) *Kant asserted that you should "always act in such a way that the maxim determining your conduct might well become a universal law."* He also said, "Act so that you can will that everybody shall follow the principle of your action," but we are entitled to ask why. Why should others act the way I choose to act? Why is my choice correct? To convey meaning, our statements must be consistent with what they refer to – that is, accuracy. Kant's assumptions or maxims are not amenable to accuracy.

(2)   Cannot any maxim be universalized, even contradictory ones? For example, consider "we should obey Hitler," or "we should obey Stalin." Both of these maxims can be universalized, but they contradict each other, and anyway we should not do either of them because they are irrational. Cannot suicide be universalized? After all, it is possible for everyone to commit suicide; we ought not to assume that everyone's death is unethical merely because we do not like it. Can't I universalize personal convenience so that I can feel free to throw a candy wrapper on a beautiful park lawn? Even the promotion of human misery could be adopted as a rule of action.

"Do this except in such-and-such circumstances" can leave us with an infinity of contradictory ethical rules. And how could such an exception be proved?

A person might be willing to be executed for bank robbery, but that might not be an appropriate punishment for others. Even trivial statements can be universalized: "You should tie your right shoelace before your left one." Why? Even the reverse can be universalized!

Picture yourself on the way to meet an appointment when you see a child drowning. "I must not destroy my moral dignity as a human being by breaking a promise to be on time for my appointment," you might tell yourself à la Kant, "so I shouldn't pull the child out of his drowning because then I'll have to go home and change my clothes and I would be late." Wouldn't this compromise your moral dignity?

"I should live only for my own happiness" can be practiced by everyone, but the opposite also meets the lame test of consistency sans accuracy. Anyway, Kant made no attempt to prove that happiness was the correct ethical goal. Happiness, especially long-run happiness, cannot even be measured.

If I have masochistic or sadistic tendencies and follow Kant's maxim, great harm to society would result – even

Kant himself would agree. If I wear a tie and suit, should everyone? Bah, humbug. To be consistent, Kant should not have engaged in a philosophical career since if everyone did so, then who would be left to farm, manufacture, or sell? He was a bachelor; wouldn't that eventually eliminate humanity if everyone followed his example?

(3) *Kant thought that he was relying only on intentions to judge his morality, but in fact he often relied on consequences to judge it.* For instance, he believed we should never tell a lie because then we would never be believed. "So what?" we may ask, and anyway he was using a consequence to judge the ethics of lying.

(4) *"Treat every person as an end in himself" was another of Kant's many ethical dictums.* Well maybe, but not always; we are entitled to ask why. When we sell goods in a competitive free market, aren't we using our customers as a means to get an income – what's wrong with that? Besides, we cannot know what this dictum exactly means; it might lead either to altruism or equal rights.

His dictums fuse means and ends, but shouldn't means be subordinated to ends? Never lie to save a life, Kant asserted (e.g., if a man obviously bent on murder asks you for the whereabouts of his intended victim, you are to tell him the truth). Fichte, a follower of Kant, remarked, "I wouldn't break my word to save the universe from destruction." Count me out. Is not lying less important than murder? If I do not lie, would I not be an accessory to murder? Lying can be a means to saving a life. The categorical principles "don't lie" and "treat every person as an end in himself" often contradict each other. If we should tell a lie to save a life, we then abandon Kantianism. But if we save a life instead, we thereby recognize the primacy of the right to life, but this requires rational proof, which he did not provide. It is maxims like these that could bring philosophy into disrepute.

(5) *Be rational, Kant asserted.* Yes, but why, what is rational, and how should it be applied to ethics?

(6) *Kant had even more maxims to offer us: "Behave as a member of society in which each regards the good of each other as of equal value with his own, and is so treated by the rest."* Why so? What is "good" anyway?

(7) *Kant says we should do duty for duty's sake.* But since duty involves respecting other people's rights, he first should prove what those rights are. His emphasis on duty may have pleased the Prussians he lived amongst, but we need more than that.

Hegelianism

Georg W. F. Hegel (1770-1831) was another leading philosopher of his time; his influence was felt well beyond his death. He was an eminent thinker, highly regarded by his many fervent followers, who these days generally tend to be postmodernists. The Hegelian dictum was "whatever is, is right." Well, let us be fair: by "is," Hegel was referring to the zeitgeist, the spirit of the times, and not to individual actions, such as murder and robbery. But we are entitled to ask, why so? How can we distinguish between the zeitgeist and individual actions? "Go with the flow" is the current postmodern equivalent of "whatever is, is right."

Why is the zeitgeist always right? Is this not trying to cross the impassable Is-Ought Barrier by deriving "ought" from "is" (the zeitgeist)? Many of his followers contradicted him and believed that "whatever is becoming, is right," but again, why so? This disagreement among Hegelians weakens any faith we might have in Hegelianism.

Other weakeners: Hegel opposed individualism and was a forerunner of German totalitarianism. Also, his prose was dense.

Utilitarianism and Pragmatism

Since the same ethical arguments apply against these two similar philosophies, they are grouped together here. They (and situation ethics, their outgrowth) deserve an extended treatment because of their considerable influence on the nineteenth century and on our own time.

(1)   *Both philosophies judge actions by their usefulness, but we can ask for a rational justification.* Truth is agreement with facts in the case of reality or with rational logic in the case of ethics; what logic could possibly prove usefulness (a reality concept) to be correct? We're more interested in truth, not usefulness. Also, different people define *usefulness* differently – that is, does it refer to social or individual usefulness? Also, what was useful to Hitler was not so to others. A lie might be useful but it is not true; the same could be said of believing in fairies. "A stitch in time saves nine" (generally true, but not always); pragmatists and utilitarians can offer no proof for why we should save nine stitches. Nor can "success," with which pragmatists often replace "usefulness," be regarded as the correct ethical standard; for instance, no matter how successful bank robbers are, they are reprehensible ethically. Adolph Hitler was surely no pragmatist, but in *Mein Kampf (My Struggle)* he wrote, "success is the sole earthly judge of right and wrong." This view is not inconsistent with the pragmatic view that whatever works is good. But what works? Even evil can work.

Some pragmatists and utilitarians looked kindly on Mussolini (he was reputed to have made the trains run on time), Hitler (he built autobahns), or Stalin (he suppressed criminals), but wrong ethical principles led them astray. These leaders murdered millions. Pragmatists and utilitarians generally favored democracy because that is how they were brought up.

Democracy was useful to Dewey and other pragmatists because they thought it brought forth many solutions to social problems, but we are entitled to ask which solutions are correct or good. Isn't democracy correct as an end in itself? Dewey et al. elevated means (majority rule) over ends (the protection of equal individual rights) – but majorities are often wrong.

I once asked a pragmatist why people should not steal. He replied that since stealing hurts society, it was wrong. "Stealing," said he, "creates distrust among people and lowers the incentive to produce goods and services. We will all benefit if we act to reduce the war of each against the other. A society without stealing would be a better society." But "better" needs precise definition and proof. Thieves should be concerned about others in society – but why? When they rob richer victims, they are not merely engaged in a just redistribution of wealth. They probably think they are helping themselves more than they are hurting their victims, who may even be unaware of the thievery (which is what thieves hope for and is often the case), but that is ethically irrelevant.

(2) *John Dewey, a leading pragmatic philosopher, once asserted: "After a polite and pious deference has been paid to 'ideals,' men feel free to devote themselves to matters which are more immediate and pressing."*[1] But when pressed by some interrogators, he allowed that we should judge goodness by standards he thought everyone would accept, such as health, wealth, friendship, honesty, happiness, freedom, beauty, and so on. That is a nice list, we learned it in kindergarten, but we do not need philosophers for it; from them we ask for *proof*. And what happens when these goals contradict each other, as when our friends are dishonest? History has seen sincere advocates of slavery, racism, classism, vested interests, nationalism, crime, nihilism, sadism, selfishness, terrorism, altruism, religion, libertarianism – just to mention a few non-Dewey-esque beliefs in a list much longer than his. History is writ in blood, particularly in the twentieth century; Dewey's assumed goals have been rarely observed in practice. Shouldn't philosophers prove their goals and not just assume them to be true? They are not teaching kindergarten. Since we live in the short run,

why should we be concerned about the long run? Let us not beg the question by assuming what we want to prove.

(3) *Happiness is no better than usefulness (or success) as an ethical guide.*

    (a) What is happiness, anyway? We can't even measure it; Jefferson had no "happistat" or "euphorimeter," nor do we. How can it be applied? Happiness is a personal psychological matter. Individual rights are sometimes difficult to adjudicate, but a judge and jury will have an easier time using rights as a standard rather than subjective happiness. Although money can be easily measured, it cannot guarantee happiness. Beyond destitution, money is no guarantee of happiness; it is safe to say that Bill Gates is not the happiest man on the face of this planet.[2†]

    (b) Happiness may be desirable, but desirability is no proof of truth; happiness is not to be equated with ethicality. The situation yielding the most happiness is when a sadist meets a masochist, but that is not desirable, nor can it constitute ethical proof. When criminals steal from their victims, their happiness may exceed the unhappiness of their victims, but ethically that is irrelevant; stealing is not therefore justified. A burglar cannot justify his actions by saying that "robbing Bill Gates will make me happier than it will make him sadder." Criminals can be happy, yet they are not ethical. Even self-delusion can lead to happiness.

    (c) Pragmatists and utilitarians should prove why we should all be *equally* happy or concerned about the welfare of others, but they do not. How can we measure equal happiness, anyway?

    (d) The government can protect freedom – with some difficulty a court can protect individual rights – but it can do little to protect happiness, which is more likely to be the result of such factors as luck, belief, emotional balance, genes, personal attitude, past lives, culture, stealing, and so on. If you want happiness, get thee religion (even a belief in the rightness of rationality will suffice). If the government protects rights and lets individuals pursue happiness, more happiness is likely to be achieved than if a government bureaucrat decides for distant citizens what will make them happy. I would not want to bet that democratic Americans are happier than dictatorized Vietnamese. The wind fills the sails of merchantman and corsair ships alike; Mafia dons can exult. If you want to be happy, you might want to see a psychiatrist; but they are not ethical arbiters nor do they pretend to be. Rights take ethical precedence over happiness. Happiness is happiness and ethics is ethics – they're entirely different. Social conflict will result if each group in society pursues happiness rather than the equal rights of individuals. Jefferson erred badly when he wrote that we all have equal rights to "Life, Liberty and the pursuit of Happiness."

(e) Nor does rational knowledge guarantee happiness. There may be some joy in being rational, but it won't cure neuroticism.

(4) *Pragmatists and utilitarians posit growth as an ethical goal.* But why so? Growth toward what? Should people grow twelve feet tall? Should traffic jams and cancers keep growing? Should evil grow as much as good? Let us have done with nice-sounding but false ethical ends.

(5) *How can pragmatism or utilitarianism successfully explain the long-term rise in crime, family dissolution, and the other cultural dysfunctions?* Are these dysfunctions to go forever unexplained?

(6) *Pragmatists often maintain that equal opportunity is an ultimate good,* thereby contradicting their generally dim view

of ultimates, but what is good and why is equal opportunity to be considered desirable? Let us not beg ethical questions, nor give burglars equal opportunity with their victims. The rich have more opportunity than the poor, but what's wrong with that? Let us elevate the poor rather than lower the rich. Yes, we want equal opportunity, but it should be limited by the equal rights of others. However, this limitation needs rational proof, which neither pragmatism nor utilitarianism can provide.

(7)   *Pragmatists assert that objective certainty in knowledge is unachievable and that subjective experience is the pathway to truth.* But a tree exists or does not exist in the Arctic whatever my personal subjective experience of it might be. Both pragmatism and utilitarianism fall victim to the Skeptic's Dilemma: If there is no objective truth or certainty, it applies to all forms of skepticism – to pragmatism and utilitarianism also.

Pragmatists and utilitarians assume that government is the correct source of rights, but when they criticize government or society, which they often do, they are necessarily appealing to a higher ethical standard they had said could not exist. But let us give credit to pragmatists and utilitarians for effectively combating natural rights, even though their reasoning was wrong.

(8)   *Pragmatism and utilitarianism pull the rug out from under transcendent virtues by hooking them to mere transitory experience,* thereby making it difficult to inspire ordinary people to pursue higher goals greater than their immediate material concerns. This generates cultural entropy (energylessness). A friend once asked Heinrich Heine, the poet, as they were looking at the grand and beautiful Amiens Cathedral: "Why don't people build like this any more?" Heine replied: "My dear friend, in those days people had convictions. We moderns have opinions, and it takes more than opinions to build a Gothic cathedral."

(9)   *Pragmatists and utilitarians deal with means rather than ends.*

But ethics, as opposed to morals, is primarily concerned with ends. Correct ends determine correct means, not vice-versa.

> *Professor Theodore Schick, Jr. (philosophy, Muhlenberg College, quoted in* Free Inquiry, *Fall 1998, p. 32): "Subjectivism implies that moral disagreement is next to impossible. Suppose Jack says that homosexuality is right, and Jill says that it's wrong. You might think that Jack and Jill disagree with one another. But you would be mistaken. According to subjective relativism, Jack is saying that he believes that homosexuality is right while Jill is saying that she believes that homosexuality is wrong. But this doesn't constitute a disagreement because neither is denying what the other is saying. In order for Jill to disagree with Jack, she would have to say that Jack doesn't believe that homosexuality is right. But it's difficult to see how she could ever be in a position to make such a claim because, presumably, no one knows Jack's mind better than Jack."*

---

(10) *Pragmatism and utilitarianism egregiously violate the famous Is-Ought Barrier because they rely on particular situations or circumstances in reality to derive "should-ness."* But they should not futilely assault the impervious, impermeable, impassable, immovable, immutable, impenetrable, undissolvable, unpierceable, unbreakable, not to mention unscalable, indestructible, unavoidable, unimpeachable, unbypassable, unbreechable, uncrossable, untrangressable, unimpregnable Is-Ought Barrier (get the idea?). Compared to it, the Rock of Gibraltar is a gossamer feather; high steel walls are mere airy collocations of separate atoms compared to this logical massivity. This barrier is the *pons asinorum*[3][†] of ethical philosophy. Try to think of

any statement about reality; it will tell you nothing at all about what ought to be. One cannot *logically* derive a statement of what ought to be from a statement of what is, yet pragmatists and utilitarians attempt to do just that. A thing *is* the way it is, but that doesn't mean it *should* be that way. 4†

It can well be asked, how could such weak philosophies as pragmatism and utilitarianism have had such a huge impact on ethical philosophy in the nineteenth century and thereafter? The answer is simple: Since no ethical principle had been proven true, usefulness or happiness was resorted to instead.

Having said all that, there is nevertheless a definite and important place for pragmatism and utilitarianism in morality (though not in ethics). Pragmatists and utilitarians may not be able to prove an ethical standard, but once this has been done, we can then apply it to particular circumstances. That is the stuff of morality, and although that is not unimportant, it is not our main focus here. Once we have proven an ethical standard, we should be pragmatic and utilitarian thereafter.

Analytic Philosophy
Analytic philosophy is an outgrowth of logical positivism, and it has its advocates to this day.5† It is mainly concerned with what philosophical terms actually mean, and as such it is a valuable antidote to philosophical imprecision. But it could easily degenerate into an uninspiring word game using the apparatus of mathematics to test the validity of various philosophical propositions. Many can grasp such formulations such as Descartes' "I think, therefore I am," but are befuddled by a modern analytic philosopher's equivalent, "To be is to be the value of a variable." This formulation leaves most laypersons gasping for meaning and could bring professional philosophy into disrepute – or into the incomprehensibility of postmodernism. Once rationality is rejected, incomprehensibility takes

over. In any case, analytic philosophy attempts no ethical proof, which is our interest here.

Altruism

This is the view (often religious) that it is our duty to serve others before we serve ourselves. But how can it be *proven* true? Why should we put the demands of others before our own, thereby violating our equal rights? Since suffering and inequity are unlimited in this world (television does not allow anyone to legitimately claim ignorance of the suffering of others) altruism would require the forfeiture of all rights to ourselves in deference to the needs of others, but why should the needs of others take precedence over our freedom? Of course, if we freely choose to defend the rights of others and not merely respect their rights, we should be allowed to do so (even encouraged), but we are not ethically *obligated* to do so.

Some government expansionists would raise revenue by taxing producers to support the downtrodden, but this form of "tax altruism" reduces individual freedom by violating the equal right of an individual to his ethical property. "Tax altruism" is a self-contradiction; true altruism is voluntary. Jesus had no gun, nor did he threaten anyone with imprisonment. Freedom and equal rights produce desirable economic results. Anyway, the downtrodden end up paying higher prices for their purchases because taxes are passed on to them, while the better-off are penalized with often-heavy taxation. Fortunately, there is a proper fund for financing government, but a full discussion of it must await Chapters 8 and 9.

The government should dispense justice, not altruism.

Equalitarianism à la Rawls

John Rawls (b. 1921) of Harvard wrote a best-seller, *A Theory of Justice*, in 1971 that made a deep impression on the philosophical world and beyond. Although technically in the realm of political philosophy, it has much to say about ethical philosophy – about what we ought to do.

Rawls assumed democracy, defined as majority rule, to be the best form of government (but philosophers should not make assumptions). The purpose of such a government is the minimization of poverty, he assumed (no assumptions, please), contrary to Locke but without proof, the maximization of private property rights, although Rawls paradoxically assumed that no innocent person should be the knowing victim of public policy (another assumption). In order to minimize poverty, the government should engage in welfare spending – he accepted the Kantian dictum, "each individual should be treated as an end in itself" – thereby requiring that each individual be the subject of *equal* concern by society (another assumption). This brings him to what he calls the "difference principle": Inequality in the distribution of primary goods can be allowed only when it also benefits the worst-off in society (yet another assumption) even if the property rights of the better-off have to be invaded by taxation.

Rawls further maintained that a just society could be constructed only behind a hypothetical "veil of ignorance," whereby everyone would be oblivious to their own interests (assumption). This would put everyone in what Rawls called a hypothetical "original position" (assumption, similar to Locke's hypothetical "state of nature") where everyone would make just decisions because no one would be influenced by the facts of his or her own life.

What are we to make of all this?

(1)   *In the first place, philosophers should not make assumptions.*

(2)   *Rawlsianism involves a huge expansion of a benign government and a contraction of individual rights.* Out-and-out despotism would be hard to avoid. Redistributing wealth and income will end up with redistribution of power to the state. The benignity of the government would not last long if private-property rights were to be violated by the taxation necessary to finance the welfare state envisioned by Rawls. It would diminish personal drive and talent by taxing them.

(3)   *It is not right or just to deny people the fruits of their labor (i.e., their property),* yet Rawls' taxation would do exactly this.

(4)   *We cannot know how people would act in Rawls' hypothetical "veil of ignorance."* It requires that people have an encyclo-

pedic knowledge of everything except their name, age, weight, race, parents, bank account, IQ, friends, and education![6] These astounding exceptions (and there are more) are necessary, according to Rawls, so that the voters would not be influenced by their personal situations (but what's wrong with that so long as they respect the equal rights of others?). Only an ivy-tower thinker removed from reality and rationality could come up with such a Rube Goldberg scheme. Hypothetical assumptions are fictional, not rational; let us not play games. A hypothesis is a myth, whereas we want to know the truth.

(5) *People might not choose justly even if it were possible to put aside their personal situations.* Justice depends on rationality, not on what we think their personal opinions might be in hypothetical situations.

(6) *Rawls' equalitarianism could never be satisfied* unless we performed strange unethical acts, like putting a tax on whiteness since whites on average earn more than blacks (but then there are Asians Americans, who on average earn the most…). We would also have to tax maleness (they tend to earn more than females), tallness (the taller earn more than the shorter), physical attractiveness, and so on. Some children have better-than-average parents – are they to be artificially neuroticized? Equality refers only to rights, not to a vague fairness.

(7) *Rawls opposes slavery but would deny Frank Sinatra his right to profit from his own vocal chords.* That's slavery, isn't it?

(8) *The millionaire's wealth does not cause the pauper's poverty.* In fact, it is millionaires who employ the poor, not Rawls.

We'll have a final answer to *A Theory of Justice* when we get to Chapters 6-8; Chapter 9 tells us how really to help the poor and avoid taxation. Have patience.

References and footnoted material for this chapter begin on page 351 in the appendices.

PART TWO

What follows is a discussion between PM, a
Postmodern Ethical Relativist, and ER, an
Ethical Rationalist or Equal Rightist.

EQUAL
RIGHTS:
a PROOF

CHAPTER SIX

POSTMODERN ETHICAL RELATIVISM CANNOT *be* PROVEN

This chapter demonstrates that ethical relativism is both self-defeating and unprovable.

Ethical Rationalist (ER):

> The cornerstone of postmodernism is *ethical relativism*, the belief that ethical statements are personal opinions only and can't be proven true or false because the individual is the ultimate arbiter of right and wrong. This view holds that only descriptive statements can be proven true or false, not prescriptive statements (i.e., ethical or moral). Since postmodernist ethical relativism is an ethical theory, then by its own admission, it *can't be proven*. Nevertheless, it is eating away at our culture like acid eating away at metal.

Postmodernist (PM):

> Aren't all ethical statements personal opinions *only*?

ER: No, not only. Obviously, ethical statements are personal opinions, but they can be either true or false. For instance, the ethical statement "widows should be burned," a practice called *suttee* in India, is as much a personal opinion as "the earth is flat" – yet both statements are false.

PM: To begin with, you had better define *truth*.

ER: For descriptive statements it is agreement with reality, and for prescriptive (ethical) statements it is agreement with rationality. Some people use the word *validity* instead of *truth* for rational or ethical truth, but such a distinction is not productive.

PM: How can you possibly prove an ethical statement to be true or valid?

ER: Ethics, as the word is generally defined and used in this book, is the study of what people do when they behave rationally as an end in itself. Aesthetics deals with their emotional reactions to objective stimuli; that's how the word is commonly used. Rationality is the ability to freely treat things as they are, as an end in itself. We shouldn't be irrational; to try to prove it, you must use the rational criteria of consistency and accuracy, thereby disproving irrationality!

If we're alive and human, to convey meaning we should be rational, as opposed to merely grunting which conveys no meaning and proves nothing. Since the dead can't convey meaning, they aren't capable of rationality (neither are animals; they're incapable of understanding ethical or rational principles). Rationality is the conveyance of correct meaning, so we should avoid irrationality; that would be incorrect.

But meaning requires consistency; "this object is all blue and all green" is inconsistent, thereby conveying no meaning at all. If we should be consistent, then we should be accurate, which is an important form of consistency between what our statements mean and what they refer to. "We should be accurate, as an end in itself" is hardly controversial. If an ethical principle is fully consistent with a true ethical statement, then it will itself be true or valid.

If ethics is dealing with other people rationally, then when we act ethically as an end in itself, we are always acting rationally. Ethical principles are provable, as are all rational statements, such as those of mathematics. Ethical relativism says that ethical principles can't be proven true, but since it is itself an ethical principle, it cannot therefore be proven true; it is self-refuting. If what it says is true, it can't be proven; and if what it says is false, then it admits unprovability. Ethical relativists are hoist by their own petard. They can't escape the Skeptic's Dilemma, which is that if nothing is true, then neither is skepticism! Nor can ethical relativism correspond to any true ethical statement, since it says there is no such thing.

Merely defining *ethical* as being a matter of personal opinion only cannot constitute a proof; nothing can be proven by mere definition or assertion. Trying to prove by definition is begging the question – assuming an answer without offering any logical or factual proof. For ethical proof, logic (not definitions) must be adduced.

If nevertheless one insists on defining *ethical* as being unprovable, then we can use another word – say, "shouldness" – which can be defined as "agreement with rational behavior"; we could then see if any basic ethical principle can meet this test. Sir Isaac Newton supposedly asked why the apple fell *down*. If he answered, "By definition, down is down; everything falls down," the Law of Gravity would have gone undiscovered for who knows how long. Fortunately, Newton wasn't dead-ended by merely defining what he wanted to discover.

Any way you look at it, ethical relativism is false. Ethical relativists say the whole ethical edifice is unprovable, but they have to present more than belief for their point of view. They should present rational proof. Belief is insufficient as proof because beliefs are often false. Two-year-olds also believe, but they aren't competent social analysts or philosophers; they don't prove their beliefs.

When you oppose murder, inequality, and robbery, aren't you granting people their rights to life, liberty, and property? We cannot rationally be ethical nihilists or relativists, who are quintessentially solipsists, an undefendable position. When it comes to the important matter of how people should treat each other, you don't want to hold an unprovable view. Then our sociocultural dysfunctions become inexplicable.

In a subsequent chapter, we prove the truth of a particular ethical statement, putting the final nail in the ethical relativism coffin.

Harold Titus (Living Issues in Philosophy, *p. 69*): *"Skepticism is self-refuting, since the denial of all knowledge is a claim that refutes itself. If nothing can be known, then how does the skeptic know that his position is a valid one? If he affirms his own position as the truth, he is attempting to distinguish between the true and the false."*

PM: But can't I say that all ethical statements are false except this one?

ER: You can say that, but you can't possibly prove it. It's not logically supportable.

PM: It may not be true for you, but it's true for me.

ER: When you say that, you mean you believe it; you surely believe your beliefs, but that doesn't make them true. Beliefs can be false. To support an ethical statement, use logic, not beliefs.

PM: Well, look. Only descriptive statements can be proven true, not prescriptive (ethical) ones. I can substantiate that the swans I've seen are white, but I can't prove they *should* be white.

ER: Of course not – I never heard anyone say that all swans

should be white; I certainly don't say that. In the nineteenth century, Comte and others put forward their belief that only descriptive and not prescriptive statements are capable of being proven true, but it was never so. Widows simply shouldn't jump onto their husband's funeral pyre no matter what their beliefs may be, because that would violate rational ethical principle (yet to be proven). Since prescriptive or ethical statements deal with rational behavior, they are provable just as are all mathematical statements (which are rational, too). Remember – ethical proof isn't correspondence to reality but to rationality.

PM: But aren't you assaulting the impassable Is-Ought Barrier?

ER: No. I would never say that reality ("is-ness") is the proper source of ethical truth ("ought-ness"); rationality is. The "ought" is in the th*ought*, correct rational thought, not in reality. I would never say because a thing is the way it is, it should be that way.

PM: If beauty (aesthetics) is a matter of personal opinion only, is not ethics also? They're both personal values.

ER: They're both personal values, but one value is provably true and the other isn't. That's an important difference. By commonly accepted definition, beauty or aesthetics is what pleases each person emotionally – the aesthetic standard is each person's set of emotions. It is therefore a matter of personal opinion only. If a person says the *Mona Lisa* is beautiful, at best we can only say that he or she is sincere. Ethicality depends on rational action, which is common to everyone. Rational logic is the standard of ethics, not emotion.

PM: Don't we often use rationality to describe reality?

ER: Yes, but the *sources* of reality truth and rationality truth (or validity) are different. We can express real truths beautifully, but that doesn't mean that reality is necessarily beautiful. Reality, rationality and aesthetics have separate sources of truth.

PM: But suppose I want to be irrational?

ER: You could, but you shouldn't. Again, to *prove* irrationality, you would have to resort to the standards of rationality (consistency and accuracy), thereby disproving irrationality. You may believe no ethical principle is true, but you can't prove it! Holding a basic view that you can't prove – doesn't that discomfort you?

You simply cannot escape the Skeptic's Dilemma: If nothing can be proven true, then neither can skepticism! Nor – and this is vitally important – could you possibly explain the high level of crime, hard-drug use, family and school dissolution, and so on.

John Silber (The Intercollegiate Review, *Fall 1990, p. 40): "I am thinking of Susan Atkins, the young woman of Charles Manson's clan who was unable to feel any remorse for stabbing and killing Sharon Tate and her unborn baby. Not only could Miss Atkins not feel remorse, she stated that what she did was right and good. 'I knew it was right when I did it,' she said, 'because it felt good.' This may be the quintessential assertion of the ethics of hedonism."*

PM: Will an ethical proof change anything?

ER: Isn't that irrelevant to the truth or falsity of an ethical principle? You wouldn't ask Pythagoras if his formula $a^2 + b^2 = c^2$ for flat right triangles would change anything, nor would you ask John Locke if his proof for democracy would change anything; rather we want to know if what they proposed was true or false. The possibility of change is irrelevant to the validity of an ethical proof. We're seeking truth, not change, although a proof is likely to lead to beneficial change. A proof of truth is worthwhile in itself – especially an ethical proof, since it determines how we should act. Aren't we more likely to be influenced by an ethical proof than by an ethical opinion? Ethical relativism is only an opinion, a false and deleterious one at that.

Nevertheless, ethics can have an important real-world effect. Calling Milosevic a war criminal and calling the Soviet Union an evil empire was important in defeating them.

PM: Look, proof is certainly possible in mathematics but clearly not in ethics.

ER: Not so – proof is definitely possible in ethics because it is the study of how people should rationally treat their fellow human beings. The relevant word for us is *rationally*. Mathematics is rational, too, which is why mathematical proof is possible; it may be more tangible than an ethical proof, but tangibility is irrelevant to proof.

PM: But ethical relativism is a meta-ethical doctrine. It is above ethics. It describes the standards for ethics.

ER: Yes, it is meta-ethical, but it still can't be proven true. Calling a statement "meta-ethical" does not absolve it from proof.

PM: But people don't always act rationally. I suppose they should, but they've got emotions, raw, powerful, surging, not-to-be-denied emotions, which, when compared with reason, are as the underwater nine-tenths part of the iceberg compared with the one-tenth visible part. One single emotion can blow away all your fine-spun rationalizations. You're talking about people, and they're irrational; that's all there is to that!

ER: People often do act irrationally, but we here are asking how they *should* act, with how they should rationally treat (deal with, act toward) each other. That's ethics. People should control their emotions. Let's find out how.

When we act ethically (as an end in itself), are we not also acting rationally? The ethical is the rational as applied to interpersonal relations; that's a position from which there is no escape.

Leon Trotsky (one-time communist leader in Their Morals and Ours *(1939), p. 15): "Whoever*

> *is not satisfied with eclectic* hodge-podges *must acknowledge that morality is a product of social development; that there is nothing immutable about it; that it serves social interests; that these interests are contradictory; that morality more than any other form of ideology has a class character."* (author's emphasis)
>
> Lawrence Dennis *(American fascist, in* Antidemocratic Trends in Twentieth Century America, *(1935), p. 156): Communism "raises issues of ultimate values rather than of facts, so it cannot be argued out."*

PM: Morally speaking, we all live in glass houses and so shouldn't cast stones. We should not judge.

ER: Why not? You just made a judgment. Is "Thou shalt not judge" the Eleventh Commandment? To think is to judge. We must judge, so let's judge correctly. If there are no provable limits to behavior, as ethical relativists say, then everything is permitted. We are now seeing "everything."

PM: If ethical relativism is so wrong, how come it's so popular?

ER: Well first, there are the three I's: Ignorance, Inertia, and Interest. Ethical relativism is easy but slipshod philosophizing. Then there is mental compartmentalization: Many people are rigorously rational and ethical in their work and everyday living, but when they formally philosophize, they take the easy way out and are not constrained by rationality; they just believe what they feel like believing. They become postmodern ethical solipsists.

These people have become so enamored of their ethical relativism that they emotionally recoil from an attempt at a proof of the equal rights they believe in. They seem much more enamored of their ethical relativism than of equal rights! Postmodernists cannot logically criticize genocide, murder, inequality of rights, robbery, the stealing of other people's property, cheating, and so on, for when they oppose those things, they imply that other people have an equal right to life, liberty, and property. When all is said and done, they embrace ethical relativism more fervently than equal rights.

PM: Well, I've never seen a proof of equal rights.

ER: Stick around, then. We'll get to it in the next chapter. A final disproof of ethical relativism must contain a positive proof of some ethical standard. Although we can't directly prove an ethical standard to be true or valid, we can prove that one ethical standard, and only one, is logically consistent with the provably true statement "We should treat things as they are." As we will see, only equal rights can do that.

PM: Maybe so, but I still remain very skeptical.

ER: I understand. As it has been written, "A man convinced against his will, is of the same opinion still."

CHAPTER SEVEN

What is ETHICAL TRUTH?

Before we can prove anything, we first must establish the basis for truth, particularly (in our case) ethical truth. That is what this chapter proposes to do. We end up with the most important statement ever made – "most important" because it is the only directly provable ethical statement that can be made.

Postmodernist (PM):

> You know, the time has come for you to start proving a particular ethical standard.

Ethical Rationalist (ER):

> Yes, quite so. So far, all we have fully substantiated is that ethical relativism has been on the rise, has deleterious cultural consequences, and is necessarily false.

Pontius Pilate: "What is truth?" said he as he washed his hands of the matter before him.

PM: So what is ethically true?

ER: A legitimate question, but there are some preliminaries to be disposed of first if the proof –

PM: Alleged proof –

ER: – is to be established. A proof is important since it provides credibility to an ethical standard and makes it easier for people to accept it.

PM: Isn't an ethical proof like trying to square the circle?

ER: No, don't pre-judge. Don't be prejudiced. Ethics is rational truth applied to human relationships: "Justice is truth in action," said Disraeli. Surely we should join the forces of rationality rather than irrationality if we're going to avoid the genocide and ethnic cleansing that's gone on in Rwanda, Kosovo, East Timor, Sierra Leone, and elsewhere, but first we must determine how rationality is to be applied to particular situations. We should examine every statement made in this book for its truth content, otherwise reading it is a waste of time. Let us not merely grouse about the growing postmodern irrationalism and ethical relativism we see in our culture today; rather must we show that these doctrines do not accord with what can be proven true.

Ralph Waldo Emerson: "We are of different opinions at different hours but we always may be said to be at heart on the side of truth."

PM: But I can't judge; I have no expertise in philosophy.

ER: That's a copout. Don't you read about politics, even if you're not a politician? Don't you vote? Don't you read about sports, even if you're not an athlete? You make ethical judgments every day and are therefore involved in ethical philosophy – shouldn't you care whether those judgments are correct or not? Philosophy is too important to be left only to professional philosophers; even they don't want that. "The unexamined life is trivial, hardly worth living," said Aristotle. Beware of any alleged proof that is complicated. It will likely be wrong.

Dennis Prager (The American Tradition of Personal Responsibility): "In my 20 years of asking high school seniors 'Would you save your dog or a stranger if both were drowning?' one-third always vote for the dog, one-third always vote for the stranger, and one-third always find the question too difficult.

"But my second question is even more interesting to me. I ask the students who voted to save the person, 'Are the students who voted to save the dog wrong?' Not one student has ever said that the others are wrong. Their argument is always the same: 'Listen, I personally feel that I should save the person, but they feel they should save their dog.'"

PM: OK, let's get on with it.

The Three Rational Purposes of Life

ER: The ancient Greeks had a great insight: They conceived the three rational purposes of life to be the Good, the True, and the Beautiful. The Good determines our proper relations with others, the True our proper relations with objects in reality, and the Beautiful (or Aesthetic) deals with our emotional reactions to those objects. These are to be pursued as ends in themselves quite irrespective of pragmatic means.

PM: What about the Sacred?

ER: It is an important aspect of reality; it asks if God exists, what He is like, whether there is an afterlife, and so on. It involves finding out what is true in reality.

F. W. Robertson: "Controversy is wretched when

> *it is only an attempt to prove another wrong. It*
> *destroys humble inquiry after truth and throws*
> *all our energies into an attempt to prove ourselves*
> *right – a spirit in which no one gets at truth."*

PM: What about fun?

ER: We all need some of it, but it is hardly a purpose in life. You can't chase happiness or fun like a collar button rolled under a radiator. Jet-setting is like eating cake made only of icing – no long-term fun in that.

PM: I can readily understand what the Good is. It's morality or ethics, and you'll have more to say about that as we go on. But explain what you mean by the True.

ER: Yes. It accurately describes the objects in reality – those things that exist independent of thought about them.[1†] Does the tree fall in the Arctic even though no one knows about it? Yes, for sure – my knowledge is completely irrelevant to whether the tree in the Arctic falls or not. There are many things that happen that we don't know about, like trees falling in the Arctic unbeknownst to us.

  Knowing reality can often be difficult. Is it holographic? Is it illusion? Is it something else? These can be difficult questions, but fortunately we needn't deal with them here since in this book we are dealing with ethical principle, which is a matter of rationality only, an easier matter. We simply needn't get involved with questions of reality at all. Ethics is over here, reality over there. The derivation of ethical principle needs reality like a moose needs a hatrack. The "ought" is in correct thought and not in reality.

  I have strongly held views about the nature of reality, but they have no place in a discussion of ethics. What, you believe that consciousness trumps reality? It has nothing to do with ethics, with what we should do.

PM: Don't people each have their own reality?

ER: No – reality, as the Greeks defined the concept and as it is commonly used, is the same for everyone. All people each have their own perceptions of it, true, but perception is one thing, reality another. Here we are primarily concerned with ethics, not reality.

*Albert Einstein (*The World As I See It, *1934, p. 60): "Belief in an external world independent of the perceiving subject is the basis of all natural science."*

PM: But descriptive truth can be subjective. I could say a real object such as a body of water is hot but you might say it's cold.

ER: True, but then we are describing our differing emotional reactions to the water and not the water itself. The water is what it is; descriptive truth is still objective.

PM: Well, don't we often use logic in describing reality?

ER: Absolutely, in order to convey meaning; we want to clear away irrelevancies. But each person's view of what reality is like has absolutely no relevance to ethical principle – to what we should do. Don't ignore the Is-Ought Barrier. Ethical principle is unaffected by correspondence or by consciousness – by whether we hold that a true statement about reality is the accurate factual correspondence between what a statement means and the objective reality it is referring to, or whether personal consciousness is the ultimate source of truth. Correspondence and consciousness have nothing to do with the object of our search – ethical truth.

U.S. Senator Daniel Patrick Moynihan: "Everyone is entitled to their own opinions, but everyone is not entitled to their own facts."

PM: I guess, after all, we had better examine the basis for ethical principle at some length. You say it is only rational logic and not empirical at all, but maybe you had better explain more fully what you think the Good, or ethics, is.

ER: Agreed. The Good or ethics deal only with what we should do.

PM: But what do you mean by *should*?

ER: *Should* is how people act when they act rationally (as opposed to an aesthetic reaction, which is purely emotional). *Should* is rational action. Rationality doesn't preclude emotion (that wouldn't be rational at all) in the same way that beauty differs from utility, although neither precludes the other. Within the limits set by rationality, emotions should flow freely and provide the motive power for action. The opposite of rationality is not emotion but irrationality.

Should applies to all the decisions we make, including our choice of ethical ends. Concerning means: If we wish to exit a room most efficaciously, we should go through the door rather than through a window or wall; the underlying principle is that we should treat things as they are.

As for "shoulds," they are hooked in a chain of means to a final ethical/rational end. It is important to choose our ends (not only our means) rationally (i.e., ethically when dealing with others). Thus, murderers might be entirely rational in their choice of means but not in their chosen end. And so this book asks, "What is the correct ethical principle for treating our fellow human beings?" Since ethics is an aspect of reason, we can be confident that an ethical proof is possible. Correct ethics is therefore how people should rationally act toward each other.

PM: But who's to say what's rational or ethical?

ER: That question is often raised, but "who says" is one thing, truth another. "Who's to say" is completely irrelevant to what is rational or ethical.

What's the difference, "who's to say"? It's completely irrelevant. A nuclear physicist tells you, "e = mc²." Are you going to ask, "who's to say"? Suppose someone says to you, "you shouldn't steal." No matter what anyone says, you shouldn't steal. We should be rational and therefore ethical in our choice of ends as well as means, no matter who says what.

PM: Don't people differ as to ethical standards, so that there are none that are correct or provable?

ER: People certainly do differ as to ethical standards, but that's completely irrelevant as to which ethical standard is correct. People differ as to descriptive statements, also; for instance, did Oswald have accomplices when he assassinated Kennedy? Either he did or didn't, irrespective of what anyone thinks or says.

Universal agreement doesn't make an ethical standard provably true. Even if everyone agreed on what is correct ethical behavior, their universal agreement would only make their agreement popular, not necessarily correct. All this can be summed up succinctly in a statement: *The rational is right.*

W.T. Stace (Concept of Morals, 1937, pp. 32-4):
"Men differ widely in their opinions about all manner of topics, including the subject matters of the physical sciences — just as much as they differ about morals. And if the various different opinions which men have held about the shape of the earth do not prove that it has no one real shape, neither do the various opinions which they have held about morality prove that there is no one true morality.... If a piece of reasoning is valid for one man, it is valid for every other. Thus it would be absurd to suggest that a piece of mathematical reasoning might be valid in France, but not in China."

PM: Doesn't *truth* refer only to reality and not ethics?

ER: No! This is a major thinking error of the past one hundred years. Don't be so nineteenth-century-ish. We're in the twenty-first century now; let's get with it.

An ethical statement is not concerned with reality but with rationality; it is not a matter of personal opinion only. If you prefer, use the word *valid* instead of *true*. Once we find a provably true or valid ethical statement, then an ethical standard logically derived from it is also true or valid. We will find that there is only one ethical standard (equal rights) that corresponds to the only provably true ethical statement there is – because it is provable, it is the most important statement ever made.

Real, ethical and aesthetic statements have entirely different standards of truth. It is perfectly legitimate and frequently said, *"It's true* you shouldn't murder or rob." Let's not do violence to ordinary speech and meaning. Although you can also legitimately say, *"It's true* that picture is beautiful," you can only mean that you sincerely like it.

PM: You say that ethics is purely logical, but isn't it based on assumptions from the real world?

ER: No – just as Euclid's many logical propositions for flat-surface geometry are all eternally true, correct propositions in ethics are likewise eternally true for all people who have free will. If neurotics and psychotics (irrationalists both) can't freely choose to follow the eternal laws of logic, they should be treated by psychiatrists, not by ethical philosophers.

PM: But weren't Hitler, Stalin, and Genghis Khan rational?

ER: Yes as to means, no as to ends. They were capable of rationality and they often chose rational means to accomplish their ends, but the ends they chose were irrational because they violated true ethical precepts (which we'll shortly develop). They might have believed the world is flat or that killing innocent people is justifiable, but their beliefs were wrong.

Ethical statements deal only with ends, not means. When it comes to a particular situation, we ask those who best know the relevant facts – social scientists, psychologists, doctors, any observers who are competent – to apply the one provable ethical standard to the particular facts of a situation. Practical people, using the proper ethical standard, should determine the proper means, while ethical philosophers should determine the proper standard.

PM: Well, shouldn't we agree that murder and thievery are ethically wrong because the law says so?

ER: No. The law often errs. We all criticize some laws, so we're applying a higher standard, an ethical / rational standard. Our laws should conform to correct ethics; if we shouldn't kill innocent people or rob them, then our laws should comply. It is correct ethics that determines what should be legal, not vice versa. Legality doesn't determine what we ethically ought to do, otherwise Eichmann's "I was only following [legal] orders" would be a valid ethical excuse. The ethical law is higher than the legal.

Henry George (in A Perplexed Philosopher, *p. 211): Some people say that all rights are derived from the state, "but they do not really think this; for they are as ready as any one else to say of any proposed state action that it is right or it is wrong, in which they assert some standard of action higher than the state."*

PM: Is ethics really all that important? I learned ethical principles in kindergarten: Don't clunk your neighbor on the head, don't steal your neighbor's toys, and so on.

ER: Yes, ethics is important; it determines how we should behave. And yes, philosophers don't improve on what kindergarten teachers generally teach unless they *prove* their ethical precepts.

PM: But when you say, "You shouldn't murder," you mean "I

SOCIETY AT THE CRO§ROADS

don't like murder" or "I wish you wouldn't murder." You are expressing only a personal like or dislike.

ER: Certainly, but I'm saying something more than that: Since it contravenes rationally proven standards, don't do it.

PM: The wicked often go scot-free. There is no necessary penalty for immorality.

ER: True, but as the old saying goes, "Virtue is its own reward." If the wicked were struck dead by a thunderbolt, that wouldn't prove ethics. Would you want God to strike minor moral transgressors dead with one thunderbolt, more major ones with two thunderbolts, and so on? That could get complicated; besides, I don't think God works that way.

PM: Yes, but if someone believes something to be true, then it's true for that person.

ER: Yes and no – that statement is terribly ambiguous. It could mean not only that someone believes something to be true but it also could mean that something is objectively true for everyone. The two are not necessarily the same. People believe what they believe – of course, no problem – but we want to know whether those beliefs are objectively true for everyone. A belief can be either true or false. For instance, some people believe it's true the earth is flat or all widows should be burned, but these statements aren't true, no matter who believes such irrational nonsense.

Lucius Garvin (Introduction to Philosophy, *p. 420, stating the Law of Consistency): "If there is something which is right for* anyone *to do who is constituted and situated as I am, then it is right for* me *to do it, since I am obviously to be counted among those who are constituted and situated as I am."*

190

PM: Isn't it arrogant to set a universal ethical standard because it is telling others what they ought to do?

ER: No, what's true is true. Let's pursue and find the truth. Truth is not arrogance. If you say everyone should follow your culture, your religion, or your ethical beliefs, isn't that clearly arrogant? And more importantly, it's untrue. The individual is not the ultimate arbiter of right and wrong.

PM: You shouldn't be the judge in your own case.

ER: Why not? You should judge everything ethically, but your manner shouldn't be arrogant. It is no more arrogant to maintain that the world is spherical or that equal rights are true, than it is to maintain that the world is flat or that rights don't exist.

PM: Well maybe, but let's get on with it. What can you say about the Beautiful?

ER: Beauty is the pleasurable impact on one's emotions when contemplating proportion, order, color, truth, or clarity. Thus, beauty is subjective and relative because emotions are subjective and personal. Yes, beauty is in the eye of the beholder; if I say an object is beautiful, I only mean that it has a pleasurable impact on my emotions. *Chacun a son goût*, or perhaps you prefer *de gustibus non disputandum est.*[3†]

PM: Wait a minute. You know what you like, but so do monkeys.

ER: Yes, so? It's irrelevant what monkeys like. What they like doesn't affect the definition of beauty.

PM: Can't a consensus of knowledgeable experts objectively determine for us what is beautiful?

ER: No. They can only tell us what they like. There is much disagreement among experts; no general consensus exists. The knowledgeable experts of 1880 would not agree with the knowledgeable experts of a century later.[4†]

Aesthetically speaking, we can only say what we like. Personally, I like the *Mona Lisa* painting more than the painting of *Whistler's Mother*, but I can't *prove* it's objectively more beautiful. I can only prove I am sincere in saying I prefer *Mona Lisa*. When I say, "This bridge is beautiful," I mean only that the bridge excites pleasurable emotions in me.

George Santayana: *"It is unmeaningful to say that what is beautiful to one man* ought *to be beautiful to another."* (emphasis added)

PM: And what do you think is the relationship between art and beauty?

ER: They're no more mutually exclusive than beauty and utility. Art is objective because it has cognitive elements that can be either true or false; beauty (or aesthetics) is subjective and is to be distinguished from art. Hence, a Nazi or Communist poem can be beautiful but will be untrue or evil. A play, for instance, could have a beautiful form but be untrue in content, or it could be ugly in form yet true in content. If actors in a play merely didactically proclaim true statements, the play would be aesthetically unpleasing not because of false content but because of uninspiring form.

PM: However that may be, which of these standards for the three purposes of life would you say are objective, and which subjective?

ER: I'm glad you asked (ha). The standard of reality is objective – empirical fact and fact alone. The standard of ethics is also objective in that there is a rational way to behave; thus, we shouldn't steal once we rationally prove that people have property rights. But the standard of aesthetics is purely subjective because it is the impact on one's personal emotions, and emotions differ from person to person. Beauty is in the eye of the beholder, but not truth or goodness.

Surprisingly, many now think it is beauty that is primarily objective (it usually turns out that what they like, they think everyone should like) and that it is ethics that is primarily subjective; but they can offer no proof – and actually the reverse is true. Relativists might say they're seeking the ethical truth but they never expect to find it and would spurn it if they should stumble upon it.

PM: Let's pursue this a bit more. Don't both aesthetic and ethical judgments deal with values, which are personal and subjective?

ER: Surely both are personal values, but aesthetic values are matters of personal opinion only, and are therefore purely subjective, whereas ethical standards are objective because by definition they're rational and therefore the same for people whenever they act rationally.

PM: Are you therefore maintaining that there are two objective standards (the real and the ethical) and one subjective standard (the beautiful)?

ER: Not quite, for there is another standard of truth – definitional. A definition is a personal stipulation to facilitate communication between people. There's no such thing as a correct definition since it is subjective. (Ambiguous definitions convey no meaning.) The subjectivity of definitions will become particularly important when we discuss what a thing is. For that, have patience.

So we have two objective standards of truth – ethics and reality – and two subjective standards – aesthetic and definitional.

PM: But you still haven't tried to prove any ethical standard.

ER: That's true, but have patience. We still have some matters to clear up before we attempt that.

The Four Sources of Ethical Truth

ER: Although there can be only one true source for discerning ethical truth – otherwise we could not escape contradiction – there are four sources of ethics:

    (1) the individual (that is to say, whatever the individ-

ual believes to be true is true because the individual believes it, or ethical relativism)

(2) culture

(3) religion

(4) reason

We have already fully examined the logical defects of item (1) in the previous chapter. It certainly is clear enough that individuals are often wrong.

PM: Well, we needn't go into that again. But isn't it obvious that culture is a correct source of ethics?

ER: No. It is a source of ethics, of course, but not the *correct* source. Confusion arises from a terrible ambiguity in the common definition of the word *ethics*. It is often defined both as what people *think* they should do and also what people *should* do. Obviously, in different cultures they think they should do different things; for instance, certain cultures think widows should be burned while other cultures think not, but merely labeling a belief "cultural" doesn't make it correct. We here are interested only in what people *should* do. What people *think* they should do is the legitimate concern of sociologists and historians; it just isn't our concern.

Surely, different cultures differ; who would maintain otherwise? The Nazi culture believed it was correct, but we want to know whether it actually was.

PM: Why do you maintain that culture isn't the *correct* source of ethical behavior?

ER: I have these seven reasons:

(1) *Cultural relativism egregiously violates the impassable Is-Ought Barrier.* This alone is enough to disprove cultural relativism.

Steven Weinberg, who won the Nobel Prize for physics in 1979, has famously supposed, "The more the universe seems incomprehensible, the more it seems pointless."[5] Alas, poor Weinberg. He thought science or reality was the source of ethics. Rationality is.

(2) *What is a culture, anyway?* What are its bounds? Why can't a culture have a membership of only one person? If I am a member of a particular religion, a suburbanite, a professor emeritus, and so on, what should I do when these cultures disagree? Government is not the correct arbiter of right or wrong – are its laws above criticism?

(3) *Why must I obey a culture?* If I commit a crime, I shouldn't say to a judge, "My culture made me do it." To the extent I'm rational, that wouldn't be so. I chose to commit the crime. Cultures are not mystical entities with a will and destiny of their own independent of the free-will individuals composing them. If my culture is wrong, then I have chosen wrongly if I choose it. Cultures often make mistakes; they once maintained the world was flat and religious heretics should be burnt at the stake. The Mafia is a culture – should it be allowed to make its own ethical rules? Several African cultures endorse female circumcision even though it is ethically wrong to do so. If the culture acts correctly – that is, rationally – then it is rationality and not culture that is the ultimate determinant of right and wrong.

(4) *Who speaks for a culture – a majority or a powerful elite?* Why so for either?

(5) *Why are others more ethically correct than me?* Why is a minority always wrong? Were Moses, Amos and Hosea, Jesus, Florence Nightingale, and Franklin Delano Roosevelt ethical reprobates because they wanted to change society? "Whatever is, is right" – do you believe that? How can it be proven?

(6) *I often change my views, but that doesn't mean I have changed my culture.* My culture certainly influences my views, but they don't determine them.

(7) *Culturalism promotes ethical relativism if it asserts*

that correct ethical principle is culture based – that is, based on what people think is right. Beg not the question.

To summarize: Culture is not the correct source of ethical conduct, and if many people characterize themselves as cultural relativists or multiculturalists, it is because they are actually saying only that cultures differ, which is obviously true but irrelevant as to what is correct.

PM: But there are no universally accepted cultural standards. They're all different.

ER: They certainly differ, but so what? That's irrelevant. Even if all cultures accepted a particular ethical standard, it wouldn't necessarily be correct. Even if everyone believed in widow-burning or the flatness of the world, those beliefs would still be incorrect. Popularity is one thing, truth another.

PM: OK, but shouldn't survival of the culture be the standard of action?

ER: Why so? Is survival the sole earthly judge of right and wrong? You don't want to identify with the man who said that (Hitler). Some cultures shouldn't survive, like the Nazi or Communist cultures. The culture of cockroaches seems to survive, even thrive, but there is no ethical or rational significance in that.

Pope John Paul II (in The Wall Street Journal, *3/8/00, p. A20): "Faith and reason are like two wings on which the human spirit rises to the contemplation of truth."*

PM: Well maybe, but let us now turn to religion. Isn't it the correct source of morality?

ER: Not any more so than it is the correct judge of beauty or reality.[6†] Religion is primarily concerned with the hereafter, ritual, and the spreading of altruism and equal rights. It could well leave the proof of rational standards of behavior to rationalists, who they can hope will be religious. It is certainly true that many of us get our ethical views from our religion, but religion's primary interests are beyond rational proof, which is our primary concern here. Religion exceeds its proper boundaries when it attempts to prove ethical principle. While we can certainly believe both in God and in a rational proof of equal rights, we shouldn't use religion to prove ethical principle, for these reasons:

(1) *It's God's will, presumably, that we be rational.* He gave us reason and must therefore have expected us to use it, so an examination of the rational is an examination of God's will; religionists shouldn't object to that. It sure beats the assumption that God wants us to think and do whatever we please.

We tend to think that our religious beliefs should apply to everyone, but why so? Isn't that ethnocentric, or at least "religiocentric"? Surely God wants us to be rational, so let's find out what is rational. As Thomas Aquinas said, sin is an act against reason.

(2) *And then there is the important matter of which came first – God or ethics.* Is the doctrine of equal rights correct because God wills it, or does God will it because it is correct? Westerners are likely to be surprised that many Asians believe the latter. This theological question is important but is beyond discussion here.

Mahatma Gandhi: "I used to believe that God was truth; now I know that truth is God."

---

(3) *The religions disagree, so what then is the correct standard of ethics?* How can contradictory beliefs called religious be considered correct? For instance, in a war both sides pray to the same God;

the old Indian religious custom of *suttee* was irrational, and so the British were correct in banning it, religious beliefs notwithstanding. When religion and rationality disagree, rationality should win out. Merely calling an action or belief religious doesn't make it right.

(4) *We shouldn't base a proof on our belief in God.* Who can prove possession of a pipeline to Heaven? Who is privy to the mind of God? Religion can certainly make an ethical standard popular and it can motivate ethical and altruistic behavior, but it cannot provide a rational proof of ethics. That is not its proper domain.

Some people think God is within us – does that mean that every time you do something good for yourself, you are doing a religious act?

(5) *Don't unbelievers often act morally?* The United States has more churches per capita than Denmark, but Americans are not therefore more ethical.

(6) *Don't avowedly religious people sometimes act unethically?* Torquemada of the Spanish Inquisition comes to mind. We shouldn't question his religious sincerity, but he was wrong to torture others. Ethics and religion often overlap, but not always.

(7) *We may have a religious obligation to support the poor, but not if force via taxation is used.* (If you don't think taxation involves the use of force, see what happens when you don't pay your taxes.)

(8) *Religion promotes ethical relativism if it asserts that ethical principle is faith based* – that is, individually based. One unfortunate result of this wrong view: If religion is not to be taught in our public schools, then neither will ethical principles.

PM: I take it from all this that you are against religion.

ER: Not at all. My experience these days has been that religious people tend to be more honest and altruistic than most. In this time of increasing ethical relativism and its consequent cultural dysfunctions, the churches have their hands full in promoting equal rights and altruism. They should welcome an ethical proof from rationalists.

Shouldn't religious people be happy if correct ethical thinking supports what they have long maintained (for instance, that we should refrain from murder, group discrimination, and robbery, thereby respecting the equal rights of others)? If rationality comes to the aid of religion by proving the ethical standard which most religions now espouse, wouldn't more people be likely to be good? Shouldn't religionists seek a rational proof of equal rights as the Word of God? Don't rationality and religion come to the same ethical conclusions? As rationality shouldn't invade the many provinces of religion, neither should religion invade the province of rationality. Religion inspires many to be good but its impact is lessened if it puts being good on a nonprovable basis only. Religion needs all the help it can get from rationalism if is to successfully counter ethical relativism and cultural disintegration. Reason has often been thought to be the enemy of religion, but that isn't so.

Alan Dressler (prominent astronomer, quoted in New Republic, 10/12/98, p. 25): "Many scientists seem to be on a crusade to run down human worth, because they think this will destroy the old religious arrogance of believing that man is the center of the universe. But nobody believes that anymore."

Gregg Easterbrook (journalist, in New Republic, 10/12/98, p. 29): "Imagine a faculty meeting at any Ivy League university or a top-staff meeting at any major East Coast news organization. In rushes a courier to announce

*that an archaeologist has just discovered proof
that the founding scriptures of all major faiths
are forgeries; there would be broad smiles and
acclaim. Then imagine, instead, that a courier
announces that a biologist has just discovered
physical evidence of the soul; faculty types would
fidget unhappily, while media types would scoff."*

PM: So you think there's still plenty for religious leaders to do even if they don't have to prove an ethical standard?

ER: Absolutely. Religious leaders objected to Newton's law of gravity saying that it drove God out of the universe and put a law in His place; the same was said of Copernicus, Darwin, and Einstein. Religion survived nevertheless because religion and science don't conflict but rather supplement each other; they're aiming at different targets of thought. Neither religion nor rationality are at odds with each other. We shouldn't use religion to rationally prove factual or logical statements.

If an ethical standard is justified by faith, can't any ethical system (e.g., egoism, rightlessness) be similarly justified? An opinion isn't true merely because it is labeled religious. When we prove an ethical standard to be rationally true, then religious opinion should apply it to reality. Churches need never fear that they'll have nothing to do:

(1) They should help enforce equal rights. Too many injustices exist in America and elsewhere.

(2) The cultural slide induced by postmodern ethical relativism should be combated. This involves the moral applications of ethical standards to particular situations in reality.

(3) Religionists have always had something to say about sex.

(4) Religions instill much-needed altruism and take care of their members.

(5) Religions must interpret their Scriptures. (Some

people think Joan of Arc was Noah's husband or that the epistles were wives of the apostles, but not so.)

(6) People want rituals and symbols.

(7) The young are to be religiously educated.

(8) Our religions should focus on the nature and definition of God.

(9) Strong religious beliefs have cured many diseases that medical science once thought incurable.[7][†]

There will always be much for religions to do.

Fyodor Dostoyevskey (in The Brothers Karamazov*): "Where there is no God, all is permitted."*

PM: Let's consider religion's age-old Golden Rule: Do unto others before they do unto you, uh no, The guy who has the gold makes the rules, uh no, *"Do unto others as you would have others do unto you."* That's it. What's wrong with that?

ER: It sounds nice, but careful consideration reveals it isn't clear, cannot be proven, and isn't always true:

- *It isn't clear*: We incarcerate those who commit crimes, even if we ourselves don't want to be incarcerated. And on and on with this: I treat women as women, but I don't want to be treated as a woman (even though I treat both men and women as people). And so forth.

- *It cannot be proven*: Those who espouse the Golden Rule never try to prove it; it's simply not in a form that can be proven.

- *It isn't always true*: For instance,

  (1) It sets up the individual as the ethical standard, and we see how wrong that can be.

   Suppose I live according to wrong ethical views; should everybody do so? For instance,

Hitler believed in the master race theory and seemed willing to die for it, but should everybody do likewise? If I like to suffer because I am a masochist, should everybody suffer? If I make others suffer, the Golden Rule would be dangerous in my hands. If I have sadistic urges, should others also have them?

(2) It can violate rights. For instance, I'd like others to give me money, but do I therefore have to give money to them? I would then have no right of property. Other people's needs shouldn't trump my right to be free. Many more such examples could be cited. The so-called Golden Rule is fine for people who are rational, but then it is rationality that is the standard and not the Golden Rule.

Hillel's negative Golden Rule (often called the Silver Rule) suffers from these same defects.

PM: What about "Love thy neighbor as thyself"?

ER: It suffers from the same defects as the Golden Rule. It simply is bad advice if I don't love myself to just the right amount – what is that amount, anyway? Exactly how should I be loving myself? We have to do better; otherwise all things will be permitted.

PM: What's wrong with the Ten Commandments?

ER: It offers no rational proof, nor is it in a form that can be proven. Also, it suffers in translation – for instance, the original Hebrew word *tirtzach* seems to have meant killing but has been transmuted into murder. This transmutation is important: Killing isn't murder, as in self-defense. Shouldn't we kill in the case of a just war? Isn't a just war just? Also, it is disconcerting that the Lutheran and Catholic versions of the Ten Commandments are different and differ from that of other faiths.

PM: What about agapë love? Millard Burrows wrote, "To love

one's neighbor is not to feel affection for him but to wish and seek his good."[8]

ER: If Burrows wants to do that, fine. More power to him, except that he and other altruists should realize that "love" loses all meaning if we are supposed to love murdering. Nor did he ever attempt a rational proof, nor did he define good. He has an unproven opinion, which anyone can have.

PM: But maybe *ignosticism* is justified. It is the view that we don't know God or His moral laws.

ER: Ignostics are always searching for the truth but never expect to find it. Now they can endlessly dispute among themselves the ethical proof offered in this book.

Thomas Paine (in The Rights of Man*): "My country is the world, and my religion is to do good."*

Arthur Schlesinger, Jr. (historian): "Reason without passion is sterile, but passion without reason is hysterical. I have always supposed that reason and passion must be united in any effective form of public action."

PM: Well, you had better wind up your views on religion and morality.

ER: Yes:

(1) Intellectuals seek answers to the Big Questions of Life, which is exactly what religious people seek. Then aren't religionists to be considered intellectuals, whether they're schooled or not? If so, they would certainly be the largest of all groups of intellectuals.

(2) Religion and rationality should cooperate and not attempt to undermine each other. Rationality is needed to prove the worth of human freedom and its limits, but then religion is needed to provide the emotive power for respecting human freedom and

its limits. Rationality is the only way to prove ethical truth. Religions shouldn't contravene rationality; otherwise people will end up believing first in nothing, and then, having no provably true ethical standards, they'll believe anything. "We do not live in a meaningless world," said Pope John Paul II, but without proven rational bounds to our behavior the world would then be meaningless; no reason = no meaning. To pursue the ethical truth is to obey God's will. Proving it is rationality's task, but living according to it is religion's task.

(3) As with culture, so with religion: We choose a religion; it doesn't choose us.

(4) When reason conflicts with religion on how we should act in this world, correct reason takes precedence. Merely calling a belief "religious" cannot justify it. For instance, it wasn't so long ago that religious (or cultural) justifications were given for slavery. I may have a religious belief in the flatness of the earth, but the earth simply isn't flat, not even for me, whether my belief is religious or not. Suttee was ethically and rationally wrong, no matter how religiously (or culturally) it might have been justified. If you commit a crime, don't tell the court your religious beliefs justify what you did.[9]† Although rationality can prove the existence of God as Creator – after all, humans didn't create people or land, yet they exist so Something must have created them – it cannot adequately describe the nature and attributes of God. That's the proper province of religion. (He's not some sort of Celestial Butler from whom we implore blessings and gifts – He does answer all prayers, although generally the answer is no; neither is He some capricious all-powerful Oriental Potentate as in Biblical times.)

Certainly, religion and culture are sources of ethical principles, but they aren't the correct sources. Those who so regard them are necessarily ethical relativists, no matter what their intentions, because they say that our personal choices, labeled cultural or religious, determine what is ethically and rationally true. Rationality is broader than ethics, but when we act rationally toward others, we are acting ethically.

PM: Yes, but culturalists and religionists often take strong moral stands.

ER: Certainly so, but strong beliefs don't constitute rational proof. After talking with many people, I have found that they often have knee-jerk reactions to the question of what is the correct source of ethics. They think, with irrational fervor, that it is culture or religion. Maybe they're thinking with their knees.

PM: But you still haven't mentioned what the ethical dictate of rationality is. You haven't yet proven any ethical standard to be rationally true.

ER: Let's get to that now.

"We SHOULD Treat Things as They Are, AAEII" – A Proof

ER: The only basic and provable ethical statement is this:

We SHOULD treat things as they are, as an end in itself (AAEII).

For example, we should treat this thing that is commonly called a table as being a table. We should treat this lamp as a lamp, and so forth. We have no choice but to always treat things in every waking moment of our lives; however, this statement tells us what we should always do. Therefore when proved it will become the most important statement ever made. It is not a mere opinion. It is the only ethical statement that can be directly proven. On the other hand, true moral statements can be literally infinite in number because they depend on an infinite number of unforeseeable particular circumstances.

"We should treat things as they are, AAEII" is the basic statement of ethical philosophy because it tells us what we should do. It is the ethical equivalent of $e = mc^2$. We mustn't expect that the most important ethical statement we can ever utter will be something esoteric and grand; it is more likely to be commonplace, often taken for granted and therefore overlooked. It is the very basis of rational behavior. Might determines the course of reality, but logic determines what ought to be (i.e., rationality).

Let's talk about AAEII. It means "as an end in itself" – that is to say, for its own sake and purpose, *sui generis*, as a principle of action irrespective of usefulness or of particular circumstances in reality. It doesn't lead to anything else. Remember, ethics can only be concerned with ends; means involve the moral application of the correct ethical end to the relevant facts of reality. Since it is awkward to append the qualifier "AAEII" to every ethical "should" statement we make, it should always be understood as being appended.

PM: Shouldn't we rather say that we should treat things as they are perceived to be?

ER: No. Suppose our perceptions are inaccurate? Actions based on wrong perceptions are wrong. If people perceive wrongly, they will act wrongly. For instance, imagine a doctor who perceives his patient to have a liver problem, but in fact the patient has a pancreas problem. The doctor will surely treat the patient according to his misperception even though he shouldn't. We are only interested here in what should have been done. (Should the doctor be blamed for having made a diagnostic mistake? Maybe, but that is another issue and not for us to say. This is not a book on medical diagnostics; the question of blame should concern doctors and criminologists, not us.) I may not know what things are and so may not treat them as they are; but ethics says I *should*. Let's not confound "perceived to be" with "should."

PM: The statement "we should treat things as they are" is meaningless unless you say what a thing is.

ER: You don't know what a thing is? You don't know what "is" is? Anyway, we're talking about how we should treat it. No matter what a thing is, we should treat it as it is. How else should we treat it? As it isn't? "A thing is what it is" is the very essence of meaning, the very basis for the study of logic, and it requires that we should treat it as it is. Rationality doesn't deny there's something out there called reality, but we're not here concerned with what it *is*, only that we *should* treat it as it is; specifically, we should treat other people, which is the concern of ethics, as they are.

PM: If we treat things as they are, we would oppose all change. That's not right.

ER: I certainly don't oppose all change. Suppose we see an injustice – sex discrimination or slavery, let us say. First, we should treat the injustice as existing (we should face the facts, however unpleasant they may be; we should be realistic, we should treat things as they are) and then, since it is an injustice, we should change it. "Treat" doesn't mean "accept" or "approve of."

PM: Look, don't we have to treat things as they are? We simply don't have a choice. How else can we treat them? You call this statement the most important statement ever made, but it's trite and trivial.

ER: If you think it's trite, then at least you think it's true, because what's trite is true. But since you've never encountered the statement before, how can it be trite? You call it trivial, but it tells us how to behave toward everything that surrounds us. That's hardly trivial. Doesn't that qualify it to be the most important statement in any language, if proven?

As for having to treat things as they are: not so. We often treat things as they are not. Can't we treat this book as an audiocassette or the sun as going around the earth? Didn't many people once treat the earth as being flat, or *suttee* as being correct? Don't scientists often err because they unintentionally treat things as they're not? Often it's not easy to treat things as they are, but nevertheless we should.

Eli J. Schleifer: "The wise man recognizes that life's most important truths are often trite. The clever man sees only the triteness."

PM: But wait a minute: Doesn't "ought" imply "can"?

ER: No. These words have entirely different meanings. We ought to (or should) do what is rational even if we cannot.

PM: Are you saying that I should do something even if I can't do it?

ER: Absolutely yes. "Can" is in the province of "is" and has nothing to do with the province of "should." (Don't try to violate the Is-Ought Barrier.) For instance, the misdiagnosing doctor mentioned previously should treat the patient for a pancreas problem even if he can't because of his limited medical knowledge. A particular person's ignorance doesn't dispel the ethical law.

PM: Well, there are some definitions we need. Start with defining *things*.

ER: If you wish. Things are whatever exist as separate entities; they are separable objects of thought or aspects of reality. They're tangible objects, conditions, or feelings; see any dictionary. Shouldn't we treat them as they are? How else should we treat them?

PM: But we can't be sure what they are.

ER: Yes, but so what? That's irrelevant. Shouldn't we always treat things as they are, AAEII? Ethical principle is over here, things or reality are over there. We're into ethics, not epistemology or physics. If you were told that this book was about things or reality, you should demand your money back from your bookseller.

PM: Isn't truth in the eye of the beholder?

ER: No – beauty is.

PM: Maybe things are holographic illusions.

ER: If so, then that's how we should treat them. Are things a certain collocation of atoms? Then that's how we should treat them. Are they an uncertain collocation of atoms? Then *that's* how we should treat them. Did Joshua make the sun stand still? Whatever, that's irrelevant to ethical principle. It's a reality problem we're not dealing with here.

I've talked with many people about this and found they think "we should treat things as they are" is a statement about things or reality. It absolutely is not; it's a *should* statement. It talks about ethical principle ("should-ness"). Reality can be difficult to comprehend, but fortunately ethical principle isn't. *Should* is the operative word in the statement, not *things*. Things are whatever they are and we should treat them that way.

PM: But, who's to say what we should or should not do?

ER: Again, "who's to say" is completely irrelevant to ethical principle. What people say has nothing to do with what actually is right and true. $a^2 + b^2 = c^2$ for flat right triangles – that's a true statement no matter who says it or denies it.

PM: But mathematical statements are about reality.

ER: So what? That's irrelevant to whether we should treat things as they are. Suppose someone says to you, "You shouldn't rob." Is your rejoinder going to be "Who's to say?"

PM: Doesn't my view of reality determine my actions toward it?

ER: Yes, but again, so what? Your view of reality is irrelevant to what we're discussing here. The libraries are full of good books on various aspects of reality, but we're discussing ethical principle ("should-ness") – that's entirely different. An ethical proof deals with rationality, not reality. Again, "we should treat things as they are" says nothing at all about things or reality.

In treating things, we can make two errors:

(1) We can misapprehend them.

(2)   We can be irrelevant.

Let's avoid both these pitfalls in both ethical and realistic reasoning.

PM: What do you mean by *treat*?

ER: Deal with, act toward, consider. Shouldn't we be realistic? Shouldn't we face the facts? Shouldn't we act toward facts as they are? Shouldn't we treat things as they are? When I thought up this statement some time ago, I thought everyone would immediately agree to it. It is the basic statement from which all "shoulds" emanate. Isn't it obviously true? Isn't it the basis of every correct action? Isn't it the general statement of what is correct to do? For the life of me, I can't understand why there is a reluctance to accept the obvious. Maybe you think we should find out what things are in order to ignore them, but count me out.

PM: Wait a moment – what do you mean by *we*, as in "We should treat things as they are?"

ER: "We" is everybody who can choose to treat things as they are. No doubt there are misguided people who regard nonmembers of their ethnic group as being subhuman, but they're wrong because they're not treating them as they are. Since they should treat all things as they are, they should treat people (who are an important class of "things") as having the same rights we do, since *we* refers to everyone.

PM: Suppose I have an incurable cancer that will lead to my early death, but I'd rather not know that. Should I be told on the grounds that I should treat things as they are?

ER: This is a problem in moral application and not ethical principle, which is what interests us here, but I'll answer anyway: You should want to know the truth, but no one should force that knowledge upon you against your will, thereby violating your right to be free.

PM: I would like to know where you're going with your ethical statement.

ER: Why? Either it's true or false, and not at all dependent on how I may use it.

PM: Well OK, but "we should treat things as they are" presupposes that we are free to choose what we'll do, within limits to be sure. It assumes free will! Well, the free will versus determinism debate is an age-old controversy with no resolution in sight.

ER: True enough. But we needn't resolve that debate here since we are investigating ethical principle and not the reality of whether we have the ability to be free. We are concerned only with people insofar as they have the free will to choose to act rationally and ethically. If they lack free will, they'll do what they're determined to do by circumstances beyond their control. But that's not our concern here.

That said, a few words here on the free will versus determinism debate are not inappropriate. It seems likely that we have at least some free will, which is the ability to choose among alternative courses of thought and action within the limits imposed by our mental and physical abilities. We all have observed that normal people can think the thoughts they think and move their bodies as they will, within those limits. We are surer of this observation than of any other we can make. In other words, we can freely choose to treat things as they are. Free will is limited by circumstances we cannot control, but it exists within those limits. We can certainly make choices. Determinists can call free will an illusion (just as any observation can be so labeled), but what evidence can they present? But ultimately, the free will versus determinism debate is for reality philosophers to resolve, not for ethics philosophers. Rationality determines how people should ethically use whatever free will they may have[10†] – that's all we need say here.

This analysis sheds light on the writing of history. To the extent we have free will, we approach the facts of the past with a particular philosophy, not vice versa. History doesn't determine correct philosophy; rather the reverse: our philosophy determines how we interpret history. We arrange and judge the historical facts according to our philosophy.

Christian deDuve (Nobel-prize-winning Belgian biologist, quoted in New Republic, *10/12/98): "Eventually we will understand that the origin of life was not a highly improbable cosmic jest but rather an* almost *obligatory outcome of chemical structures, given the right conditions" (emphasis added).*

Arthur Compton (renowned nuclear scientist, quoted in Living Issues in Philosophy, *1959, pp. 180-1): "One's ability to move his hand at will is much more directly and certainly known than are even the well-tested laws of Newton."*

PM: Let's talk now about ends and means. Surely you don't think the end can justify the means?

ER: I most assuredly do. What are ends for but to justify means? Because means enact the end, they are part of it. When we justify a means we use a relevant end to do so. The real questions are these:

    (1) Are we choosing a correct rational/ethical end?

    (2) Is the chosen means relevant to that end?

    (3) Is the chosen means the most effective for reaching it?

Since there's no clear litmus test for determining the appropriate means, we can easily err by choosing means which are in themselves irrational and unethical. [11†] Immoral means cannot be justified by altruistic ends if those ends are not relevant. Once we determine what the proper ends of human behavior are, we are better able to choose the proper means.

We are faced with many alternative means for enacting an ethical principle. We can't avoid them. To choose the best of them, we need the reports of competent observers, be they politicians, psychiatrists, businessmen, social scientists, doctors, relatives, and so on. Ethical philosophers should deal only with ends.

Hitler, Stalin, Genghis Khan, and others like these were often rational in their choice of means, but their ends were irrational. We should be rational as to both means and ends.

Jacques Maritain (in Man and the State, *1954, p. 50): "Means must be proportioned and appropriate to the end, since they are ways to the end and, so to speak, the end itself in its very process of coming into existence."*

PM: One last stab at this: People interpret "things" differently. Who's to say who's right?

ER: Here we go again with "who's to say." That's irrelevant to what we're discussing, which is ethical principle. We're primarily interested in what people *should* do rather than in what they think they should do, or say.

What people really mean when they ask, "Who's to say?" is "Aren't religion or culture the *correct* sources of ethics?" No, rationality is, for the reasons given.

The Big Question

PM: But the Big Question is still not answered fully: You say we should treat a thing as it is; maybe we should, but how can you *prove* it?

ER: Let's be perfectly clear about this, for this is the very core of this book. There are two ways to prove the statement "We should treat a thing as it is." The first way is this:

(1) *Since a thing is as it is, we should treat it as it is, AAEII.*

Twenty-four hundred years ago, Aristotle put forward

the statement "a thing is as it is" (a = a). It forms the basis of the study of logic.[12] It's called the Law of Identity.

PM: Wait a minute. Not so fast. Here is a chair (pointing to what most people subjectively define as a chair). I think it's comfortable to sit on, but others may not. Sometimes we may want to stand on it (to reach something high) or even burn it (under certain conditions). Some people may regard it as a throne, or even as an elephant. A thing is what we think it is.

ER: Well, I suppose I'll have to substantiate even the obvious, that a thing is as it is.

In the first place, quite obviously some of our thoughts are *false* (we're not always right, as when most people thought the world was flat or equal rights is unprovable), so a thing isn't what we think it is. Second, the things you stated about the chair seem perfectly true, but they are *irrelevant* to the statement that a thing is what it is. The thing you're pointing to has a certain size, weight, composition, and so on; that's what the thing is, however we may define it. What, "A" doesn't equal "A"?

"A thing is what it is" tells us that the thing exists. It's the Law of Identity. Does that bother you? Do you have trouble with existence, with "is"? That statement doesn't tell us anything about chairs or genomes or black holes or whatever; we need other sentences to do that, but in no way do any of them affect the truth of the sentence "A thing is as it is."

You can't have rational or logical discourse without assuming that a thing is as it is, that it exists. It's a tautology, but tautologies are true. Offer some logic to disprove it if you can, but it's too obviously true and important for you to plead ignorance.

If a thing is as it is, shouldn't we treat a thing as it is, AAEII? Shouldn't we take the Law of Identity seriously? If a statement is true, shouldn't we treat it as being true? If we did otherwise, we would be acting on the premise that a thing isn't as it is, and that's obviously false.

Here then, is the first proof: If a thing is as it is, then *we should treat it as it is, AAEII*. This is the basic Law of Ethics, since it tells us what we *provably* should do! It's so obvious, it has been overlooked. For whatever his reasons, Aristotle never made the logical leap from the Law of Identity to the Law of Ethics.

Shouldn't we face the facts? Shouldn't we be realistic? Shouldn't we recognize an unjust situation as existing in order to change it? In short, shouldn't we treat things as they are, AAEII? Since the Eiffel Tower is in Paris, shouldn't we treat it as being there instead of, say, in Florence? "Should" statements are true, valid, rational, and basic, but this has to be carefully explained to a postmodernist.

Expect a basic ethical principle to be extremely simple; we should be suspicious if it were difficult for an average person to understand. If you still insist on treating things as they are not, counter with logic, not a sidestep.

Lionel Ruby (Logic: An Introduction, p. 264): "Does the reader believe that a proposition can be 'true for one man and false for another,' or that 'what is true in one age of history is false in another age'? If so, he rejects the law of identity, for the law means that if a proposition is true, it is true for all persons, in all times, and in all places. But, the reader may urge, was not the statement 'The earth is flat' true in the middle ages and is it not false today? The answer to the first part of this question is No. The earth was not flat in the middle ages, and to have called it such was to utter a false statement. People believed that the earth was flat, but believing a thing is so does not make it so. Their belief was false." (Ruby's italics)

What an oversight Aristotle committed by not connecting his Law of Logic with the Law of Ethics! (Actually, he went off in another ethical direction altogether, a dead end.) We've gone 2,400 years in the ethical dark!

PM: But aren't you trying to bust the unbustable Is-Ought Barrier?

ER: No. I didn't say that because a thing *is* as it is, it *should* be as it is. That would be deriving "ought" from "is," but I didn't do that. That would be asserting that whatever is (exists), is right (should exist), and therefore all change is bad; I would never say that.

PM: But "should" or "ought" statements are false or invalid – matters of personal opinion only.

ER: To think so is self-contradictory. You say we *should* believe that, yet you say "should" statements are false or invalid!

Let me ask you to make a statement that you think can't be denied.

PM: I exist.

ER: By that you mean we should treat you as existing. OK, but that doesn't contradict "we should treat things as they are, AAEII." Your existence is *irrelevant* to that statement.

PM: Enough already. You said there's another way to prove "we should treat things as they are." Let's hear it.

ER: Yes, you may prefer this approach. The second way is this:

(2) *We should be accurate,* AAEII, *and accuracy requires that we should treat reality as it is.*

The AAEII qualifier is important, because sometimes we should deceive someone by describing a thing inaccurately, as when we should lie to a prospective murderer about the whereabouts of the intended victim. But in that case, our end or purpose is deception, not accuracy or truth. Ends are the only concern of ethics.

Accuracy is the very essence of truth, but doesn't it require treating a thing as it is? We couldn't be accurate if we didn't.

We have finally arrived at the most important statement ever made – *"we should treat a thing as it is,* AAEII.*"* This is the only "should" statement that can be *directly* proven true!

Let's face it – there can be no logical support for ethical relativism. If you embrace that illogical doctrine, you suffer, society suffers, and it makes no sense to read this book if logic be damned and you're not going to abandon relativist views.

There are those who say, "Who needs logic?" (or in matters of reality they say, "Who needs evidence?") "I don't change my views for anything; I am a stone." But what's the sense of knowing more and more about things, as science tries to do, unless we treat those things as they are? Shouldn't we act rationally and ethically? Shouldn't we treat Caesar as having crossed the Rubicon River with an army in 49 B.C.? Postmodern existentialists tend to treat things as they are in their own businesses (be they geologists, lawyers, economists, businesspeople, historians, and so on) or in solving everyday problems (like cooking food or exiting a room), but when they get philosophical, they go solipsist and criticize "We should treat things as they are" by saying "I don't understand" or "We should act however we please."

If we should treat a thing as it is, then we surely have a right to be free to do what we should do (should = right to be free), in which case the right to be free to treat things as they are is *proven*. However, we'll have to leave the full proof of this for the next chapter. Now we need only say it is proven that we should treat a thing as it is, AAEII.

PM: But didn't Ralph Waldo Emerson say, "Consistency is the hobgoblin of little minds"?

ER: No, he didn't say that. He said, *"Foolish* consistency is the hobgoblin of little minds" (emphasis added). I've got no problem with that. Down with foolishness.

It would seem that many people are more enamored of ethical relativism than of equal rights, averring that people should do whatever they wish, even if irrationalism or solipsism has to be embraced. They hold onto their ethically relativistic outlook with irrational fervor even after it has been proven false. They're not aware that for almost all of recorded history, ethical principles were regarded as being provable (although, to be sure, the proofs offered were invalid). Postmodern ethical relativism is peculiar to our time, and actually to only a small but vocal minority in the world, however unaware postmodernists may be of this.

PM: What about peace? Isn't that a correct ethical standard?

ER: No. Peace at any price may not be ethical or just; it probably won't be. If we all blindly followed a leader like Hitler, we would have peace but not justice. He would order us to do unjust things. Besides, it can't be proven that peace is a correct ethical standard.

PM: Then justice is the correct ethical standard.

ER: OK, but justice needs definition and proof.

PM: Well, how about being moderate? Why can't we be a little relativist and a little absolutist? Why one or the other?

ER: Moderation is often good moral advice, but ethical principles are either true or false, rational or irrational, or as with computers 0 or 1. Let's have no fuzzy thinking. You can't be half-pregnant. Ethical or mathematical principles are either right or wrong.

PM: But isn't it ethically empty to say that we should treat things as they are? It gives us inadequate ethical guidance in our daily lives. For instance, what can it tell us about the morality of abortion?

ER: Agreed – "treating things as they are" doesn't directly address abortion or any of the other moral problems we face daily. But have patience – we are now ready to prove an ethical standard of human behavior that can be morally applied to particular circumstances in reality. Our next chapter addresses this. Suffice it to say now that we have arrived at a true ethical statement (a "should" statement), and all that remains for us to do is to *logically derive* from it a useful ethical standard. That won't be difficult. Then we will have put the final nail in the postmodern ethical relativist coffin and clearly see that it is mere opinion only, a false and dele- terious one at that.

Henry David Thoreau: "There are thousands hacking at the branches of the Tree of Evil for every one who is striking at the root."

References and footnoted material for this chapter begin on page 351 in the appendices.

CHAPTER EIGHT

EQUAL
RIGHTS:
The PROOF

Chapter 7 proves a particular ethical statement to be true, but it is not in a form that can guide us in solving the leading ethical problems of our day. This chapter addresses that subject.

Postmodernist (PM):

> I conceive it as my task here to help you bring out your ideas and raise commonly held objections, rather than to argue steadfastly and long for my position that nothing ethical can be proven. One can offer nothing more than moral sound and fury, signifying naught but personal opinion.

Ethical Rationalist (ER):

> And I conceive it as my task to show that acting ethically is synonymous with acting rationally, and therefore an ethical proof is possible; we needn't submit to the deleterious impact of ethical relativism. There is a rational alternative. We're not en-

gaged in a mere intellectual exercise: If we disregard ethical rationalism, cultural disintegration inevitably follows.

Abraham Maslow (eminent psychologist): "The ultimate disease of our time is valuelessness.... This state is more crucially dangerous than ever before in history."

PM: OK, let's get on with your alleged ethical proof.

ER: Well, to begin with, let us assume that we have already proven an ethical "should" statement to be true. Those of our readers who don't think so should reread the previous chapter. Its main contention is "We *should* treat things as they are, as an end in itself (AAEII)." This is the most important statement ever made because it tells us what is true for us to do. All that is required of us now is to find an ethical standard that corresponds to it. It logically follows that everyone has a right to one's own life, liberty, and property limited only by the equal right of others, AAEII. This is the second most important statement ever made.

PM: Some lists of rights are longer. The United Nations (UN), for instance, lists thirty rights.

ER: That's true, but the UN's list of rights is based on these basic three. Actually, the rights to life and property are derived from the right to liberty (or freedom).

We should always respect the equal rights of others if it is provably correct to do so. Our sun may someday burn itself out, the Ice Age may come again, might always triumphs in history, but we should always respect the equal rights of others.

PM: Perhaps, but prove it.

Albert Camus: "Without liberty heavy industry can be perfected, but not justice or truth."

> William Jennings Bryan: "No question is settled
> until it is settled right."

The Equal Right to Be Free (Liberty): A Proof

ER: First of all, let us dispense with the Jeffersonian vagary that people are equal. Equal as to what? I am not Mozart's equal in music, Jordan's equal in basketball, and so on, nor even equal as to opportunity with others. (The rich rightfully have more opportunity than I do insofar as they came by their riches honestly.) We are equal only as to rights.

PM: What about equal opportunity as an ethical standard?

ER: No good. We shouldn't accord equal opportunity to the burglar and burglee (the victim). Equal opportunity should be limited by the equal rights of others.

PM: Yes, but prove it.

ER: OK. The following reasoning is presented as a series of steps for purposes of clarity, but since each step logically follows from the previous proven step, then they're all simultaneously true. They are all based on the statement that *we should treat things as they are*, AAEII. Here we go:
[§1] *We have a right to be free to treat things as they are*, AAEII.

If we should treat things as they are, AAEII, as proven in the previous chapter, then surely we have a right to be free to do so. If we should do something, then we have the right to be free to do it. *Should = the right to be free.* If I should clear the snow off my sidewalk, then I have the legal right to do so and others have the duty to respect my right.

PM: You had better define *right*.

ER: Yes – a right is *an ethical claim others should respect*. But since people are things (important and sentient, to be sure, but things nevertheless), then it follows from [§1]) that:
[§2a] *We have a right to be free to treat people as they are, AAEII, since people are clearly a certain class of things.*

There couldn't be another correct way to treat people –

if there were, it would necessarily violate the equal rights of others.[1†] To state this precept more simply:

[§2b] *Our right to be free is limited by the equal right of others to be free.*

Q.E.D. When you oppose racism or sexism (group discrimination in general), are you not according to other people their equal right to be free?

PM: But since each person is different, shouldn't we treat them differently?

ER: They certainly are different in many nonethical ways, and so we should treat them differently in those ways, but ethically they are the same; we should all treat things as they are, AAEII. "We" means *all* people, including those we are treating; they have the same right to be free that we do. We have a duty to respect their proven rights.

PM: Well yes, but you're a logic chopper.

ER: I see. Maybe you'd be happier if I said only 75% (or some such percentage) of all people have equal rights. There'd be no logic-chopping in that – but no logic, either. Don't you want a proof for what you already believe in?

PM: I suppose so. But you don't mention lying; isn't it ethically wrong?

ER: Yes, because it violates the right of others to treat things as they are.

PM: How do you relate *rights* to *duty*?

ER: *Duty* is the converse of *rights*. If you have a right, I have the duty to respect it.

William Hazlitt (Freedom House pamphlet, 11/55, p. 7: "The love of liberty is the love of others; the love of power is the love of ourselves."

PM: Shouldn't we be altruistic rather than merely respectful of the equal rights of others?

ER: No. First we should be free; then we could be altruistic if we wish. Insofar as altruists actively defend rights, they deserve our praise and encouragement. But we shouldn't force people to be altruistic; force is wrong. Other people's needs don't override our rights. If they have needs, we could choose to voluntarily help them; in any case, equal rights provides a justifiable governmental income for them, as we subsequently demonstrate.

PM: What if I voluntarily make a contract to give up my right to be free and become a slave?

ER: Such a contract would be irrational and ethically void; you would be denying your own future rights. Legal regulations should prevent such a contract because it contravenes equal rights; we should not contract irrationally. The right to be free is inalienable and not something you can rationally or ethically give up.

PM: Others before you, like John Locke, concluded that we have equal rights. What have you added to their efforts?

ER: An airtight proof.

PM: Maybe, but isn't an ethical proof rather theoretical?

ER: No doubt, but so what? The relevant question is "Is it true?" The doctrine that individuals have no rights and should do whatever they wish – that's also theoretical.

PM: Well, I'm willing to grant other people the equal right to be free, but there are some who don't.

ER: Then they're wrong and you're right. Honest people don't differ as to ethical principles, just as to the means of achieving them. By definition, they embrace ethical principles (that's why they are honest), which are simple to know, but they can disagree about means because means involve all the relevant circumstances of reality, which are often difficult to know.

Judge Learned Hand: "Liberty lies in the hearts of men and women; when it dies there, no constitution, no law, no court can ever do much to help it. While it lies there it needs no constitution, no law, no court to save it."

Let me try another line of reasoning – the "duty" approach. If we should all be free to treat things as they are, then we all have the duty to do so, since obviously we have the duty to do what we should do. Q.E.D.

Thomas Jefferson: "The God who gave us life gave us liberty at the same time."
  Motto seen at the University of Pennsylvania: "Law is but the means, Justice is the end."

PM: Doesn't everybody agree to equal rights? Can't we take it for granted?

ER: Unfortunately not. We have to face the facts and should treat things as they are. The doctrine is hardly self-evident. In fact, only a minority in the world today accept the equal rights doctrine; few think it provable. Nor is equal rights won for all time – it must be constantly defended, and a proof would be helpful. History is writ in blood, especially in the twentieth century, with its racism, sexism, labor taxation, ill will, dictators, genocides and wars, also increasing ethical relativism.2†

PM: Well, let's move on to your alleged proof that we have an equal right to life.

Benjamin Franklin (letter to David Hartley, 12/4/1789): "God grant that not only the love of liberty, but a thorough knowledge of the rights of man, may pervade all the nations of the earth, so that a philosopher may set his foot anywhere on its surface, and say, This is my country."

The Equal Right to Life: A Proof

ER: If each of us has an equal right to be free limited by the equal right of others, then logically,
  [§3] *We have a right to our life limited by the equal right of others.*

Without the right to life, we couldn't have an equal right to be free. Our right to life is the sum total of all our rights to be free. If we have these rights, then we have a right to life. Q.E.D. If we murder people, we violate their right to be free. When we oppose murder, we accord others an equal right to life.

PM: Try telling that to the Columbine murderers.

ER: They weren't the correct arbiters of right and wrong. The weakest pupils in class are not the determiners of truth and falsity. There were fewer murderers when everyone assumed that the right to life was more than a personal opinion.

PM: If we have a right to our life, are you saying we have a right to commit suicide?

ER: No. That's murder – self-murder. I don't own my life that I can kill it; no one owns it, no one owns my soul – souls are unownable. I only own my *right* to life; that's significantly different from owning my life or soul. Suicide infringes on my right not only to my life but to my future liberty: Without life, I couldn't be free. We cannot justifiably do whatever we want with our lives; we shouldn't rob or murder, for instance, nor should we "slow-murder" ourselves, as we might with drugs.

The ethical principle that we shouldn't commit self-murder (suicide) is clear enough, but the moral application of this principle may not always be. For instance, suppose we can't be rational because we face a bedridden future riddled with reason-obliterating pain as do many sick people on their deathbed (few will die painlessly); suicide or assisted suicide may then become a rational choice. We could morally excuse the actions of a soldier who unwillingly reveals secrets under imminent threat of torture and death. There may be circumstances that could justify a particular decision to commit suicide, but when all is said and done, we have an equal right to our life, and so murder *as an end in itself* is unethical.[3][†] Moral considerations may make for a "slippery slope," but it is unavoidable.

Horace Mann (first president, Antioch College Commencement Address, 1859): "Be ashamed to die until you have won some victory for humanity."

PM: You say everyone has an equal right to life, but since food is necessary to life, does everyone then have an equal right to food?

ER: Everyone has an equal right to obtain food through production or purchase. Only those who can't possibly do so should get a properly funded government handout.

PM: The right to welfare seems connected to the right to life.

ER: Yes, there should be welfare for the deserving poor; fortunately there is a proper government fund for it (to be described later). It may not be always clear who is deserving, but one thing is sure: We'll never get rid of poverty by subsidizing it. Certainly, there'll be less poverty if we provide equal opportunity to work (which the equal-rights doctrine can guarantee – see later).

PM: Isn't the equal right to life more important and more inclusive than the equal right to liberty?

ER: It certainly is, in the same way that the whole is greater than its parts. But we must first prove the equal right to liberty before we prove the equal right to life.

PM: What about discourtesy and verbal abuse? They seem wrong.

ER: They certainly are, because they limit another person's equal right to life and liberty.

PM: What about health?

ER: It is clearly part of the right to life. If some people can't pay its costs, the money for it should come from a proper equal-rights source (see later).

PM: Perhaps so. But now let's talk about the equal right to property.

The Equal Right to Property (Labor): A Proof

ER: [§4a] *We all have an equal right to our labor, limited as always by the equal rights of others.*

Labor is exertion to produce wealth in order to satisfy our material desires. If we have the equal right to be free, then we have the equal right to exert ourselves in the manner mentioned; that is, we each of us have a right to our labor. Another way to look at the matter: Since our labor is the product of our brain, nerves, muscles, and so on, it (and the product thereof) should be ours.

If we all have an equal right to our own labor, then we all have an equal right to the product of our labor, those products being an extension of each of us. Since our labor is in what we produce, we own what we produce. Who else should own the products of our labor? Those products become our ethical property (hopefully our legal property also). When you oppose robbery, are you not thereby according to others an equal right to property? In other words,

[§4b] *We have a right to property limited by the equal rights of others.*

If we own our labor (see §4a), then we own what we produce with it – that is, our property. *Labor exerted is the sole justification for private property.* We can't think of another justification, and if there were, it would necessarily limit the right to our labor. To deny our right to property is to deny the right to our labor.

Our equal right to life requires an equal right to property. Property is also necessary to liberty. Robbers make you their slave for as long as it took you to make the thing they stole from you, or if you had bought it, then for as long as it took you to earn the money needed to buy it. You have been forced into temporary slavery. In effect, they *forced* you to work for them, thereby denying your equal right to be free. The same holds true for poor burglars robbing a rich homeowner; they aren't engaged in mere income redistribution. Burglary is ethically reprehensible. It is equally reprehensible for society (others) to take your property by taxation and then redistribute it. The imprimatur of the majority lessens the injustice not one whit.

John Locke argued somewhat differently – but validly – for the equal right to property. He pointed out that when we make a chair, our labor is embodied in it. If we own our labor, then we own that chair and can sell or bequeath it. Our equal right to property is as valid as our equal rights to life, liberty, and labor.

John Locke (in his Second Treatise*): "Every man has a property in his own person. This nobody has any right to but himself. The labor of his body and the work of his hands, we may say are properly his. Whatsoever, then, he removes out of the state that nature hath provided and left it in, he hath mixed his labor with it, and joined to it something that is his own, and thereby makes it his property."*

David Hume: "Whatever is produced by man's art or industry, ought, forever, be secure to him."

PM: Aren't property rights set by society?

ER: Legal property rights certainly are, but not ethical property rights. Let us make a clear distinction between the two. The higher law is always the ethical, never the legal.

PM: Property rights are clearly not the equal to our rights to life and liberty.

ER: They are not as comprehensive, but they are as valid. They are necessary to life and liberty, and are as alienable as life and liberty. All rights can be violated: We can be murdered (denied life), discriminated against or imprisoned (denied liberty), or robbed (denied property).

Somebody has to own things – to control their use, even if only to destroy them; shouldn't it be the person who made them or who has bought a *just* title from the producer or his or her assignees (intermediaries)? In the legitimate purchasers is vested the just title of those who made the property in the first place. Ultimately, *labor exerted is the sole justification for private property.*

Remember, we should distinguish between life, liberty, and property and the rights to life, liberty, and property. Thus, those who are murdered sink into the grave, their life lost, but their *right* to life was intact. Rights are inalienable, although life, liberty, and property are not.

PM: But consider the social fund theory of property as expressed by that once well-known economist, E.R.A. Seligman:

> Individual labor has never by itself produced anything in civilized society. Take, for example, the workman fashioning a chair. The wood has not been produced by him; it is the gift of nature. The tools that he uses are the results of the contributions of others; the house in which he works, the clothes he wears, the food he eats (all of which are necessary in civilized society to the making of a chair) are the result of the contributions of the community.... Nothing is wholly the result of unaided individual labor.... Society holds a mortgage on everything that is produced.[4]

ER: Seligman's conclusion is wrong. When we draw on the social fund of knowledge and experience, we give back to it at least as much as we took from it. Isn't the social fund enhanced when the chairmaker makes his chair? It has one more chair than before; previously it had only some odd pieces of wood and maybe glue. The social fund is thus reimbursed, as is the chairmaker when he sells his chair. In addition, the chairmaker legitimately owns his supplies, having bought them from willing suppliers. The chair purchaser is recompensed because he now has a chair he needed. Everyone is happy, except possibly E.R.A. Seligman.

Let us imagine a villainous old reprobate who has secured the guardianship of his ten-year-old niece and robbed her of her rightful inheritance and then gloats over his deed. Won't you say he acted unjustly, whatever society might allow?

PM: Yes, but in his own eyes he may be guilty of no injustice – not in my eyes, of course. It's all a question of eyes.

ER: I would say, let reason and not eyes determine what is right and wrong.

PM: It would seem you're a supporter of Karl Marx's Labor Theory of Value.

ER: Not at all. Marx didn't believe in private property. Furthermore, he asserted that the value of a product is the amount of its socially useful labor. But what is socially useful? (even pragmatists can't answer that.) And why anyway is that the proper standard of ownership? It is better to say that the value of a product is the amount of labor it saves the purchaser. But anyway, a theory of value has nothing to do with a justification for private property.

PM: But your alleged proof has a serious problem: In a modern industrial economy, chairs are produced by many people in a factory, not by one individual.

ER: That's a complication but not an obstacle; it requires only another step in our reasoning. In a free market, the workers make a bargain concerning wages with the stockholders (i.e., the owners, some of whom are workers). Stockholders are recompensed with a dividend share of the profits for their capital contribution to the productive process. Free competition prevents them from taking too much.

Let people be free to buy and sell, limited only by the equal rights of others; that's what happens in a free market. That's the precise dictate of rationality and ethics. Let freedom be the standard, not force. (But when taxes take 45% of the U.S. national income [more elsewhere], Americans seem to be living in an economy based on force.[5])

"To each the fruits of one's labor" is the free-market dictum, and to take away those fruits against the will of the worker or capital-owner (capitalist) and redistribute them according to the will of some government bureaucrat, as tax-socialism would do – that is naught but slavery. True free enterprise decentralizes economic power into the hands of producers and consumers.

Equality of opportunity, limited by the equal rights of others, is served by free enterprise and the absence of monopoly. On the other hand, in a socialist economy, government bureaucrats have greater power than others in determining who gets what and at what price.

In a free market, workers own their labor and what it can produce. They can legitimately exchange their labor for that of others, and what others are willing to give them for their labor is their just wage. Wages and profits are the measure of how well the worker and capitalist satisfy the needs of others.

Since capital (e.g., factories, machinery, desks) is the product of labor, its private ownership is completely justified. Isn't it saved-up past labor?

In a free market, the more goods you produce, the more you satisfy others and the more you are rewarded monetarily; so requires justice and efficiency. The free pricing system induces labor and capital to flow to where they are most needed, if not like water seeking its level then like hot molasses doing likewise. (It can take a little time to redistribute labor and capital throughout the economy.) For instance, if computers are in short supply, then computer companies will have high profits and wages and will attract labor and capital from other sectors of the economy – appliances, let us say, or shoemaking –

where wages and profits are lower; in fact, low wages and profits would positively repel labor and capital from inefficient sectors. This efficient allocation of labor and capital is done automatically. The best a government agency could hope for is to duplicate the free market.[6][†] Once people lose their allegiance to the free market as the objective determiner of wages and profits, then it is each person for himself and the devil take the hindmost, or rather each special interest group for itself and to hell with the interests of society as a whole (particularly the poor).

PM: That's very nice theory, but in reality, we don't have free enterprise. Huge global mega-corporations set prices and dominate our economy. Free competition is a myth.

ER: Not so. Let's look at the facts:

(1) In 1972, the U.S. Federal Trade Commission's Bureau of Economics found that in a sample of one hundred concentrated industries where monopoly was claimed to exist, prices exceeded costs by a mere 3.16%. That's small enough, and the Bureau got this result with assumptions that tended to bias this percentage upward.[7]

(2) Arnold C. Harberger, a highly regarded economist specializing in economic concentration, concluded in his detailed study (1960s) that eliminating monopoly in the United States would raise income by no more than 1/13 of 1%.[8] Six other studies show that the impact of monopoly was similarly slight.[9] These studies were confirmed by many European ones.[10]

(3) High-barrier industries do exist and can tend toward monopoly, but in the 1970s in the U.S. they accounted for about 10% of total manufacturing output, which itself was less than a third of total gross national product (GNP), and the other two-thirds of the economy has been considered more competitive.

234

(4) Since net profits after taxes were only about 8% of GNP (probably less) in the U.S. and monopoly or semi-monopoly profits could only have been a small part of that 8%, the impact of monopoly cannot be very great.

(5) High-barrier industries have not increased over the years. In the early 1970s, the leading authority in this matter, Professor M. A. Adelman of Massachusetts Institute of Technology, reported that the concentration of industry in the United States varied slightly from year to year, changing "at the pace of a glacial drift."[11]

(6) The market percentage of value added for the four largest firms in the 50 largest U.S. industries was virtually unchanged from 1947 to 1970.[12]

(7) According to one experienced observer, Henry M. Schachter, "In almost no major consumer goods category…is there a brand on top today [1970s] which held that position ten years ago."[13]

(8) Of several top brands in 100 product groups in 1923, only 23 were still leaders in 1997.[14]

(9) Competition is constantly buffeting our biggest businesses. Of the 100 largest industrial corporations in 1909, only 36 remained on the list in 1948. Of the top 100 corporations in 1948, only 65 continued to hold that ranking in 1968. Carl Kaysen and Donald Turner, writing on antitrust in 1958, complained about the "monopoly power" of the big magazines *Life*, *Look*, and the *Saturday Evening Post*, but fifteen years later they had all ceased publishing.[15]

(10) From 1969 to 1976, small businesses with seventy or fewer employees generated 66% of all new jobs in the United States.[16]

(11) Affluence and better transportation have increased competition. With the car, consumers now have many more stores to choose from. Pro-

ducers now customarily invade each other's markets. Constant growth allows room for new competitors; new inventions and management techniques threaten old leaders.

(12) New companies are constantly appearing or expanding. (Microsoft comes to mind; new technologies are likely to cause it to face serious competition.) Many older companies have been downsizing.

(13) Price competition is not the only kind of competition; for example, U.S. auto makers, though few in number, compete vigorously on style, sales, advertising, service, quality and technology.

(14) Considerable inter-industry competition exists (and is growing); for example, competition exists between televisions and furniture for the consumer's dollar, also between autos and fur coats, cotton-wool-artificial fibers, oil-coal-gas, paper-glass-aluminum-steel in the container business, supermarkets and drug stores, discount stores, and so on.

(15) Considerable competition exists within corporations for jobs and advancement. Corporate executives are under high pressure.

(16) Then there's countervailing power: Big buyers neutralize big producers (e.g., General Foods can't intimidate Safeway, nor can GM intimidate Goodrich).

(17) Growing imports threaten monopolies. Automobile and steel companies, among many others, demand tariffs and import quotas – evidence that they face important competition.[17†]

We had better stop here; otherwise we'll unbalance this book. Much more hard evidence could be presented.[18] Let us say that perfect competition does not exist, but the perfect ought not to be the enemy of the good-enough. Competition is still the dominant force in our economy; vigorous and rational antitrust action can continue to keep our economy competitive. Socialism isn't necessary.[19][†] And if we had equal access to land and no taxes on production (more fully discussed later) our economy would be even freer and more competitive.

World Research, Inc:
> *"You're gouging on your prices if*
> *You charge more than the rest.*
> *But it's unfair competition*
> *If you think you can charge less.*
> *A second point that we would make*
> *To help avoid confusion:*
> *Don't try to charge the same amount,*
> *That would be collusion!"*

This is not to say that our economic system contains no abuses of free enterprise. It unfortunately does; for instance, newspapers too often twist the truth or cover it up to please their advertisers,[20] and there is here and there less than totally-free competition; clearly, our economy needs appropriate regulation. But it approaches the worthy goal of free enterprise for which there is no reasonable alternative. Cooperation might be better than competition, but not if forced by government edict or threat of jail. That's not true cooperation; Jesus threatened no one with guns or jail. Justice should precede charity; true charity flows from justice.

PM: But surely we need unions to defend the rights of workers and to improve working conditions. Fully 9% of the private U.S. workforce is unionized, yet aren't unions antithetical to free enterprise?

ER: Unions have been useful in establishing acceptable working conditions (though this is more properly a government function). But they don't produce anything, often

237

tend to violence, and often unjustly raise prices beyond what a freely competitive economy would set, thereby robbing consumers and stockholders.

PM: Surely we need government welfare for the poor.

ER: Yes we do, especially in a high-taxes-on-production economy, so let us *properly* fund government welfare (to be discussed later). In any case, the poor aren't as poor as they used to be, or seem to be. A study by MIT economist James Poterba showed of 1985 data that only 61% of Americans in the bottom income-tenth were also at the bottom in terms of consumption.[21] In 1975, only 5.1% of the poorest fifth of income earners were still in that category in 1991[22]; for instance, medical students may be in the bottom statistical fifth of income in a particular year but yet live reasonably well by borrowing against their future incomes. Eventually, they'll be out of the bottom fifth.

Rich people provide more jobs than do poor people (few of the latter employ anyone). The trouble with the rich is that there aren't enough of them to support the rest of us; they shouldn't be required to do so.

PM: But surely you'll agree that corporate profits are too high.

ER: Not in a free economy. They average about 5% or 6% of sales.[23] That's paltry, and if profits were unjustly confiscated by legislation, property rights would be violated and there would be nothing to confiscate in ensuing years (no one would produce taxed-away profits); without jobs or wealth production, the poor especially would suffer.

Remember, too, that an increasingly large percentage of stockholders are workers who have invested their pension money and other savings in mutual funds and stock; we are rapidly attaining worker-owned capitalism. To paraphrase Pogo, "We have met the owners, and they are us." Don't shoot ourselves in the foot.

Frederick Bastiat (in The Freeman, *12/99, p. 53):*
The state is "the great fiction by which everyone

seeks to live at the expense of everyone else."

Milton Friedman (prominent economist, in Capitalism and Freedom, p. 15): "Underlying most arguments against the free market is a lack of belief in freedom itself."

Monsignor John A. Ryan (in Distributive Justice, p. 47): Why "...has the shoemaker a right to the value that he adds to the raw material in making a pair of shoes? It is because men want to use his products and because they have no right to require him to serve them without compensation.... They are morally his equal."

PM: What's wrong with holding property in common, as in Israeli kibbutzim or religious monasteries?

ER: Absolutely nothing as long as the participants do so voluntarily and are free to leave at any time. If people wish to give their property to a community, they should freely be allowed to do so.

PM: Can anyone truly earn a million dollars a year?

ER: Yes – millionaires should be judged according to the facts of their case. They're innocent until proven guilty. Some people are lucky or have a talent for making money, just as some people win a jackpot or have an astounding musical talent like Mozart or Frank Sinatra. I can hardly play "Come Back to Sorrento" all the way through, and then I hear professional pianists playing long pieces from memory – very disconcerting. I can't jump as high as Michael Jordan and he shouldn't have to share his fabulous income with me or anyone else. Talented people shouldn't be our slaves. Talent isn't distributed equally; only rights are.

PM: Pierre Proudhon said that property is theft.

ER: Yes, he said that, but it isn't so. Look, I extract an apple from nature by plucking it from a tree, thereby exerting labor on it and legitimately making it mine. (Oil companies, farmers, and miners do likewise.) If Proudhon or his followers deny us the right to eat an apple or any other food, we would soon die. His ethic better not be right; fortunately, it isn't.[24]

The taxation of labor and the products of labor – that's theft and bad economics. Russia's high taxes make it too expensive to be law-abiding there.

PM: Mere purchase alone cannot justify ownership of property. You can purchase slaves or stolen property, but they are not therefore justifiably yours.

ER: Certainly so. That's because in those cases I didn't purchase a just title. "Just" – that makes the purchase ethical. Those things weren't bought from anyone who made them. When a deficient ethical title is bought, that's all the purchaser has – a deficient ethical title. It might be legal, but it surely isn't ethical.

If labor is the sole justification of private property, then land is not justly ownable since it isn't a product of labor unless the owner pays everyone else for that privilege. (We'll later discuss how to do this.) Since everyone else created the value of that privilege, they should own it. The unethical taxation of production to support government would not then be necessary.

PM: But some property is inherited. Surely inheritance isn't justified.

ER: Why not? If I justly own some property, can't I justly give it away, now or after I die? Shouldn't I be allowed to sell my property to my heir for nothing? It's a type of a gift, effective after death. You don't like gifts?

PM: What about monopolies due to patents or copyrights?

ER: It's easier to guarantee the right to physical property than to inventions or songs, the fruits of one's own brain, but it can be done. Patent and copyright law attempt to approximate a person's property right in those creations for as long as it can be reasonably estimated that no one else would have come upon them. That's why copyrights exist for longer than patents.

PM: Well, let's get back to landownership.

ER: Yes, let's. Private landownership is supremely practical, but private land *rent* ownership is ethically wrong for these reasons:

    (1) Labor is the sole justification of private property.

    (2) If we all stand equally before God or nature, we should all have equal access to the opportunities they afford.

    (3) Land owners don't produce land rent.

    (4) All land titles have their origins in force or fraud and are therefore ethically void.

    (5) The Bible says so.

Let us discuss each item in detail.

Private Property Justified Only by Labor

People are entitled to the full fruits of their labor. If you make something, be it a product or machinery, it's rightfully yours. Who else but you should own it? Since you generally don't want to continue owning all you can make, you sell some of it. So you transfer your just title through intermediaries to the ultimate consumer, and in that ultimate consumer is vested your just title.

But labor can justify neither landownership nor slavery. Both land and people were produced by God or nature and not by human labor, so neither can be justifiably owned unless we abolish slavery or tax land rent instead of taxing produced goods and services. Both landownership and slavery are completely unethical insofar as they infringe the labor of others. We can get rid of slavery by abolition, whereas it would be completely impractical to abolish private ownership of land.[25†] We can allow private property in land – it's highly practical to do so – if we tax it according to its annual rental value; the revenue so obtained can fund the government instead of onerous and unjust taxes on producers; thus, all would share equally in the advantages of landownership. If the government doesn't do this, it must unjustly limit everyone's private property rights by the taxation of labor and the products of labor. If landowners get an income without producing, then some producers are producing without getting their full income; that's a conclusion that is mathematically, rationally, logically, and ethically unavoidable.

When taxing the annual rental value of land, it is important to tax the imputed as well as the currently collected land rent. If I rent a piece of land to someone else, the rent is clearly collected, but what happens if I use the land myself? I don't bother to transfer the land rent from my building-owner's pocket to my landowner's pocket, but the land rent exists nevertheless. It's *imputed*, and the government should collect it in taxation. The U.S. government already taxes imputed income, as when it taxes the imputed tip income of waiters or the imputed value of parking-space privileges of factory workers. If all land rent (including imputed) were eventually collected in taxes, leaving no net rent to the landowner, then eventually all land *prices*, but not annual rental value, will decline to zero. This would be of great benefit to potential land purchasers since they would pay nothing for land sites, nor would they be taxed for their land improvements, nor would they have to pay for land elsewhere.

The doctrine of equal rights absolutely requires getting rid of both slavery and private land *rent* ownership; they are both denials of the ethical dictum, "To each the fruits of one's labor." Land-use benefits accruing to private landowners will be exactly offset by their land-rent tax to the government (i.e., to all of us).

PM: You morally equate slavery with private land *rent* ownership, but slavery isn't only a violation of the equal rights doctrine, it is personally degrading to both slaveowner and slave alike. It still very much exists in the world today.

ER: All true, but bear in mind that slavery affects only a portion of society, whereas private land *rent* ownership permeates the entire economy and in the long run hurts everybody by negating opportunity and prosperity. The poverty and inequality resulting from land *rent* owning is as personally degrading as slavery.

PM: But many landowners are nice people and philanthropic; shouldn't we be nice to them?

ER: We should always be nice, but niceness doesn't justify land *rent* owning. Slaveowners may be philanthropic and nice, too. But niceness and philanthropy justify neither slavery nor land *rent* ownership.

Arthur Yeatman: "It is as ridiculous to say, 'you have the right to eat but you may not have any access to producing food' as it is to say, 'You can make a living but you may not have any access to land.'"

PM: Aren't you advocating socialism?

ER: Absolutely not. Taxing wages and profits – now *that's* real socialism! When the government does that, it socializes part of what you have earned and gives it to others. I stand for the private ownership of land. I repeat, *I stand for the private ownership of land.* (There, that ought to do it, but experience teaches me it won't.) Alas poor Russia: It will never succeed economically until it learns this.

The price of land is our enemy. It is the measure of the injustice of the private collection of the rent from land.

John Dewey (famous philosopher, first president of the Henry George School, quoted in Significant Paragraphs from Henry George's Progress and Poverty, *p. 76): "It would require less than the fingers of the two hands to enumerate those who, from Plato down, rank with Henry George among the world's social philosophers. No man, no graduate of a higher educational institution, has the*

*right to regard himself as an educated man in
social thought unless he has some first-hand
acquaintance with the theoretical contribution of
this great American thinker."*

PM: Shouldn't the government protect the vested interests of landowners?

ER: No. No one has a vested interest in picking someone else's pocket (i.e., in living off someone else's labor). It is the duty of government to dispense justice, not protect vested interests. But a land value tax should be instituted gradually. That much we could do for land *rent* owners. Give them time to adjust their investments to the new tax situation.

PM: Let's get on to your next argument against the ethics of private land *rent* ownership.

ER: Yes.

Equal access to Opportunities God or Nature Affords

Since landownership is necessary to gain this access, then we all have an equal *philosophical* right to land, though once again *practicality* demands private landownership with public land *rent* ownership.

Insofar as the earth is a gift of God to all of us equally (He had no dispossessed children), equal access to it is required. The Eleventh Commandment should be, "Everyone should have equal access to land."

Private landownership can be justified only if the full land rent for each site is paid to society (all of us). We've become accustomed to owning most of the ocean and air in common; now furthering equal rights requires owning the land rent in common via taxation.

When 1% of the local population controls at least 53% of the total land surface in eighty Appalachian and upper South counties, we can conclude that there is no equal access at least there.[26] But so it is elsewhere: In the United States, less than 1% of all landowners hold 40% of all private land.[27] In the United Kingdom, 1% of the population owns 52% of all land.[28] And so on.

PM: Well, let us now get to your third argument against the private ownership of land rent.

Landowners Don't Produce Land Rent

ER: Land rent is created by Nature, as when it provides certain sites with beautiful views, rich mineral deposits, fertile soil, and good location; or they can be created by *Society* which provides jobs and shopping opportunities nearby; or by *Government*, which provides such services as roads, schools, protection (police, fire, military), and so on. Landowners don't produce land rent. Only if land values are fully taxed can we all equally share the bounties of nature, government, or society. The revenue from such a tax could fund public services (in place of unjust taxes on production), or it could fund a land-rent dividend distributed equally to all. (Yes, let the government pay taxes to its citizens, even though it sounds too good to be true.) Without land value taxation, landowners will enjoy more benefits of landownership than others while non-landowners are tax-penalized.

PM: Doesn't demand produce all value? For instance, a watch wouldn't be worth anything without a demand for it, so maybe society has a moral claim on it.

ER: No. Don't overlook an important distinction: The value of the watch may be *measured* by the demand for it, but the watch itself is *produced* by the watchmakers. Private ownership is justified by production, not measurement.

Winston Churchill (1909 and 1918 speeches, quoted in Incentive Taxation, *6/83, p. 2): "Land monopoly is not the only monopoly, but it is by far the greatest of monopolies – it is a perpetual monopoly, and it is the mother of all other forms of monopoly…. I have made speeches by the yard*

245

> *on the subject of land value taxation, and you*
> *know what a supporter I am of that policy."*

PM: But sometimes certain large landowners make the surrounding land values valuable, as in Florida's Disneyland or Long Island's Leavittown.

ER: Not so – these landowners merely recognize the potential locational value of those land sites before anyone else; they didn't create those values. Without government-built highways and the demand of homeowners, Leavittown would have been an expensive failure.

PM: Now let's get to your fourth ethical argument for land value taxation.

Land Titles Ethically Void

ER: The original inhabitants unjustly appropriated land that belonged to all humankind; they appropriated part of the earth that philosophically belonged to everyone who has ever lived or will live. These appropriators were often despoiled of their titles by foreign conquerors who themselves were eventually conquered, and so on. Only common land *rent* ownership can reestablish everyone's equal right to land.[29†]

PM: Wait a minute – didn't the original settlers establish a just claim to their land sites by cultivating the soil, by growing crops?

ER: No. Almost no landowners today can trace their legal titles through inheritance to the original settlers. But more important, the original inhabitants found only a piece of the land that belonged to everyone. They certainly had a just claim to the crops that embodied their labor, but they could justly claim ownership of the land only if they paid land rent to society (which at the time of discovery was zero). They didn't produce either the rent or its future increase. Could Balboa have legitimately claimed ownership of the Pacific Ocean? Could the U.S. legitimately claim ownership of the moon because an American walked on it first?

By all means, let the original inhabitants own the piece of land they discovered, to use or dispose of as they wish. But the rent of it belongs to the community.

W. J. Cadman (Land & Liberty, 4-5/68): "If a man plants a field with seed and in due time reaps the harvest, that harvest is undoubtedly his private property, for his labour has produced it. But does the act of sowing the seed give him the right to claim that field as his property, forever?"

Biblical Justification

PM: What is your fifth justification for land value taxation?

ER: This one will interest religious people.

Leviticus 25:10 established the concept of the Jubilee Year – the fiftieth year in which the land was to be given back to the original owner. (It may have been lost due to nonpayment of a debt.) Since the original division of land was essentially equal, the Jubilee reestablished land *rent* ownership equality. That was good enough justice for a nation of small farmers, but in today's urban society only the taxation of land values would suffice to maintain the same Biblical principle.

In short, to deny that land rent should be collected by government in lieu of labor taxes is to deny equal rights.

PM: To be fair, shouldn't landowners be compensated?

ER: No, what for?

(1) *Land titles are not being confiscated, so why compensation?* In addition, most landowners generally have other sources of income that will be much less taxed; most of them would actually end up paying *lower* taxes! And they'd be living in a better and more just economy.

(2) *If the implementation of land value taxation is gradual enough (politically it will have to be), landowners would have ample notice that they will be taxed more on their land rent ownership and less on their wages and capital income than previously, and so they would have time to adjust their investments accordingly.* They wouldn't be disadvantaged. As it happens, gradual imposition is mathematically equivalent to compensation.

(3) *Legal changes don't lead to compensation.* If they did, legal improvement would be too costly to be implemented. And just as slaves are more entitled to compensation than their masters, so workers and capital-owners are more entitled to compensation than landowners, but practicality requires us to forego that claim.

PM: Suppose new developmental possibilities suddenly descended upon a particular neighborhood. Land prices there would start to escalate, and so would land taxes. Purchasers wouldn't want the existing building anymore at that location, and the land would have a low price since it would be highly taxed. Existing property owners might not be in a position to take advantage of the new developmental possibilities and would face confiscation of their property!

ER: Don't worry about that. First of all, for many years the land value tax (LVT) would be too low for that to happen. Second, local law should specify that no property owner need pay more than 3% or 5% in addition to the inflation rate over what was paid in the previous year. Owners could easily adjust to that; it's more protection against sudden tax hikes than they have now. Third, the government should recompense property owners for the reproduction cost of their buildings if they were demolished (subject to certain reasonable conditions); property owners would then have complete protection (more than now).

PM: Who would want to own land if it were subject to a high tax?

ER: Those who want to use the land. If you own a piece of land, you can determine and make money from its use – that's important. Also, new land purchasers wouldn't have to buy it with a huge pay-now-and-go-into-debt lump sum; small businessmen and homeowners for whom credit is expensive would find that particularly advantageous. What's more, their improvements would be completely tax-free.

PM: Why do you seek to tax landowners so exclusively? Why not spread the tax burden equally?

ER: Landowners produce nothing; workers and capitalists produce everything. We shouldn't unjustly burden everyone equally. Why unjustly burden anyone? Abolish unearned land-rental income instead. If producers should own all they produce, there'd be nothing for private land *rent* owners to own!

PM: How is land speculation different than stock or bond speculation?

ER: There is a vast ethical difference. Land speculation emanates from private land *rent* ownership and thus is inequitable – that's not so for the ownership of labor-made capital as represented by stocks and bonds. Also, land speculation is inefficient because it leads to the underuse of land and therefore joblessness.

PM: But isn't it impossible to determine the value of land separate from the value of the improvements thereon?

ER: No, not for those in the real-estate business, not for businesspeople buying and selling land all the time and necessarily ascribing a value to land parcels.

Look, 30% of the assessed value of my residential property is land value. The location is worth something to me: I simply don't want to live in the woods or on some mountainside. I like living in the community where I reside instead of living miles away. I like having a paved right-of-way to my house instead of slogging through muddy fields in rainy weather. But many real-estate neophytes incorrectly merge the value of land into the value of the building on it and think only farmland and empty lots have value. They may not know the value of land, but they can easily get to know it. Overlook land only at your peril (and society's peril).

PM: Isn't it unlikely that the taxation of land values would provide enough revenue to fund all other governmental duties?

ER: I think it would; it certainly would have as late as the 1930s. Studies indicate that the annual rental income of land throughout the U.S. comes even now to at least 24%-28% of national income.[30†] Land rent pervades the entire economy. That the government could spend more than its proper income should not surprise us since its victims are convinced they should be taxed (robbed) on their labor. Individuals and groups generally spend more than their proper income if given the opportunity; the government is no exception. If the free enterprise system is allowed to work properly, then it could solve our economic problems without Big Government or heavy taxes; but to do so it needs land value taxation.

In any case, land rent should be taxed irrespective of whether the revenue it produces could replace all other taxes. If we'll need other taxes, then I suppose we'll have to adopt the "goose" theory of taxation ("pluck the goose [taxpayer] with the least squawk").

PM: Doesn't government perform services for us in return for the labor taxes it takes from us? It provides roads, schools, hospitals, and protection (police, fire, and military), and so on.

ER: That sounds good, but consider the following:

(1) *We get those services whether we want them or not.* We wouldn't countenance an automobile salesman pointing a gun at us and saying, "Buy this car, or else – ." We'd get a car, true, but we would nevertheless rail against the injustice of being forced to buy it.

(2) *We pay more for government services than we should,* if only because income and sales tax payments bear no relation to services received. Also, unlimited labor taxation fosters political corruption. The taxation of labor is corrupt to begin with and can easily be increased, whereas an LVT belongs to all of us and is independently fixed by the free market (although to be sure, even that revenue could be misspent).

(3) *If the government taxes land values, it needn't tax producers at all.* It would substitute a land value tax for labor and capital taxes. Since the land rent fund expands and contracts as the economy expands and contracts, it should be sufficient for government needs; in emergencies, borrowing is always possible.

PM: What's wrong with the voters deciding which government services should be provided?

ER: Nothing, if government services are funded *properly* as with the taxation of land values. But it's wrong for other people to take some of your income from you by force, even for allegedly good purposes and even if approved by a majority. That's surely communism.

T. S. Eliot:
"The last temptation is the greatest treason,
To do the right deed for the wrong reason."

Will Rogers: "Taxes have made more liars than golf."

Cartoon: Boss, handing envelope to employee; "It's finally happened, Hosgood. Your withholdings exceed your salary. Here's your bill."

PM: But surely the taxation of labor and the products of labor can be justified by majority vote, no?

ER: No. How can a majority justifiably (speaking ethically rather than legally) impose taxes on labor? How can others justifiably take your property? People don't have an ethical right to take someone else's money by threat or force, either for themselves or for others, so how could they grant the government that right?

Imagine a majority doing something we all know to be wrong – say, enacting a law enslaving a particular group. We would all agree that the majority shouldn't do that, thereby showing that we really believe there are proper limits to majority rule. Obviously, the majority is often wrong. Should Copernicus have put his theories to a majority vote?

Walter E. Williams (More Liberty Means Less Government, p. 240): "Americans who make the pretense of Christian faith act as though God's law to Moses, "Thou shalt not steal," really means, "Thou shalt not steal unless you do it legally through a majority vote."

Don't shove this matter of land value taxation aside. Face it. Face the facts. Be realistic. Treat things as they are. *Without land value taxation, there can be no equal rights* The prosperity that full land value taxation would engender is well-nigh unbelievable to those who have become accustomed to the taxing of labor or labor-products. (It's like getting used to sitting on tacks.)

Much more can be said about taxing land values rather than producers. If it is ethical, we should expect it to be practical, which Chapter 9 shows to be so. We will demonstrate that here is a tax that actually promotes economic growth: *The more it is raised, the better the economy!*[31]†

Ralph Waldo Emerson (quoted in Freedom House

pamphlet, 11/24/55, p. 16):
  "For what avail the plow or sail,
  Or land, or life, if freedom fail?"

Dwight D. Eisenhower (quoted in Freedom House pamphlet, 11/24/55): "A people that values its privileges above its principles soon loses both."

Adlai Stevenson (quoted in Freedom House pamphlet, 11/24/55): "The history of freedom in our country has been the history of knocking down the barriers to equal rights."

Why Democracy?

PM: How can you apply the equal-rights doctrine to the need for government?

ER: If the equal rights doctrine is unproven, then Hitler, Stalin, Genghis Khan, and the others like them have as much right to rule as anyone, but not so if equal rights is provable. If there are no provable rights, then laws will be printed on rubber, constantly stretched to fit changing circumstances.

William Penn (quoted by Rev. William Blair, Indiana Evening Gazette, 12/13/76, p. 2): "Right is right if no one does it and wrong is wrong if everyone does it."

An economy that lacks an equal-rights tax system, no matter how capitalistic it may be otherwise, is not truly free and cannot solve our social problems. Government will inevitably grow (conservatives, take note). People will look to Big Brother for economic solutions. Today, government is the biggest violator of equal rights through labor taxation, repression, overregulation, and unnecessary wars. Libertarians are correct in asserting that throughout history, government has been the chief denier of equal rights. It has constantly preyed upon its citizens even while performing certain necessary services for them.[32†]

PM: Well, I'm glad you see the necessity for government.

ER: Yes, I do. We need a government to do these things:

(1) Provide for the national defense. It's a dog-eat-dog world. Our equal rights must be protected from international criminals. Private armies are not likely to do the job properly; they shouldn't be allowed to roam around our cities and countryside.

(2) Handle foreign affairs.

(3) Provide a system of justice (police, courts, jails, social workers, etc.) to contain the criminals within our midst.

(4) Regulate the money supply to ensure a constant price level.

(5) Ensure that people don't bargain away their equal rights via private but unethical contracts (e.g., laws are needed to protect children and the handicapped, and to prohibit unsafe working conditions; security regulations are needed to protect financial property rights).

(6) Provide needed welfare to the deserving poor.

(7) Provide some scientific research that would exceed the capabilities of private enterprise.

(8) Provide consumers with protection against monopolists and duopolists. Natural monopolies (e.g., roads, sewers) must be regulated. This can easily be overdone: For instance, U.S. newspapers are exempt from antitrust prosecution but don't seem to be making excessive profits (probably because there is considerable inter-industry competition from television, radio, movies, magazines,

books, direct mail, suburban papers, shopping papers, Internet, etc.).

(9) Ensure that the food and drug supply is safe (e.g., consumers can't test every can of food they buy for botulism); the government employees who do this are like police officers (even if they don't wear a blue uniform).

(10) Provide rational protection for the environment.[33†]

(11) Establish land-use zoning (less needed with land value taxation).

(12) Assess and collect the LVT.[34†]

Free enterprisers don't usually carry on these activities because they entail much expense and little or no prospect for profit, so government is needed. Although we can have too much regulation, we can't go into detail here about exactly which regulations are needed and which are not.[35†]

Stephen Leacock: "Socialism would only work in Heaven where they don't need it or in Hell where they already have it."

PM: OK, we need government. But how can you *prove* that it should be democratic?

ER: The purpose of government should be the preservation of the equal rights of all individuals. The majority should choose the means for achieving this purpose by passing the necessary laws; since all people are equal in rights, the majority should outweigh the minority. If a minority prevailed instead, then the individuals composing it would be superior (not equal) to those in the majority. Above the small-town level, practicality requires representative rule.[36†] The end or purpose of democracy is equal individual rights, but the means for doing this is majority rule. If a proof for equal rights has not been provided to the public, democracy is thought to be majority rule only. This will become mob rule without rational limit, the inevitable long-term result of ethical relativism.

PM: Many people think that government should manage our economy and own enterprises, but that is not on your list. Why so?

ER: People should be free to produce and purchase. Government has proven itself incapable of efficiency in business; free enterprisers are more motivated than government bureaucrats. Where socialism has been practiced, it has been accompanied by a terrible despotism, as in communist Russia. Today, socialism hangs on as a romantic theory in some academic corners that have had no direct experience with its despotism. Imagine that a building in town needs a new drainpipe; should its approval come from city hall? Don't politicians have enough to do without getting involved in such decisions?

Moral Applications

PM: Let's now apply the equal-rights doctrine to moral problems in the real world.

ER: OK, but this book is not primarily about moral applications in reality. Whole books, good books, have been written on this important subject. Although we'll have to talk a little about moral applications, they shouldn't overshadow the main focus of this book, which is the *correct* ethical standard to approach these real-world circumstances.

If we apply the correct ethical principle – equal rights – then we'll be more apt to act morally. We should not assume that everybody naturally accepts equal rights; a majority now don't nor in history ever did. Let's not project our views on others, mindlessly thinking they have the same ethical views we have.

Certainly, we need more than the correct ethical principle to treat moral problems successfully. We need also to know the relevant facts. Correct moral action includes the entire chain of the expectable consequences of our actions.

Technically, moral applications have a definite right answer. The correct ethical principle can be known, and so can the facts of reality. But since honest people can disagree about the relevant facts, it is hard to know what the right moral application is.

PM: Yes, there's no moral litmus test. We have only personal opinions to fall back on.

ER: Well, there are some guidelines to follow. Although we may not know all the relevant facts, we should try our best to muster them and apply the proven ethical principle to them. We should make sure that the means we choose to solve a real-world problem will further equal rights as much as possible, keeping in mind that the right to life is more inclusive than the rights to liberty and property, and therefore generally takes precedence over them; similarly, the right to liberty generally overshadows the right to property.

We won't present here the last word on moral applications, but neither can we ignore them altogether. A knowledge of ethical principle can at least enable us to offer the first word on them.

PM: Let's start off with President Clinton and Monica Lewinsky. How can you apply equal rights to that issue?

ER: Some pundits give the impression that it was Kenneth Starr who had an affair with Monica, but no. In the United States, the president is regarded as a role model, especially for children. But the issue revolved around perjury, not sex, and perjury is always wrong; but it could be argued that removal from the presidency was an inappropriate punishment for Clinton's perjury. Philandering is wrong because it involves lying to one's spouse. But when all is said and done, what Monica and Bill did doesn't seem to be adequate grounds for presidential removal. Different means should have been chosen.

PM: Here's a complicated moral application for you: What should we do with Kosovo?

ER: That *is* complicated. Americans got themselves into a deep foreign entanglement, but as many times before, their luck held out and the military opposition collapsed. I suppose the irregulars of the Kosovo Liberation Army (KLA) will now have to be supported. They're not choir boys, and let's hope they (or their successors) won't be seeking revenge; but they're more motivated than are NATO ground troops, and they seem to have been effective in routing out many ethnic-cleansing tanks from hiding places for NATO planes to destroy. Unarmed Kosovar civilians were being massacred, so arm them: That's cheaper and more effective than war or an extended no-end-in-sight occupation.

PM: Should the United States have dropped A-bombs on Hiroshima and Nagasaki in 1945?

ER: It depends on the relevant historical facts. For instance, the Americans had few A-bombs at their disposal in August 1945, so weren't more lives saved as compared with those maimed or killed as a result of the A-bomb drop?[37] Could conventional warfare have caused the Japanese to surrender? Would the Soviet Union have communized more countries than North Korea if the United States hadn't dropped the A-bombs? And so forth.

PM: How does equal rights apply to abortion?

ER: A woman has a right to her own body, but she shouldn't use it to murder or rob. No one should use one's body in any way they wish.

Is an abortion to be considered no more than an appendectomy? Psychics and mystics testify that fetuses have thoughts and feelings.[38] When women find out they're pregnant, they say "I'm having a baby," not "I'm having an embryo." Some other considerations:

(1) Too little attention been given to the adoption option.

(2) The Center for Disease Control reports that in 1972, the year before the *Roe v. Wade* decision,

there were just 39 deaths from illegal abortions and 27 from legal ones.[39]

(3) When nice people commit abortion, jail or the death penalty are inappropriate.

(4) Public policy should certainly not promote abortion. In any case, it should be subject to community or state law, not national law.

(5) Abortion is not only a woman's issue: A father and grandparents are involved, and it isn't the only condition that is group-specific (e.g., sickle-cell anemia particularly affects blacks, Tay-Sachs particularly affects Jews and Bretons, prostate cancer affects only men, only women undergo hysterectomies).

(6) Abortion should surely not drive people to ethical relativism (but I think it does for many).

PM: What about contraception?

ER: It is not immoral because no killing is involved. (For some it may be irreligious, however.)

PM: You say we shouldn't murder, but shouldn't we lie to a potential murderer about the whereabouts of his intended victim?

ER: Of course. We shouldn't murder because others have an equal right to their life, AAEII. Neither should we lie, AAEII, but clearly lying in such a situation is preferable to participating in a murder. As the whole is greater than its parts, so does life take precedence over lying. We must consider all the expectable consequences of our actions. Tell that to the followers of Immanuel Kant.

PM: What about capital punishment?

ER: When criminals are executed, they lose their lives but not their right to life. Clearly, we have violated their right to life, but if it saves more rights than it extinguishes, it is moral.

Some other considerations:

(1) We also imprison criminals; few doubt we should do that, but are we not violating a criminal's right to freedom? (Clearly so, but it is morally justified if

we protect more rights than we are violating.) Aren't capital punishment abolitionists advocating a life of torture in jail for their objects of sympathy?

(2) When the courts levy fines, are they not violating the finee's right to property? That can be justified if more rights are being protected than are being violated.

(3) To be consistent, capital punishment abolition also militates against just wars, but just wars are clearly just. Don't just wars save more rights than they violate?

PM: Suppose the rights of different people conflict?

ER: They often do, which is why we have courts of law to decide such cases. Depending on the relevant circumstances, they must determine where the preponderance of rights lies. Difficult though that sometimes is, it is clearly easier than judging feelings.

PM: This brings us to the Elian Gonzalez case. He was five years old when he landed in America, half-drowned. Should he have been returned to his father in Castro's Cuba?

ER: No. There was a conflict of rights here, to be sure, but Elian's equal rights to life, liberty, and property, which Castro & Co. won't respect, take precedence over his father's rights to bring up his son. Elian was only a little kid; he shouldn't have been consigned to a life in a virtual prison. If U.S. law says otherwise, change the law; it's wrong. What kind of a father, anyway, would consign his son to a virtual prison? Why did he wait so long to see his "dear" son? Didn't Elian's mother die for her freedom and her son's?

If freedom is nothing but an unprovable personal opinion, then Elian should have been returned. If provable, he should have been allowed to stay.

PM: Should the Eskimos leave their old people to die in the cold?

ER: Yes, if the alternative is the death of the whole tribe. The same reasoning applies to two people in a one-person lifeboat.

PM: A parched straggler crawls in from the desert; only we are present. Aren't we morally obligated to help?

ER: I would say so. In that untypical situation, we are the government and must therefore assume governmental responsibilities. But emergency situations shouldn't determine what we should normally do.

PM: Should we imprison a Jean Valjean who stole a loaf of bread for his poor starving children?

ER: No. He should have received a lighter punishment than he did. In emergencies such as this, those who can act as the government should do so when the government will not. His children's right to life takes precedence over the baker's property right, so the baker should willingly have given Valjean the bread. But in fact, most thieves don't steal to forestall child starvation. Also, there are many relevant facts about such a situation that we need to know; for instance, why didn't the government help him and his children (using its proper income, of course)? Did J.V. try other ways to feed his children, such as borrowing or begging? If he stole half a loaf, would that have sufficed to forestall his children's starvation? Did he ask his friends (or the baker) for help? Would he have repaid the baker someday when he could? Did he offer to do so, or could he have worked off his debt? And so forth.

PM: Isn't polygamy or polyandry sometimes justified?

ER: Ordinarily not, but in isolated societies they might promote equal rights where the sexes are not equal in number.

PM: Shouldn't we remedy past injustices by punishing ethical transgressors?

ER: Yes, if the past transgressors can be properly punished and their victims properly recompensed, but this cannot often be done. Remedying past injustices may be socially disruptive; the government or society that allowed the injustices in the first place may be at fault, and there's no such a thing as collective guilt – only individual responsibility. Moral grievances or rights can't be inherited. Let us concentrate on eliminating present and future injustices; that's difficult enough. All this would seem to have particular application to affirmative action.

PM: Don't we have a right to be wrong?

ER: Philosophically no – wrong is wrong. But practically, it is often difficult to tell wrong from right, so let people be free to think and act as they wish provided they don't contravene the equal rights of others.

Benjamin Franklin (quoted in Freedom House pamphlet, 11/55, p. 6): "Abuses of the freedom of speech ought to be repressed, but to whom dare we commit the power of doing it?"

Take pornography as an example. We don't like it, but how wrong is it? What about borderline cases such as soft porn? What is the proper punishment?[40†] These questions, and there are others, require care in combating pornography lest freedom of expression be invaded. If verbiage or pictures verge on action, then society should get involved.

Lucius Garvin (A Modern Introduction to Ethics, p. 541): "The most stringent protection of free speech would not protect a man in falsely shouting fire in a theater, and causing a panic. It does not even protect a man from injunction against uttering words that may have all the effect of force. The question in every case is whether the words used are used in such circumstances and are of such nature as to create a clear and present danger that they will bring about the substantive evils that Congress has a right to prevent."

PM: Can a war possibly be just? Isn't peace at any price better?

ER: If a war preserves more rights than it extinguishes, then it is just. If you want peace, seek justice. The ethical law says, do not aggress; it cannot say, do not resist.

PM: How about gun control?

ER: There is good evidence that gun ownership saves more lives than it destroys, but nevertheless certain gun safeguards are necessary. Rational proponents and opponents of gun control usually agree with both these points, but they often talk past each other.

I personally don't own a gun, but there is evidence that U.S. counties with personal right-to-carry gun laws have less crime than counties with strict gun-control laws.[41] Right-to-carry laws seem to deter criminals who can never be sure their intended victims aren't armed. For instance, on October 1, 1997, an assistant school principal disarmed at gunpoint a teenage killer in Pearl, Missouri, who had a gun. The killer was soon arrested; he had killed two students and wounded seven and was intent on killing more.[42] A potential Columbinesque massacre was avoided.

Since criminals steal guns, it makes no sense to deny law-abiding citizens the right to defend themselves, with guns if necessary. Anyway, it would seem to be too late to prohibit guns; there are too many guns out there – in the United States, probably more guns than people.[43] No doubt there are accidents with private gun-owning, but they are sporadic and reducible and are not to be equated with intentional and much more numerous gun-induced crime deterrence.[44†]

But in the final analysis, there should be safeguards to minimize accidents; criminals and psychotics ought to be denied the right to purchase guns, assault weapons should be banned, guns should be legally sold only by licensed gun dealers, and so on. But only the elimination of ethical relativism will ultimately reduce gun misuse.

History offers us an interesting perspective on this issue. The introduction of the gun reduced the prevalence of brutally cruel and bloody hand-to-hand combat. It

minimized brute strength and raw courage, thereby leading eventually to female equality. (It wasn't for nothing
that the gun was called "the Great Equalizer.") Before the
gun, cruelty; after, respect for equal rights. Be careful
what you wish for; you may get it.

PM: What about gay-lesbian rights?

ER: Almost all gays and lesbians seem innately that way, and
like everybody else, they should have an equal right to be
free provided they don't violate the equal rights of others.
However, public displays of sex are in bad taste, even
when done by straights.

Concerning marriage, it would be most practical to reserve it for the two old-time sexes in order to keep it sanc-
tified, but certified gay and lesbian couples ought to have
all the legal privileges that married couples enjoy; let there
be equal rights for all.

PM: Shouldn't we be vegetarians?

ER: There's no ethical compulsion to be so. Torturing animals
is surely to be deprecated but wantonly killing them
shouldn't be equated with killing people. Because animals
lack the capacity to reason from general principles (i.e.,
they can't always treat things as they are, nor can they respect the equal rights of humans) there is no way to prove
that they have rights (equal to humans) to life, liberty, and
property. Most species are genetically programmed to kill
and rob; they don't have free will in the matter, they cannot reason fully; hence, there's no such thing as an evil dog
(or a moral one).

Some animals might be domesticated because their
human masters have implanted their will upon them and
made them theirs; animal domestication is really a form
of human labor. Also, doesn't the eating of vegetables require killing, and shouldn't maleficent bacteria be killed?
But if we can't prove equal rights, then we're no better
than animals, and we should all be vegetarians.

Another consideration: There are more animals because we eat them. For instance, there were about 30,000 turkeys in the United States in 1930, but because Americans have developed a taste for them, they now number 4.2 million.[45]

Concerning necessary animal experimentation, it seems ethical enough since human health should take precedence over animal life.[46†]

Where do we draw the line between animals and humans? Not at life, but at abstractability – that's a difference in kind, not degree.

PM: Women are different than men. Don't they then have different rights, not the same or equal rights, as men?

ER: Women are surely different than men but that is irrelevant to rights, which don't depend on gender.[47†] All people have equal rights, whatever their gender, intelligence, culture, religion, and so on. For instance, we shouldn't accord fewer rights to the less intelligent.

PM: What about children and the handicapped?

ER: They have equal rights, too, but require special consideration.[48†]

PM: How is the writing of history affected by the equal rights doctrine?

ER: Historians have two professional responsibilities: They should find out the following:

(1) What happened
(2) What should have happened.

For example, we may want to know what caused World War I, but it is also legitimate to ask whether the United States should have entered it; that is, did the United States' entry advance or retard equal rights? In both cases, historians are needed to correctly marshal the relevant facts. We should treat things as they are (or were in the case of history); that is, we must ask whether a particular action in history advanced or retarded the world toward the goal of equal rights. It is often difficult to determine this, and professional agreement may not always be possible, but we should attempt it nevertheless.

What It All Comes To

PM: My head is swimming. Sum it all up briefly.

ER: Why should it swim? Are you experiencing logic renunciation? That could bring on mental discombobulation. Look – *if we should treat things as they are, we have the right to be free to do so*. There it is in one sentence. We have the right to be free and, therefore, the right to life and property. You don't understand the genome project, yet you accept it! But ethics – is it too simple for you? Do you want something more complicated, even though it will be wrong and socially deleterious?

Well, here's a complication that may please you: It's impossible to prove any ethical principle of behavior *directly*. But one of those standards – equal rights – is totally consistent with a provably true "should" statement: *We should treat things as they are*. Therefore, it is provably true.

PM: Doesn't everybody agree with equal rights?

ER: Certainly not. Few do. Once again, don't project your ethical views onto others. Not only history but contemporary life is writ in blood with little concern for equal rights. Genghis Khan killed millions, and there were others like him; yet now he's revered in Mongolia as a god; the Aztecs and the Mayans seemed to be unaware of the equal-rights doctrine. The relativized twentieth century has been the bloodiest century of all.[49†] Crime, hard-drug use, and so on are obviously on the increase; ethical principle is often considered by many to be merely a matter of personal opinion *only*. Taxation based on force is rampant. Equal rights is hardly self-evident. Not only is it generally believed to be unprovable, but people (especially the young) believe increasingly in benevolent dictatorship, the futility of voting, ability-to-pay taxation, natural rights, animal rights (but not vegetable rights), PC multiculturalism,

ethno-rights, and envy of the rich. And why not, if nothing ethical can be proven true?

PM: Do you think a proof will change the course of history?

ER: It will help, but we should seek an ethical proof as an end
in itself irrespective of its impact on history or society.
Shouldn't we apply reason to ethics?

PM: How did you get to be so hung up on proof?

ER: It all started in my first semester of college history teaching. We were discussing the American Civil War in class,
and I uttered what I thought was an incontrovertible pro-
nouncement that slavery was wrong, when a bright
young student raised her hand to object, "Who's to say?
We think slavery is wrong, but the Confederates didn't." I
couldn't reply convincingly, and ever afterward I sought a
reasonable answer to her objection.

PM: The fact is that ethical proofs convince those who want to
be convinced, fail to convince the others, and so are not really proofs at all.[50]

ER: Convincing others does not constitute proof.

PM: You oppose ethical relativism, so I presume you believe in
absolute rights.

ER: No, I don't. I believe in equal rights. We do not have an absolute (unbounded) right to be free, or to live or hold
property. Our rights are limited by the equal rights of others. Call me a universalist, if you must; I find that word
less objectionable than *absolutist*.

PM: I think you're running against the thought trend of our
time, the zeitgeist, the spirit of our age.

ER: Perhaps so. Nevertheless, let us pursue the unvarnished
Truth.

*References and footnoted material for this chapter begin on page 353 in the
appendices.*

CHAPTER NINE

FULL EQUAL
RIGHTS –
the ONLY WAY *to*
ECONOMIC
PROSPERITY

The economy will prosper in the long run only
if the government lives off what it creates instead of what individuals create.

Postmodernist (PM):
> Shouldn't we be considering only ethical and not
> economic doctrines here?

Ethical Rationalist (ER):
> Well, if we act ethically, we should expect our economy will prosper. That requires us to follow equal rights to the point of taxing land values (LVT) rather than production. However, this should be fully substantiated.
>
> We have already proved that the government should collect the annual rental income of land in taxation; *we can't have equal rights without it.* The government could use the revenue derived from a

land rent tax in place of other taxes to either distribute services or an equal per-capita annual land-rent dividend. But it's legitimate to ask if it's *practical* (economic) to do so. Keep in mind that two-rate LVT falls on all land, both vacant and built-upon sites.

Many cities in Australia, New Zealand, Denmark, and elsewhere throughout the world are already taxing land more than buildings with uniformly good economic results. In the United States, twenty jurisdictions (more soon) have shifted some of their local property tax from building assessments to land assessments, and new construction and maintenance have *always* followed adoption of the shift in *all* seventeen jurisdictions that I personally have been able to study. (Other researchers have fully corroborated these findings.[1])

PM: Well, that's not rocket science. If you untax buildings, you'll obviously have more buildings.

ER: So let's do it. Also, if we increase the tax on land, we encourage landowners to use their land sites more fully. By increasing the holding costs of vacant or underused land, we encourage landowners to develop their land sites or sell them to someone who will. In my many years of experience, even a little up-tax on land values has resulted in much new construction and renovation – if land rent is taxed and the land site is underused, there's an endless money drain. Money drains tend to motivate. In other words, here is a tax which actually lowers taxes on labor and labor products, thereby promoting economic growth and jobs. *The more the land tax, the more the growth and jobs.* This can be completely revenue neutral and costs near nothing to implement.

PM: Substantiate all that.

ER: Well, if we tax land values, we obviously can reduce taxes on labor and labor products; hence, the revenue neutrality. In addition, there are seventeen empirical studies of the jurisdictions that adopted the two-rate LVT building-to-land switch in the local property tax, and *every* study shows that spurts in new construction and renovation occur within three years of two-rate LVT adoption, and the two-rate jurisdictions have *always* outconstructed and outrenovated their one-rate but otherwise comparable neighbors. Here are some examples of those seventeen studies:

(1) Pittsburgh, Pennsylvania, has taxed land assessments more than building assessments from 1913 to 2000. In 1979 and then again in the following year, it made a substantial two-rate building-to-land switch in its local property tax. In 1980-82, its office-building construction increased 293% over 1976-78, whereas new office-building construction nationwide increased only 54% during the same time.[2†] These increases were also confirmed by the facts presented in a study of the Pennsylvania Economy League, a prestigious economic-research organization.[3]

(2) *New Castle, Pennsylvania,* saw the dollar value of its building permits issued jump 70% in the three years after it adopted a two-rate building-to-land shift, whereas its neighboring and comparable cities of Farrell and Sharon experienced actual declines: 66% and 90% respectively.[4]

(3) *McKeesport, Pennsylvania,* likewise outconstructed its neighboring and comparable cities after it adopted two-rate LVT in 1980. It had a 38% increase compared to declines in Duquesne of 20% and 28% in Clairton.[5] Both Duquesne and Clairton have since adopted two-rate.

(4) *Scranton, Pennsylvania,* experienced a 23% increase in the dollar value of building permits issued in the three years after it significantly transferred some of its property tax on building assessments to land assessments as compared to its three-year-

prior period, versus a 47% decrease in neighboring and comparable Wilkes-Barre for the same time periods.[6]

(5) *Aliquippa, Pennsylvania,* made a substantial two-rate building-to-land switch in 1987; it then experienced a 97% increase in the dollar value of building-permits issued for the period three years after as compared with the three years before, even though the neighboring and better-situated cities of Ambridge and Beaver Falls (the county seat) experienced substantial declines during the same period.[7†] When its school district went two-rate LVT, a similar jump in new construction and renovation occurred. [8]

And so forth. I presume you get the idea. These property-tax shifts from buildings to land were completely revenue neutral. Many other studies by well-known researchers come to the same conclusion that here is a tax that not only provides revenue for the government but also produces economic growth and presumably jobs. If it happened in one or five two-rate LVT cities, maybe it could legitimately be said that irrelevant factors might have caused these spurts in new construction and renovation as compared with their comparable neighbors, but in *all seventeen* localities? Note that these seventeen empirical studies are fully corroborated.

I must admit that every time I started to do a study, I trepidated: Will the two-rate LVT city promote economic growth and jobs and outdo its comparable neighbors? Then I go ahead anyway with the study and I am surprised that in every instance, seventeen cases out of seventeen, they do! I must admit to continual astonishment. It just goes to show what happens when you abide by equal rights. In the few cases where I was able to identify irrelevant factors, they generally worked against the two-rate LVT jurisdiction.

272

> *Marian Hahn (letter to the editor,* Pittsburgh
> Press *, 12/31/81): "The site-value tax is the best
> of all possible taxes primarily because it channels
> land rents from the owner-speculator who collects
> rents but performs no services, to the community
> which offers services and needs taxes."*

PM: Why were all your studies in Pennsylvania?

ER: I taught and lived there for nearly twenty-five years. I was able to visit nearby cities in my spare time, got some city councils to go two-rate LVT, and then returned three years later to measure their new construction and maintenance and that of their comparable neighbors. *Always* the two-rate LVT jurisdiction does well, better than comparable neighbors, but it is still uphill work to spread the two-rate property tax. It's been like offering candy to a baby who says, "Naah, thanks anyway – I'm busy reading Proust, I've been told he wrote something about cookies and I'm interested in cookies." Two-rate LVT is still little known, even though locally powerful homebuilders should strongly support the proposal since it untaxes what they produce – buildings – and reduces the cost of the land they must buy. Maybe some day the urban experts and then the local politicians and the voters will start seeing that here is a no-extra-tax-cost way to promote urban rejuvenation. It could happen suddenly when a "tipping point" is reached.

> *Milton Friedman (1976 Nobel Prize winner in
> economics, quoted in* Human events *, 11/18/78,
> p. 14): "In my opinion the least bad tax is the
> property tax on the unimproved value of land."*

PM: How did you measure new construction and maintenance?

ER: Every city hall keeps records of building permits issued, which measure new construction and renovation. I examined those records.

> Urban Land Institute (Research Monograph No. 4, p. 28): Land value taxation is "the golden key to urban renewal – to the automatic regeneration of the city, and not at public expense."

PM: Why did you limit your search to the three years before and after?

ER: Construction and maintenance changes are likely to be manifested within three years; any longer time and irrelevant factors might creep in.

> Lawrence Abbott (Economics & the Modern World , p. 654): "Instead of having to pay $10,000 for land with a $600 rental value, the buyer would pay nothing, invest the $10,000 in securities, and use the dividends to pay the $600 tax!" (In addition, the building needn't be taxed at all.)

PM: I suppose LVT was OK for the nineteenth century and before when land was more important to the economy than it is now. I'm not so sure it would have much effect today.

ER: But it *has* had such an effect, as we see from all the previously mentioned studies and what we could logically expect. If these cities had employed a bigger building-to-land tax shift, the effect would have been even greater. This is no tempest in a teapot; land values today are very high, even though the current property tax depresses them somewhat.

> Old Proverb: "All else passes away, the Land only remains."

In fact, the continuance of civilization depends on LVT.

Equal rights requires LVT. Only it can ensure the long-run success of the free economy, which is central to the maintenance of our civilization, but for the foreseeable future it can be spread only if localities (where decisions on next year's LVT rates are being made) follow certain formulas and procedures. This should remind us of the old children's story: For want of a nail the horse was lost, the king couldn't ride, the battle was lost, so was the war and the kingdom. (Similarly, formula-and-procedure knowledge leads to LVT in one locality after another, which can lead eventually to popular support and a national single tax, which will bring continued economic prosperity and the continuance of a free society.) The proposed LVT can put society on a rational and prosperous basis, thereby banishing ethical relativism and its sociocultural dysfunctions.

Anonymous:
> *A misguided economist planned*
> *To see if he could do without land*
> *He would have succeeded*
> *But found that he needed*
> *Some place upon which to stand.*

PM: Does LVT have any application in underdeveloped countries?

ER: Yes. It will break up large underdeveloped estates and bring in revenue, not raise governmental debt such as land redistribution does.

PM: How can we separate land values from building values?

ER: It may be hard to do it perfectly, but the perfect shouldn't be the enemy of the good-enough. The market in land is reasonably active; businesspeople are constantly buying and selling land – they obviously know its price. So do professional assessors. Don't display neophytism by exaggerating the difficulty in assessing land value.

PM: Won't LVT result in overbuilding and congestion?

ER: This is the reverse of the objection that it will have little impact. When we tax land values, we key land use to land demand. If the government builds a bridge, land values jump; shouldn't it tax the land values it creates rather than taxing producers?

Mortimer Zuckerman (editor, U.S. News & World Report *, quoted in* Incentive Taxation *, 7-8/90, p. 3): "The Eiffel Tower looks like the Empire State Building after [building] taxes."*

PM: Our cities need land for parking.

ER: Parking lots on back streets can be a good use of urban land; also, parking garages generally pay less with a two-rate building-to-land tax shift.

Flat parking lots on busy streets don't employ many people, but buildings on them do. For instance, there used to be a parking lot on Pittsburgh's main street, employing a few low-paid workers. It was replaced by the Oxford Towers, a 60-story office building employing hundreds.

PM: Won't landowners be bankrupted if they have to pay a higher LVT for a site for which there is no market?

ER: If there is no market for a site, its value would be zero, and so should its assessment and LVT. Landowners will like that, and in addition, their buildings won't be taxed.

PM: Vacant lots don't require city services; therefore they should pay no tax.

ER: Not so. City services such as roads, schools, police and fire protection, and so on make those lots valuable. Their owners can make huge land speculation profits when they sell out. Should the taxpayers be subsidizing them?

PM: LVT increases the tax rate on land. Won't this frighten the voters?

ER: Not if they and newspaper reporters are properly in-formed. Few voters know what their property tax rates are. They haven't been frightened in the nineteen current two-rate LVT jurisdictions. Most voters will get tax reductions – that won't frighten them.

PM: Some homeowners will pay more.

ER: Most won't – literally dozens of studies I have personally conducted show this. Job-producing properties generally pay less in taxes. The few pay-mores tend to own underdeveloped sites that harm the local economy by holding back its economic development and causing urban sprawl into the nearby clean and green countryside. Income-producing properties tend to pay more, but they have income to meet the increased tax cost. If we shift taxes from buildings to land gradually year by year, the few pay-mores will be thoroughly protected. They'll have ample time to adjust to the new tax situation.

PM: There's no public support for LVT.

ER: Often not, primarily because people don't know about it. Are *you* telling them about it? Since the great majority of taxpayers will get tax reductions, attitudes will tend to be positive once they get to know about it. Many governmental innovations are introduced without public knowledge or support; why not a better property-tax system also?

PM: Isn't the land in most cities already developed?

ER: Cities are more porous than you think.[9] Besides, cities need constant improvement; should they wait until dilapidation sets in? Are they perfect now? Should homeowners be tax-penalized for maintaining their property (say, for putting on a new roof)? Every city, even Beverly Hills, can benefit from having its buildings down-taxed and its land up-taxed.

PM: Do you oppose zoning?

ER: No, but the need for it would be much less with LVT. Now, much money can be made by getting a land site up-zoned; this temptation to break zoning would be gone with LVT.

PM: Won't two-rate LVT increase tax defaults?

ER: No – why should the down-taxing of buildings increase tax defaults? Defaults might be encouraged if land is assessed too high, but that's not a two-rate LVT problem. [10†] Actually, tax defaults have *fallen* in the nineteen existing two-rate jurisdictions. [11]

PM: Isn't a reassessment needed before LVT can be implemented?

ER: No, why? Two-rate LVT involves a tax-rate change, not an assessment change.

PM: How will poor people be affected?

ER: They will be the biggest benefiters:

   (1) Most people will pay much less in taxes with a production-to-location property-tax shift since they are producers more than they are location owners. Most people have a taxable income, but few own much land value. Poor people would especially pay less because they own almost no land value (otherwise they wouldn't be poor). [12]

   (2) A two-rate building-to-land tax shift generally lowers significantly the property taxes on apartment buildings (reason: big valuable buildings on moderately-priced land). These taxes are passed on to tenants, many of whom are poor. [13†]

   (3) The cost of land increases the cost of housing for the poor. LVT will lessen land costs.

   (4) The alternatives to the LVT hurt the poor: Sales taxes raise the prices of their purchases and income taxes reduce their income. Building taxes raise their cost of housing. Taxes on labor and the products of labor make it more expensive to be poor.

   (5) Wouldn't the poor benefit from a healthy economy, which is likely if locations are taxed rather than production? Wouldn't there be more jobs and opportunity for them?

   (6) An LVT fund could easily cover the costs of welfare to the deserving poor. Producers didn't cause the poverty of the poor and so shouldn't be asked to pay for antipoverty programs. [14†]

> *George Gilder (in* Reader's Digest *, 4/92, p. 181):*
> *"High tax rates do nothing to stop people from being rich; the rich can always manipulate funds and properties in ways that avoid taxation. British aristocrats and Swedish tycoons have demonstrated this for decades. High tax rates, however, are effective in preventing poor and middle-class people from getting rich through working harder and more resourcefully than the classes above them."*

PM: Aren't you making a mountain out of a molehill? The property tax is not an important part of our economy.

ER: It's much more important than you seem to think. Property taxes in the United States today average about 2.5% of selling price. If you can hope to earn 6.79% on your real-estate investments (about the current interest rate[15]) then the average property tax is about 26.9% of what you can earn on a property investment (2.5% divided by [2.5% + 6.79%] = 26.9%). That's not inconsequential. In half our cities, it's more. Our urban economies would be rejuvenated if not only the building-assessment tax but all other local taxes were replaced by LVT.

Clearly, the property tax is the best tax in the world, and the worst. Worst, in that the tax penalizes buildings, a necessity of life, and causes urban decline and sprawl; best, in that it falls on land value with the aforementioned positive results.[16†] If an urban fiend wished to kill a city, he or she would devise a building tax and not an LVT.

Now we pay twice for a location: Once when we buy it ("It's a nice neighborhood," says the seller) and again when it is assessed ("It's a nice neighborhood," your assessor also says). In addition, the building gets taxed.

PM: Won't elderly homeowners pay more with a property tax

like LVT? Wouldn't retirees be better off if there were a wage tax?

ER: No, for these reasons:

    (1) Empirical studies show most elderly homeowners pay less with a two-rate tax shift from buildings to land. Reason: Usually they don't own much land value.

    (2) Their two-rate LVT could be deferred until time of sale or bequeathal to their heirs. (This deferral could even be made available to the certified unemployed or poor.)

    (3) We could specify that no one's two-rate payment need be more than 3%-plus-the-inflation rate above the previous year's payment, at least for the elderly.

    (4) Non-LVT taxes could pay the excess of the two-rate property tax over the one-rate, at least for the elderly.

    (5) A government loan fund could do likewise.

In other words, no one, elderly or otherwise, need pay more taxes. Also, we shouldn't tax-penalize wage-earners, some of whom are elderly, nor should we levy taxes on their purchases.

Joey Adams (in Reader's Digest *, 3/67): "We may never cure poverty, but with prices and taxes the way they are, we're sure going to cure wealth."*

PM: How will mass transit be affected?

ER: It will be greatly benefited because underdeveloped urban land will be developed; there'll be more people around the mass-transit stations. Taxing land values enhances mass transit.

PM: Well-situated but currently underusing property owners, called holdouts, prevent large developments from occurring because they demand huge payments for their property; they're hurting the local economy. How would LVT affect that situation?

ER: These antisocial holdouts would be more inclined to sell if their valuable locations were taxed.

PM: Isn't LVT inelastic as a source of a locality's revenue? It may not expand as fast as a city requires.

ER: Don't worry about that. If the locality's economy increases, so will LVT. If a locality had to, it could increase other taxes, or it could float bonds. In the near future, if a locality needs less revenue, it should reduce the tax rate on buildings (or on other producible things); if it needs more revenue, it should increase the tax rate on land assessments. That's real elasticity.

Even if we were to gather up all the land rent and dump it in some voodooistic ceremony into the nearest ocean, it would be preferable to not collecting the land rent at all. Efficient land use would then be required.

PM: The problem with your land-tax theory is with farmers. They own a lot of land; won't they pay more with a building-to-land tax switch?

ER: You would think so, but here are fifteen considerations for thinking otherwise:

(1) Every study I've seen shows otherwise. Two-rate LVT is based on land value, not land area, and farm acreage is not very valuable compared to urban land.[17†] LVT opponents should present studies to substantiate their viewpoint (if they can).

(2) Throughout the world, farmers have led the movement to spread LVT (cf., Australia, New Zealand, South Africa, Denmark). Farmers can readily see that a farmer owning a fertile piece of land should earn no more than a neighboring farmer who works just as efficiently but is less well situated.[18†]

(3) Wouldn't farmers be better off if the economy improved and their customers had more money?

(4) Farm production and farm buildings would be down-taxed.

(5) If the two-rate LVT were adopted only in urban localities where there are no farmers, farmers wouldn't be affected at all. As of this writing, the current two-rate jurisdictions are all urban; they have no farmers at all.

(6) If two-rate LVT were adopted in purely farming localities, some farmers would pay more while other farmers would pay less, but as a group, farmers would pay exactly the same.

(7) In 1997, farmers were 2.62% of the U.S. workforce[19] yet still produced a surplus; few of them are full-time small-family farmers. Should 97.38% of the workforce be taxed for the benefit of 2.62%, especially since many farmers get most of their income off the farm?

(8) Even without LVT, farmers are leaving the farms.

(9) Farming pollutes the environment more than any other economic activity and is the biggest cause of deforestation.[20]

(10) Surprisingly, farmers generally have more assets than nonfarmers; should poorer taxpayers subsidize those who are richer?[21]†

(11) We shouldn't be subsidizing farmers who want to sell out and retire on their land-speculation killings. Shouldn't we rather be kinder to young farmers wanting to enter farming and are looking for inexpensive farmland? Why burden these young farmers with huge land mortgages even before they begin to farm? They'll spend a lifetime paying those mortgages off.[22]†

(12) Farm subsidies the world over are no substitute for LVT. In the United States, most of the subsidies, because they're based on production, have gone to well-off farmers, probably elsewhere also. In the

long run, farm subsidies enhance land values by making farmland ownership more profitable. [23†]

(13) Many farmers sincerely want to keep their land in farming or in conservation. This would be facilitated if land were used efficiently, as with LVT; there would be less urban sprawl (the chief enemy of farmers) into the clean and green countryside because people would build on city lots rather than on farmland. Urban sprawl also increases governmental costs because distant spaced-out sites must be serviced with roads, sewers and utilities; it also increases commuting time.[24†] Rural sprawl also has bad effects. In short, farmers are hurt when labor is taxed rather than land values.

(14) We'll always need farmers. People won't eat less if land values were taxed.

(15) If private ownership of land rent is unethical, it's unethical for farmers, too.

But there are some legitimate things we should do for farmers:

- We could exempt about $1,000 per acre of farmland assessments from taxation in order to roughly reimburse farmers for the in-land improvements they make, such as grading, fertilizing, tree-breaking, ponding, fencing, and so on; the values of these in-land improvements are generally included in the land assessment, although they shouldn't be.

- We could make it easier for farmers to pay their LVT bills by tax-billing them after harvest time when they can more easily pay.

- We could index their LVT bills to farm prices or production.

- Farmland could be zoned for agricultural use only.

- The government could sell farmers much-needed bad-weather insurance.

PM: If open-space land were developed, wouldn't that harm the environment?

ER: Yes, but LVT would actually preserve open-space land. If the tax system discouraged urban sprawl, the pressure to develop such land would be *reduced*.

PM: Wouldn't LVT be bad for the environment?

ER: No – it would be good for it, for these seven reasons:

     (1) Environmentalism and LVT share the same philosophical rationale: They both emphasize that land is not human-produced.

     (2) It would cause urban land to be more efficiently used, thereby reducing the urban-sprawl pressure on open-space land.[25†] There would be less rural sprawl also.

     (3) It protects rational zoning by removing the profit from spot rezoning.

     (4) It would promote mass transit by densifying our cities.

     (5) It would eliminate absentee landownership, a significant cause of land misuse. (Absentees won't own land if their income is taxed away.)

     (6) It could provide a plentiful revenue source for legitimate environmental programs.

     (7) When people are affluent, they're more likely to be environmentally conscious.

PM: Do you want Brazil's rain forest, "the lungs of the world," to be developed?

ER: No. That rain forest is annually shrinking in size in part because land speculation underuse elsewhere in Brazil sends farmers into the rain forest in search of affordable land. [26†] Both farmers and environmentalists need equal rights and land value taxation.

PM: There still are some unresolved problems with the taxation of land values. For instance, if you tax land values more, the selling price of land will disappear. You'll end up taxing more and more of less and less until the government would end up with nothing.

ER: Not at all. A building-to-land property-tax switch should be gradually increased each year until the land tax rate equals the interest rate. At first, we can assess on land price, as in the United States, but leave a little land value to be assessed; eventually we could switch to assessing on what the land can be annually rented for, as in England.

PM: It doesn't matter what is taxed; it all comes out of the same pocket. What's the difference if we pay $400 land rent tax or $400 in other taxes?

ER: There are major differences: Producers will pay less tax with two-rate LVT but more with non-LVT taxes. Don't we want to help producers (workers and businesspeople) rather than land speculators (nonproducers)? If we tax locations rather than production, we'll enjoy economic growth and a plethora of jobs; non-LVT taxes hobble the economy. For instance, tax builders and they'll leave town, but tax land and it won't; it'll just be used more efficiently.

PM: Suppose a millionaire doesn't own any land. He'll pay no taxes under your scheme.

ER: Yes, so? But if you insist on soaking millionaires, then devise fiendish taxes for them until the two-rate LVT can become the only tax – a single tax. That will take some time.

PM: Won't historical or aesthetic buildings be tax burdened?

ER: Not if they're tax-exempted in whole or in part.

PM: Isn't the taxing of downtown office skyscrapers a source of revenue too juicy for localities to overlook?

ER: No. Greed is bad ethics and bad economics. These buildings contain juicy jobs every locality needs. Why tax them out of town?

PM: Are you a liberal or a conservative?

ER: Both – I believe in equal rights; so do both liberals and conservatives. Liberals should like two-rate LVT because it can painlessly fund welfare and contain urban sprawl. Conservatives should like it because it can replace taxes on producers. I personally could go both ways, or either way.

PM: How could owners of small businesses afford the higher tax on land values?

ER: When they want to buy land, they'll pay less for it (because it would be taxed more) and what they produce on it will be down-taxed. Because they won't have to pay a huge down payment for land at interest rates higher than what big businesses pay, they'll benefit even more than big businesses.

PM: If land rent were fully taxed, who would want to use land?

ER: Those who want to pay less for it and make a less-taxed income from its use.

PM: How can we divide LVT revenue among the various levels of government?

ER: Land values are likely to be assessed and taxed locally at first, but when the state and central governments start to tax them, the LVT revenue could be distributed among the various levels of government as now. In the United States, that would mean that localities and state governments would get about 20% each and the federal government about 60%.[27] Other divisions are possible.

PM: But since two-rate LVT is a property tax, the U.S. federal government can't levy it.

ER: Not so. The federal government has taxed land values in 1798, 1813, 1815 and 1861.[28] The Sixteenth Amendment to the U.S. Constitution specifies that "Congress shall have the power to levy and collect taxes on incomes *from whatever source derived*...." (italics added). Congress could then tax land values and exempt all wage and capital income. As a demonstration, the U.S. Department of Housing and Urban Development could fund a new town that could give away all land sites to private users with the proviso that they would pay the full annual land rent in taxation. Such a new town would be completely free of all taxes on production!

In fact, I can highly recommend a study (I wrote it myself) titled *Legal Suggestions for Enacting Land Value Taxation*. This study contains thirteen specific suggestions for implementing a U.S. federal land value tax. As a bonus, there are thirty additional suggestions for other levels of government (non-U.S. governments could also implement them).29†

PM: Well, OK, but there's no harm done if we don't adopt LVT.

ER: Yes, harm is done. Ethics is violated. Poverty bites. Opportunity suffers. You seem to have no idea how extremely prosperous our economy can be if we were to apply equal rights fully.

Winston Churchill (in a 1906 speech to Parliament): "We do not want to punish the landlord. We want to alter the system."

PM: Let's take a look at some economywide problems. What about unemployment? One scholar estimates unemployment at more than 50% of the U.S. workforce (more than ten times the official amount) by counting the underemployed, the temporarily and part-time employed, and those who have dropped out of the work force.30

ER: OK, so let's not tax jobs. (The social-security tax falls only on jobs!) Tax locations, not production. Apply equal rights to our economy.

PM: How would a country's exports be affected?

ER: The proposed LVT would enhance them. Exporters would pay less to buy land, and they'd pay less tax on their exports. They'd be more competitive. This is the way to increase world trade.

PM: Surely LVT has nothing to do with causing recessions and inflation.

ER: It certainly does, although there can be other causes. Limited space prevents us from fully discussing how LVT can alleviate these problems. 31†

PM: I suppose you think the Asian economies are suffering because of a lack of LVT?

ER: Yes, how did you know? Land prices in Asian cities have
gone sky-high. At one time, Tokyo's land values were
higher than in all of the United States. Banks there made
real-estate loans based on those inflated land values; when
the land values deflated, the banks went bust, dragging
the economy down. The proposed LVT would have controlled such excessive land speculation. To be sure, there
were other causes of Asian distress.

PM: American voters today don't seem very concerned about
high tax rates.

ER: They should be. Stealing is stealing, and poverty hurts.
When a recession hits, their concern is likely to become
monumental.[32]

PM: If land value taxation is such a good idea, how come it isn't
widely practiced and better known?

ER: Well, it's widely practiced in Australia, New Zealand,
Denmark, and we find it even in the United States. [33†] But
the main reason it isn't better known is that so far only two
people in the U.S. know fully how to implement two-rate
LVT in the foreseeable future and have actually done it. If
almost no one knows how to do it, it won't be widely
adopted and few will know about it.

PM: Will two-rate LVT cure ingrown toenails and accidents?

ER: No.

PM: Don't you regard it as a panacea?

ER: No. There are no panaceas.

PM: What's wrong with the other taxes we have?

ER: Plenty:

> (1) They're unethical. They violate the right of pri-
> vate property. Conservatives can rail for years
> against high taxes, but they won't get them re-
> duced without LVT, since a shaky economy leads
> voters to hang on to their government handouts
> even at the cost of high taxes, much like castoffs

adrift on the high seas holding on desperately to nearby driftwood. As for liberals, they should realize that most taxes end up raising prices for poor people or lowering their income.

(2) Non-LVTs penalize economic growth and job making by taxing them. Since taxes in the United States are 46.7% of the national income, what wives in a two-income household earn goes to pay the average family's tax bill. Taxes on labor require wives to go to work. (Feminists take note: After taxes, many wives are taking home less than the minimum wage.)

PM: The income tax falls mainly on rich people, so surely it's OK.

ER: No.

(1) Let's not embrace the ethics of burglars; they shouldn't steal from richer householders, nor should we. If there's nothing wrong with being rich, why should income be taxed?

(2) The income tax penalizes initiative and hard work. It makes liars of many of us[34] and tax slaves of all of us. (The government takes what we've produced; slaveowners do likewise.)

(3) The income tax is complicated. Even the one-time director of the Internal Revenue Service (IRS), Jerome Kurtz, says the income tax is difficult to administer properly.[35] When a prominent tax lawyer and a New York City accountant maintain that the income tax code (now the size of about eight Bibles[36]) is too complicated, you know Kurtz was right.[37]† *Money* magazine recently sent a hypothetical income report to forty-five accountants and got forty-five different answers as to what the income-tax liability of a particular U.S. income-tax return would be.[38] A brief study by *The Wall Street*

Journal found that IRS advisers gave more wrong than right answers to telephone inquiries.[39]

(4) Then there's audit-phobia. One of life's greatest stresses for Americans is the fear of an IRS audit.[40†]

(5) The IRS has recently been called to task for its too-aggressive collection tactics. But in China they kill tax evaders; at least the IRS doesn't do that.[41]

IRS (IRS superiors to three whistle-blowing IRS agents, quoted in Newsweek *, 8/7/989, p. 15):
"The Organization will get you, you whores."*

---

(6) An IRS official testified in 1989 that U.S. taxpayers averaged 11.6 hours to prepare their income-tax return,[42] but in 1988 a University of Michigan economist estimated that the average household took an average of 21.7 hours to do federal and state returns at a cost of $275; and recently, the income tax has become even more complicated.[43] The proposed LVT wouldn't incur these costs. Because of the U.S. income tax, the income-tax-less citizens in Hong Kong fare better economically under Chinese than under U.S. rule.[44]

We'd have to put up with the income tax if the government had no alternative for raising revenue, but it does. We'd do better taxing those who produce nothing rather than taxing our producers according to what they produce in order to cadge a few bucks off the rich.[45†]

Aside from these objections, the income tax is OK.

PM: I can see you don't like the income tax.

ER: I guess not, yet it may be the least worst of all the taxes on labor. Unfortunately, space limitations preclude full consideration of the other taxes – maybe some other time. Just remember, good ethics is good economics.

PM: The implementation of LVT must be very complicated.

ER: Not at all. There are two main formulas, both simple, for implementing LVT in the foreseeable future, although it would be best to know the other thirty-two simple formulas also. Only the mathematically impaired would have trouble with them. They are contained in two pamphlets (plus additions) issued by the Center for the Study of Economics (CSE); one also needs to know the simple procedures of implementation.[46†]

PM: What are the two main formulas?

ER: First you must know that since the LVT is a reform of the local property tax, its rates for the next year are being set by any locality levying a property tax, such as city councils, county councils, and school boards. Therefore, the first target for reformers must be localities, not state or central governments. The implementation must be gradual. (Experience dictates a 20% per year maximum reduction on outstanding assessments so that in five years, buildings will be completely property-tax-exempt; this will prevent some property owners from getting suddenly larger property-tax bills and facing imminent bankruptcy. They are likely to go into howling opposition to LVT and win the support of the unknowing electorate and their politicians.) This approach can be called *local gradualism*.[47†]

The first thing to do is to tell your prospects the suggested tax rates on land and building assessment. They'll be mystified if you only tell them to tax land more. They're not likely to understand that; they'll want to know what you're urging them to do and so they're not likely to act. Afterward, you can tell them what the benefits of LVT are.

In order to maintain revenue-neutrality for the government, determine PBTR (proposed building tax rate) and PLTR (proposed land tax rate), using these simple formulas:

$$\text{PBTR} = \text{OBTR} - (20\% \times \text{OBTR} \times y),$$

where OBTR = the building tax rate in the last one-rate year and y = the number of years after the switch from one-rate.

The 20% comes from experience, not logic. Faster reductions may be politically possible in ensuing years.

To suggest tax rates on land assessments to your prospects, use this formula:

$$\text{PLTR} = (\text{CBTR} - \text{PBTR}) \times \text{BA} \div \text{LA}, + \text{CLTR}$$

where CBTR = the current building tax rate, PBTR = the proposed building tax rate and is obtained from the first formula, BA ÷ LA = the total locality-wide building assessments divided by the total localitywide land assessments, and CLTR = the current land tax rate. CBTR = CLTR for the old-fashioned one-rate property tax.[48†]

The world is full of the mathematically challenged who can't handle even these simple formulas. This may be why the LVT has been so little employed in the U.S.

In two-rate LVT jurisdictions, the proposed building tax rate will always be less than the current property tax rate, and the proposed land tax rate will always be more. It is not possible in the foreseeable future (beyond which we shouldn't try to peer) to attain the single tax (a tax on land values only) but it is an *eventual* goal that is ethically required. Two-rate LVT is at least a move in the right direction. It's all that we can hope for in the foreseeable future. "'Tis better to light one candle than to curse the darkness"; also, "the longest journey begins with but a single step."

PM: I can understand those formulas. I'm not mathematically impaired. But aren't there other ways to gradually levy LVT?

ER: Yes, there are four other ways:

(1) We can obey the law and update assessments regularly (using the building-residual technique of assessment).

(2) We can exempt all buildings in whole or in part (a

dollar exemption would be kinder to poor property owners than even a percentage exemption). This could be particularly kind to poor property owners.

(3) We can assess land closer to market value than building assessments.

(4) We can keep the current (regressive) property tax and replace it and other labor taxes by a separate LVT, using existing assessments.

PM: Who is actively advocating LVT?

ER: The annual conference of aficionados in the United States draws about one hundred participants, and there are hundreds more who donate annually to the three major LVT organizations. Eight recent American economists who have won the Nobel Prize have endorsed LVT,[49†] but they don't know how to implement it in the foreseeable future and the three major organizations don't much advertise it; it is the Great Economic Secret. But at least CSE has induced some LVT adoptions.

There are other LVT advocates and organizations the world over.

PM: Don't all these non-CSE advocates want to learn how to implement the tax?

ER: Unaccountably no. The Nobel-prize endorsers are more interested in other matters, and the LVT aficionados favor an immediate single tax, but it's not likely to be adopted in the foreseeable future; they tend to reject gradual measures and so get no adoptions.

PM: Wait a minute – the two-rate LVT idea has already been successfully implemented in twenty jurisdictions, you say. How could the aficionados reject success by not learning how to do it? Who can reject success?

ER: Aficionados.

PM: You'll have to explain.

ER: I don't have a sufficient explanation. Many of them say the voters don't like taxes (certainly true enough) so instead they use the phrase "rental revenue for government" instead of LVT or the single tax, but this mystifies prospects (local politicians have no problem with taxes); also, people are repelled because they think it means government ownership of the land. No wonder these "rental-revenuers" have had no success at all. In their zeal to collect all the land rent at once, they reject the two-rate LVT steps toward a single tax that is all that can be adopted in the foreseeable future. (It is also possible that they have become land nationalists, unbeknownst to themselves.)

Furthermore, the aficionados believe in *natural* rights, which is passè and anyway wrong, as we have shown. They believe we each own ourselves, but that's much contested and not to be assumed. Also, they themselves have been so infected with ethical relativism that they mainly restrict their advocacy to economic arguments, whereas most voters and politicians first make up their minds on ethical grounds and then seek economic arguments to support their ethical point of view. But when all is said and done, all this doesn't add up to a sufficient explanation for rejecting success. There's no sufficient explanation for that.

One good thing about the single tax is that any *one* person (such as a reader of this book) can get it adopted; that can't be said of most other reforms. All one has to do is to see a city council or school board member, and induce some two-rate LVT. That would be a start in the right direction. In the beginning, abjure assessment reform (very difficult to obtain) – stick to tax-rate reform – and abjure education. (It can take forever to educate millions of people about the virtues of the single tax; just do it for their sake.) To be sure, in some U.S. states, the state legislature must first authorize a two-rate local option.

PM: If the two-rate LVT won't be adopted, won't the single tax organizations wither away for lack of popular support?

ER: No, not likely. The two largest organizations are sitting on

millions of dollars, mostly bequested by long-dead aficionados or gained in a surging stock market. These organizations fund studies that few read and run classes that
few attend. They are the custodians of one of the three
greatest ideas the world can ever know. But they write in
water, and few know what the single tax is and what its
benefits are.

PM: Well, the idea might be OK, but a snowball in hell will
withstand melting before the LVT will be adopted.

ER: Surprisingly not. The single tax may not now seem possible in the foreseeable future. Success in all two-rate jurisdictions has not yet made U.S. urban experts aware of it,
and the voters won't support an idea they think stands no
chance of adoption in the foreseeable future, no matter
how effective it has been or promises to be. But let a few
more jurisdictions go two-rate, and a tipping point may
suddenly be reached. Then the urban experts could get
the politicians to support two-rate LVT, which would then
spread like a grease spot in water, replacing one tax after
another. Popular support would soon follow.

Tipping Point
  Pound and pound a ketchup bottle,
  None'll come, and then a lot'll.[50]

And then there's something else: Most governments in
the world will face monumental expenses in the not-so-
distant future. For instance, in 2007 the huge U.S. baby-
boom generation will start to retire. How will the government get the tax money to pay Social Security and
Medicare-Medicaid, not to mention mounting entitle-
ments and national-debt interest?[51]† This problem is exac-
erbated by the huge personal, corporate, and foreign debt
in the United States, which far exceeds the current budget
surplus. And what happens if a recession or foreign "police action" intervenes before 2007? The only alternative

to impossibly high taxes, unacceptable inflation, or governmental bankruptcy will be a revenue source that will actually promote rather than hinder economic growth – that is, the taxation of land values. *The more the tax, the better the economy.* Only this tax can fully fund these future obligations without encountering these undesirable alternatives. Sheer desperation might drive the voters to support LVT – provided the readers of this book can make it a well-known politically viable alternative by 2007.

PM: I can't hold my breath on that. The single tax is nowhere on the political horizon, and the whole idea swims against the current ideological tide. To think otherwise is sheer lunacy.

ER: You might be right, despite the ethical and economic imperatives. After all, the CSE, which has done indispensable research on the implementation of LVT in the foreseeable future, teeters on the edge of financial insolvency and desperately needs contributions, yet the future of the world depends on its research. But what will be, will be; the future is not for us to see. We can only do our duty. It could be that "people convinced against their will, will be of the same opinion still."[52][†]

Ralph Waldo Emerson is reputed to have said in despair about America in 1859: "No man living will see the end of slavery."

References and footnoted material for this chapter begin on page 359 in the appendices.

CHAPTER TEN

ETHICAL CERTAINTY *in a* POSTMODERN WORLD

This chapter summarizes the main ideas of this book and shows how they can counter the ethical-relativist causes of our sociocultural dysfunctions.

The Old Man on the Mountain was wrong: All things are not logically permitted, and we can rationally recoil from the concepts and actions of the Order of Assassins.

The great fallacy of our age is that no ethical principle can be proven true and is a matter of personal opinion *only*. This postmodern ethical relativism is the chief cause of high crime, hard-drug use, family and school dissolution, shock-jock entertainment, suicide, illegitimacy, and the undermining of science. The rise in these social malfunctions is amply demonstrated in Chapters 2 and 3 of this book; our zeitgeist is making people "eyeless in Gaza." By renouncing rationality, they are engulfing themselves in a "death culture": Only the dead can truly renounce rationality.

If no ethical standard can be proven true, then neither can equal rights. If no one has a proven right to life, liberty, or property that others need respect, criminals can feel free to commit crimes. Why shouldn't they murder if their victim has no provable right to life? Why not group-discriminate or rob if no one has provable equal rights to liberty or property? What can a society expect if it tells its potential criminals that their victims have no provable rights? It will surely engulf itself in numerous dysfunctions!

James Stovall: "Integrity is doing the right thing, even if nobody is looking."

For instance, drug addicts live in their own world; their addictive urges trump their rationality. There will be little common outlook to hold a family together. Illegitimacy will increase. If morality is a matter of personal opinion only, basic physical urges need encounter no restraints, and entertainment will sink to sex and violence. If there's no provable ethical goal worth striving for, then life has no real purpose, and suicide becomes attractive. Why engage in scientific research if it is merely personal belief? Habit and pursuit of profit might motivate, but not for long. The same can be said of students, though vocationalism might motivate them for a while. Relativized students feel their teachers have only unprovable ethical opinions that are no better than what they already have. If their parents also sanction this relativism, no wonder that schools do less well and seem purposeless.

At root, ethical relativism is the prime cause of the ills of modern society. Any attempt to remove these ills must counter this acidic ethical outlook. An airtight ethical proof must be presented, though other measures will also help. But all these measures will ultimately fail if ethical relativism is not properly addressed. One is either an ethical rationalist or an ethical relativist. There is no middle ground.

Although modern society stands at the pinnacle of scientific and technological progress, it is nevertheless beset by intractable ethical problems. In this concluding chapter, let us summarize what has gone before.

> *Charles Kettering (inventor): "This problem when solved will be simple."*

An ethical principle is provable in exactly the same sense as is a mathematical principle. Both principles are aspects of rationality, of logic. Both accord with consistency and accuracy, the two criteria of rational proof. Both are consistent with true statements. Rational principles are therefore provable and not merely nice sounding. The realization of this is the main contribution this book can make.

Truth is not descriptive only; it can also be prescriptive (although some would prefer the term *validity* to *truth)*. Let us not unconsciously accept the contrary nineteenth century belief.[1†] It is as true to say that $a^2 + b^2 = c^2$ for flat right triangles as it is to say that *suttee* should be abolished or that people have certain rights. Truth in mathematics is universal: Ethical and mathematical principles are the same for the French, Italians, or Germans, whatever their beliefs may be. Both mathematical and ethical principles are as universally true as rationality. Correct ethical values are discovered, not created. We err significantly if we don't extend rationality to human relations.

As we have seen, the one and only ethical standard that can be proven true is this: *Each of us has a right to life, liberty, and property limited only by the equal rights of others*. It is true because it logically follows from "we should treat things as they are." This is the most important statement ever made because it is the only provable ethical statement. See Chapter 7 (particularly the Big Question section beginning on p. 213) and Chapter 8.

When we oppose murder, slavery, and robbery, we accord to others their equal rights to life, liberty, and property. We ought to welcome a proof of that. All other ethical standards are wrong and false, even if widely embraced. Let's be tolerant, but not of error.

All this is so obvious, yet many people who vigorously oppose murder, slavery, and robbery will nevertheless deny that people have equal rights to life, liberty, and property. They seem actually to embrace their self-contradictory, unprovable, and deleterious relativism more than they embrace equal rights.

Once we realize that the case for equal rights can be proven and is not merely a matter of personal opinion or cultural-religious whim, then apathy, alienation, and violence, the three main intellectual challenges of our time, the Three Horsemen of the Apocalypse (there used to be a Fourth), become less viable alternatives. If others provably have equal rights, it is our duty to respect them; apathy will then vanish. If it is generally recognized that a common ethical standard and purpose rationally exist for all humanity, then alienation and violence will lessen. Order and purpose become provable rational alternatives to postmodern relativistic chaos.

If others have no provable rights, war and violence are more likely. There are some conservatives who think they stand for order and sanity as opposed to chaos but contradictorily assert that ethical principle is a matter of personal opinion only (or dependent on their view of God, which comes to the same thing). They may think they know what's right and wrong, but in fact all they really know are their own opinions; so did Hitler, Stalin, and Genghis Khan.

If we choose an ethical-relativistic outlook and maintain there are no impartial ethical standards to which rational people can appeal, we isolate ourselves from others, unable to truly communicate with them, shouting at them from our own little islands of belief, able to settle our disputes only by force. How effectively can we argue for the equal rights standard if our only argument is that *we* happen to like it? If we reject a rational proof of equal rights, we can never account for the many shortcomings of our culture or society, nor will we ever find their underlying rational solution.

> *Mortimer Adler: "When men no longer have confidence that right decisions in moral...matters can be rationally arrived at...the institutions of democracy are like the walls of an empty house which will collapse under the pressure from without because of the vacuum within."*

If we should respect the equal rights of others, then let's get doing it! It's not just a philosophical exercise, a mere brain-twister or personal opinion, but *an ethical imperative*. If we fully believe in equal rights, then we should tax land values fully, which as it happens, will bring us continuous prosperity. Without land value taxation, we won't have *full* equal rights and will eventually have inflation and economic decline instead. That prosperity follows from *full* equal rights shouldn't surprise us, for the more the government taxes land values, the more revenue it will have and the more economic prosperity and jobs we will have.

Is ethical rationalism liberal or conservative? Well, either the equal-rights doctrine can be proved, or it can't; liberalism or conservatism have nothing to with it. Isn't that doctrine conservative in its respect for the rights of private property and in its denigration of ethical relativism? Only a proof of equal rights can make low-tax conservatism viable, since the voters will be reluctant to give up their tax-supported governmental goodies. If there is no proof, then equality of result will eventually eclipse private property rights and individual liberty.

But ethical rationalism is also liberal in its concern for the welfare of the common man. Liberals should realize that ethical rationalism can provide a legitimate way of funding welfare; they should also realize that taxes on production increase poverty because taxes are generally passed on to the poor in the form of higher prices for what they buy. What liberals think is important because they tend to activism.

Often, both liberals and conservatives are more interested in goring each other than in finding out where the correct target is and how to reach it. Rather than pursuing conservatism or liberalism, let us pursue the unvarnished Truth, whether it is on the right, left, or center; actually, it is beyond the usual discourse. Let us transcend conventional conservatism or liberalism. The real question is, "What is the valid ethical proof?" not "Is it liberal or conservative?" It's both.

We might expect the question "What is the rational purpose of life?" to be as difficult as the questions "What is God or the Universal Force?" or "Where does consciousness come from?" Well, those questions are truly difficult; this book does not address them because they deal with reality, whereas this book deals primarily with rationality as applied to ethics. "What is the rational purpose of life?" is an easier question. The answer is neither mystical nor complicated.

If we all have equal rights, then the rational purpose of individual life ineluctably follows. We have the freedom to do whatever we wish within the limits imposed by reason. If there were any other limits, they would necessarily limit reason and our equal rights. Ethically, the only rational limit to doing whatever we want is that we should respect the equal rights of others. That's all that can be proven, but it's enough to tell us what the rational purpose of life is, even though some people expect a more complicated answer and are dissatisfied with anything less. They seek what isn't there.

Some might ask, "Well yes, but what should we do with our freedom?" Rationality replies, "Do whatever makes you happy, whatever you want to do, limited only by the equal rights of others." There's purpose enough in that. It will keep you busy your whole life through. Some people will want to use their freedom to pursue art or biology; others will want to raise children properly, or pursue a hobby, and so on. Everyone should be free to do whatever interests them, limited only as already mentioned.

The truth of all this can most easily be seen by comparing it with the postmodern outlook as reported in an interview with Hillary Clinton:

> The Western world, she [Hillary] said, needed to be made anew. America suffered from a 'sleeping sickness of the soul,' a 'sense that somehow economic growth and prosperity, political democracy and freedom are not enough – that we lack at some core level meaning in our individual lives and meaning collectively, the sense that our lives are part of some greater

effort, that we are connected to one another....'

She spoke of ...a nation crippled by 'alienation and despair and hopelessness,' a nation that was in the throes of a 'crisis of meaning.'[2]

Such postmodern connectedness necessarily leads to a bleak outlook.

There is no guarantee that rationality will lead to happiness, which depends on many factors, especially the personal and psychological. It may be that the pursuit of rationality will make people happier than they otherwise would be, but for this there can be no guarantee.

It may even be more important for women than for men to find this provable purpose of life. Society today expects a man to earn a living; such machismo at least provides a purpose to his life. But many women try frenetically to balance both work and child care; they would greatly profit from having found a proven life's purpose that could justify their frenetics.

The equal rights doctrine has interesting connotations for reincarnation, which many postmodernists generally deride because they get their view of it from charlatans or supermarket tabloids; few of them have read the thorough research (800 carefully verified cases all over the world) of Professor Ian Stevenson, the recognized authority in this field; in fact, they may not even have heard of him. Not having examined any genuine reincarnation evidence themselves, they're in no position to criticize. We can only say here that there is much empirical evidence from many reliable sources for reincarnation,[3†] although what is reincarnated is not a dead body, which clearly crumbles away into dust, but the soul (the derivation of the term *reincarnation* being somewhat misleading). In fact, reincarnation proves the existence of a soul. It can also dispel the despair that must come if we expect nothing but oblivion at the end of our lives. And some people say reincarnation is unimportant![4†] One can wonder what evidence would convince them of its reality.

If previous souls experienced a pain or frustration, recall and acknowledgment of those pains and frustrations can correct current-life phobias, philias, or other personal problems (just as recall and acknowledgment of this life's pains and frustrations can do likewise). There is no evidence that ethics is involved at all; the Is-Ought Barrier applies here, too.[5] That's because reincarnation is an aspect of reality, not rationality or ethics. If your personality in a previous life thought it was wrong to enslave but enslaved anyway, that personality will *feel* guilty, and your health is likely to suffer in this life, but not if that personality thought it was right to enslave. You simply are not ethically responsible for the actions of others, whatever their guilt may have been. If, for instance, your soul was reincarnated from a predatory Viking warrior, you don't inherit his sins (they're his, not yours). Neither, of course, can you claim a previous personality's ethical worth. Objective reason determines what is *ethically right* to do in any given life – whether past, present, or future – while reincarnation deals with *health* challenges. Present-life illnesses are bad health-wise, but that has nothing to do with ethics.[6†]

These are some major ideas dealt with in this book:

(1) *Part I explains how ethical relativism is undermining our culture.* There are other causes of the undermining, but they are superficial. Part II presents the equal rights doctrine as a provable alternative to ethical relativism.

(2) *We should always be rational.* We should always treat things as they are, AAEII. There are no exceptions. Equal rights is thereby required.

(3) *Mere belief shouldn't trump evidence or logic.* If it does for you, this book can't offer you much.

(4) *Ethics can be defined as what people think they should do or as what people should actually do.* This book uses only the latter definition. Therefore, it's irrelevant to ask, "Who's to say?"

(5) *The United States is more affected by ethical relativism than are other countries,* primarily because it is newer and has many cultural traditions. In the United States, tradition offers a weaker resistance to the escalating ethical relativism than elsewhere. But many Americans accept postmodern ethi-

cal relativism *unthinkingly*, even though they may not even have heard of the words. Prior to 1968, that wasn't so; the climate of opinion was entirely different. It had been generally assumed there were answers out there. (People were objective in their outlook.) Now they don't think so (they're subjective); they might seek ethical answers but they don't expect to find any. They've been postmodernized, relativized.

(6) *Russian society today is distorted by centuries of Czarism and communism.* Equal rights has shallow roots there, so neither private enterprise nor democracy can really work. Russia especially needs an airtight proof of equal rights. Americans, on the other hand, still *assume* equal rights to be true.

(7) *In the last analysis, ethical beliefs are what we live and fight for.* They should therefore be correct. Obviously, a proof can strengthen ethical beliefs.

(8) *Ethical relativists seem to assume that others share our equal-rights views, but not so.* History is writ in blood, particularly the century just passed, and only a minority in the world today believes in equal rights or their provability.[7]† We ought not to project our view on others.

(9) *If you violate equal rights, that's as wrong as treating the world as being flat, but in neither case does God strike you dead.* He doesn't work that way.

(10) *Ethical rationalism can provide a firm philosophical basis for democracy by proving that we have equal rights that governments and majorities should uphold,* whereas existential postmodernism unthinkingly elevates majority will as an end in itself.

(11) *The equal rights doctrine provides a valuable guide for historians.* Ethical principle is the string on which we put the facts of reality. It's like the beads of a necklace: No string and the beads scatter. Ethical principle gives meaning not only to individual life but to history. It can lead us to ask important questions of history.

(12) *The derivation of the word* philosophy *is love of reason.* If it abandons reason it becomes an academic sideshow that few will take seriously. It becomes misology.

(13) *A word here about guilt:* If you have infringed the equal rights of others, you absolutely should feel guilty. But that's the beginning and not the end of feeling. Now act. There is healthy (rational) guilt and unhealthy (irrational) guilt. Remedy the infringement and do not let guilt eat you up.

(14) *Postmodernists discount both evidence (for reality) and logic (for ethics).* Concerning reality, they should be empirical realists. Concerning ethics, they should be ethical rationalists.

(15) *Means versus ends:* Social theorists should make a clear distinction between the two. We approach particular circumstances with an ethical principle, an end in itself; we are then more likely to make the correct moral choice. For instance, a poor father steals bread for his starving children (extremely rare). He shouldn't steal, but let us say that otherwise his children will die. But this is a moral dilemma as opposed to an ethical one, and we are not primarily concerned with moral dilemmas here. Ethical principles can deal only with ends, whereas moral applications apply those ethical ends to particular circumstances in reality.

(16) *Equal rights versus legal rights:* Another clear distinction is called for here, particularly (but not only) as to property rights. The law should conform to ethics, not vice versa.

(17) *The correct source of ethics is rationality, not religion or culture.* The Is-Ought Barrier is unbreachable. Religious believers should be happy that rationality can come to their aid. As for culture, only secular postmodernists believe it is the correct source of ethics.

(18) *It has been my experience that most people are so welded to their preconceived ironclad notion that equal rights can't be proven, they won't change it even in the face of hard logic,* even though they may give lip service to rationality. But surely any

reader who has come this far in this book is not one of these unfortunates.

Now let us consider postmodernism at some length. Once reason is rejected, then so are reality and ethics. Let's talk first about the rejection of reality: I once was walking with an English professor who refused to accept the statement "A thing is what it is." In desperation, I said, "There's a lamppost (we were walking past a lamppost) – it is what it is, isn't it?" "Oh, no," he responded, "in French it's called something else. Besides, we cannot say what the definition of 'is' is."[8][†]

Judge Gilbert Ramirez (New York Times, 3/13/92, A30): "There are those who will not see what they are not prepared to believe."

This rejection of reality has adverse practical ramifications. For instance, Walter Olson reports:

Some Navajo schoolchildren, like many other children, have trouble in math class. According to an article published in a leading journal for mathematics educators, one reason may be that "the Western world developed the notion of fractions and decimals out of a need to divide or segment a whole. The Navajo world-view consistently appears not to segment the whole of an entity." Teachers in the rural Southwest might therefore want to begin with concepts more "naturally compatible with Navajo spatial knowledge," such as "non-Euclidean geometry, motion theories, and/or fundamentals of calculus," and de-emphasize or postpone "segmentation...into smaller parts."[9]

In other words, Navajo children should be taught calculus before fractions!

You ask, "How can postmodernists deny reality?" Well, consider what Anita Hill said in her speech at Georgetown University Law Center, marking the first anniversary of the Hill-Thomas hearings: "Because I and my reality do not comport with what they [presumably senators] accepted as their reality, I and my reality had to be reconstructed."[10] This is campus deconstructionism: Reality is different for everyone: It is a construct of words, a mere word game, not what's objectively out there; truth is whatever one says it is, especially in ethics.

---

*Dorothy Gilliam (*Washington Post *columnist and former president of the National Association of Black Journalists, quoted in* Two Steps Ahead of the Thought Police, *p. 58): "Part of the mold that needs to be broken is the illusion that journalism is a quasi-science. It isn't. Journalism is a subjective, value-driven exercise. There is neither one truth or one way to frame reality."*

Professor Stanley Fish, a prominent deconstructionist and executive director of Duke University Press, has written that "there is no such thing as literal meaning" and then went on to tell his readers not to worry because truth didn't really matter.[11]

Duke Alumnus (bumper sticker): "Subvert the Dominant Paradigm."

Postmodernists argue that there is no objective knowledge or facts, only personal interpretation; reason is just another myth. They believe the prevailing version of reality is constructed by ruling social groups for their own welfare and that power replaces rights. These postmodern theories (also called poststructuralism) undermine science and social reform as well as equal rights itself. Essentially, postmodernists believe we can know nothing (not even postmodernism?). Somewhat contradictorily they accept gravity, the periodic table, astrophysics, and so on[12†] but in general they view science as just another way of knowing, another way for the ruling class to dominate others for its own purposes. They tend toward Afrocentrism, "constructivist" social anthropology, "critical" social science, deep ecology, and ecofeminism. Postmodernism bears considerable resemblance to Marxism. It may be that postmodernists are cognitively challenged.

> *Allan Bloom (in* Closing of the American Mind, *p. 38): "Openness used to be the virtue that permitted us to seek the good by using reason. It now means accepting everything and denying reason's power."*

Because existential postmodernists deny that objective reality exists, they deny that an ethical principle can be proven. Ethical relativism is a prime cornerstone of postmodernism in that it denies personal responsibility. This book devotes extensive space to its disproof; nothing new can be added in this last chapter.

Although most people in the Western world don't know what existentialist postmodernism means or what its implications are, they unthinkingly accept its premises, particularly its basic premise of ethical relativism.

Not only ordinary folks but many reputable intellectuals also seem to adopt postmodernist ethics without realizing the full implications. For instance, in 1947 the American Anthropological Association objected to the United Nations Universal Declaration of Human Rights because "standards and values are relative to the culture from which they derive so that any attempt to formulate postulates that have grown out of the beliefs or moral codes of one culture must to that extent detract from the applicability of any Declaration of Human Rights to mankind as a whole."[13] (See what this book has to say about the Skeptic's Dilemma.)

Only an airtight proof of an ethical principle can hope to turn back the postmodernist tide. If critics of postmodernism reject a proof of equal rights, they are themselves ethical relativists and cannot answer postmodernism effectively.

One postmodernist writer had this to say:

"You and I stand on the surface of the little star [!] and shout, 'racism is unjust.' The cosmos yawns and takes another spin. There is no cosmic record of our complaint.... The stars pay us no heed, a complaint lodged against an indifferent world, under stars twinkling in a void. The call of unjust suffering, of little, ontic [the word wasn't in my dictionary], concrete disasters falls on deaf ears. [The universe] knows only greater or lesser discharges of energy, only self-accumulating and self-destructive forces, but does not know about the call of justice."[14]

But existentialist postmodernists shouldn't be looking for justice in the nature of the universe; "should-ness" can't logically come from "is-ness." When they reject equal rights, they are forced to replace it with either equality of results or with power.

Because postmodernism deconstructs (undermines) reason, its prose is dense and opaque. Here is a typical postmodernist quotation taken at random:

It is not a non-knowing installed in the form of "I don't want to know." I am all for knowledge [laughter, presumably Jacques Derrida's], for science, for analysis, and...well, okay! So, this non-knowing...it is not the limit...of a knowledge, the limit in the progression of a knowledge. It is, in some way, a structural non-knowing, which is heterogeneous, foreign to knowledge. It's not just the unknown that could be known and that I give up trying to know. It is something in relation to which knowledge is out of the question.[15]

Enough is sufficient. Readers can substantiate the charge of postmodern opaqueness for themselves. But it would be an obvious inconsistency to expect a proof of irrationalism. Do expect incomprehensibility, darkness, pessimism, bleakness, wild disconnectedness, despair, and stress on disaster. (Postmodernists love to point out that this latter word comes from *dis-astrum*, loss of a guiding star.) Postmodernism is existentialism taken to an extreme; both logically stem from ethical prooflessness.

The critical words of Ziauddin Sardar seem particularly appropriate here. He asserts that the seven defining principles of postmodernism are "...no truth, no reality, only images, no meaning, multiplicities, equal representation, and doubt."[16] He claims it is ultimately nihilistic.

However, if by this time our philosophers have not come up with an adequate ethical *proof*, then postmodernism has to be their only logical alternative. But there is one important and good thing about existential postmodernism: It thrusts forward the ultimate challenge of complete skepticism. It requires us to take nothing for granted and to prove our beliefs. In that, it does us a distinct service.

Adolph Hitler (in Free Inquiry, *Fall 1998, 20, citing* Conversations with Hitler *by Herman Rauchning): "We stand at the end of the Age of Reason. A new era of the magical explanation of the world is rising. There is no truth, in the scientific sense. That which is called the crisis of science is nothing more than that the gentlemen are beginning to see on their own how they have gotten onto the wrong track with their objectivity."[17]†*

Jiang Zemin (Chinese president, justifying his country's human rights record at the United Nations): The U.S. and China "differ in social system, ideology, historical tradition and cultural background, the two countries have different means and ways in realizing human rights and fundamental freedoms."[18]†

Now we have come to the end of our long quest for ethical certainty in a postmodern world. A thing is what it is; we should treat it as it is, AAEII, thus, we have the right to be free to do what we should do, Q.E.D. But there is no guarantee that this simple truth and the logical corollaries stemming from it will do any more than grace these pages. Ethical relativists don't drop their ethical relativism easily; it may be that ethical rationalism is running against the ideological tide of our time and is therefore doomed to history's dustbin of discarded ideas. However, maybe not.

T.H. Huxley: "Sit down before fact like a little child, and be prepared to give up every notion, follow humbly wherever and to whatever abyss Nature leads, or you shall learn nothing." (The same can be said for ethics, only substitute logic *for* fact.*)*

Crime, hard-drug use, and so on are likely to escalate if ethical principle is postmodernly regarded as mere personal opinion only. Security measures, no matter how strict, will not deter lunatics from committing all sorts of crimes they can excuse as their irrefutable personal opinion, especially if society sanctions their belief. Such postmodernism will logically produce a dysfunctional society, and the Great Democratic Experiment will slowly commit hari-kari. In the United States, the sacrifices of those who died on D-Day, in the bloody Civil War, and in the idealistic American Revolution will end in the nihilism of postmodern relativism. Will we go down the pathway taken by the Weimar Republic? We can live off the ethical capital of the past out of mindless habit – but only for a limited time.

Writing a book is an act of faith, but then so are the effort and time involved in reading it. Maybe it is too late to affect the course of events – it may be five minutes to midnight. Is an ethically relativist democracy like a sand castle facing the imminent onslaught of a rising high tide? Let us hope not.

For most of history, it was thought that ethics was susceptible to proof, but not today. Only an ethical proof can basically counter the social dysfunctions of our time; we may not succeed, but the effort will be worth the writing and the reading. The world doesn't need another encomium to equal rights; there are already many eloquent ones. What it needs is an airtight proof so that never again need people say, "Ethical principle can't be proven; it's a matter of personal opinion only."

Each of us should do what we can do to solve the problems of our time irrespective of material success. When our time has come, we will not be asked whether we have succeeded, only if we have done our best. More than that we cannot be expected to do.

Pogo: "We have met the enemy, and he is us."

Who can really say what the ideological tide of the time is? Don't read the requiem for rationalism just yet. Perhaps we cannot be as optimistic as Thomas Jefferson, who said, "Let truth and error grapple; who could doubt the result?" Although such doubt is very possible, we should nevertheless recognize that equal rights is far from being dead; for instance, the nations of the world risked much in invading Kosovo, not out of love of lucre, or of oil, and certainly not out of ethical relativism, but out of concern for the equal rights of Kosavars and Serbs. It is up to us to provide a rational proof for those equal rights.

There may be an unexpected benefit from the long-term rise in social dysfunctions: Maybe street-corner crime, mind-altering drugs, shock-jock entertainment, the tax invasion of private-property rights, jaundiced journalism, family dissolution, and school slide will yet motivate people to seek an ethical *proof.*

George Orwell (quoted in Transaction Publishers' Newsletter, *1999): "To see what is in front of one's nose requires a constant struggle."*

Meanwhile, you and I, dear reader, should engage in the task of applying reason to find out why our society and culture are dysfunctioning. Even if this book disappears as if written on water, we are at least engaged in the last great feat of pure logic left in the world to do. The pursuit of reason is an end in itself. In applying it to ethics, truth is more important than evanescent popularity.

What do you, dear reader, intend to do now that the truth has been laid upon you? When you began this book you should have taken the oath to follow the truth wherever it may lead. Now what do you do: Do you join the forces of apathy and ethical relativism on the one hand, or of equal rights on the other? When you fall into the grave, will it be said of you that you were part of the problem and not of the solution, and that you unthinkingly embraced the reigning acidic ethical view?

The fate of this book lies in the hands of its readers. It may only be an act of faith at this juncture to think the world can be turned around, but the ethical truth must be pursued for its own sake. What will be, will be. The stakes are high: Weapons of mass destruction don't merely loom on the horizon, we have them now and ethical relativism won't contain them.

The readers of this book still have much to say on whether this is going to be the Age of Ethical Rationalism or the Age of Irrationality. It could be that people convinced against their will, will be of the same opinion still.

But maybe not.

Bible (1st Thessalonians, 5:21, King James version):
"Prove all things, hold fast to that which is good."

References and footnoted material for this chapter begin on page 365 in the appendices.

PART THREE

ENDNOTES
& INDEX

ENDNOTES

Introduction

1†   Columbine is the state flower of Colorado.

2   *Wall Street Journal*, 6/11/97, A22.

3†   There are many competent jeremiads delineating our cultural collapse: Martin Anderson, *Impostors in the Temple: American Intellectuals Are Destroying Our Universities and Cheating Our Students of Their Future* (1992); William Bennett, ed., *The Book of Virtues: A Treasury of Great Moral Stories* (1994); Bennett, *The Devaluing of America: The Fight for Our Culture and Our Children* (1992); Allan Bloom, *The Closing of the American Mind: How Education Has Failed Democracy and Impoverished the Soul of Today's Students* (1987); Robert Bork, *Slouching Towards Gomorrah: Modern Liberalism and American Decline of Today's Students* (1996); Lynn Cheney, *Telling the Truth: Why Our Culture and Our Country Have Stopped Making Sense - and What We Can Do About It*

(1996); Andrew Debanco, *The Death of Satan* (1995); Dinesh D'Souza, *Illiberal Education: The Politics of Race and Sex on Campus* (1991); Richard E. Friedman, *The Disappearance of God* (1995); Roger Kimball, *Tenured Radicals: How Politics Has Corrupted Our Higher Education* (1990); Neil Postman, *Amusing Ourselves to Death* (about TV); Laura Schlessinger, *Ten Stupid Things Women Do to Mess Up Their Lives*; also *How Could You Do That!? The Abdication of Character, Courage, and Conscience*; Peter Shaw, *The War Against Intellect: Episodes in the Decline of Discourse* (1989); Charles Sykes, *Profscam: Professors and the Demise of Higher Education* (1988), also *The Hollow Men: Politics and Corruption in Higher Education* (1990). One must admit these titles display literary flair.

4   *Wall Street Journal*, 10/10/00, A26.

5   *New York Times News of the Week in Review*, 4/19/70, 16 on American views of individual rights; *Wall Street Journal*, 12/29/99, A31, citing a Freedom House study that 42% of current humanity is living under dictatorship.

6† Some people use the words *ethics* and *morals* exactly otherwise.

7† For instance, *U.S. News & World Report*, 2/14/00, 4 – lists 19 staff members in library and information services (exclusive of those in photography) plus 9 in research and 117 writers and editors, to which should be added the unlisted support staff.

Chapter 1

1†.   One can argue with the precise dates I have assigned to these thought periods in Western history, but that wouldn't alter any conclusions.

2.   *U.S. News & World Report*, 8/16-23/99, 79.

3.   See Locke, *Second Treatise of Civil Government*, Section 57.

4†.   Locke wrote in his *Second Treatise* (II, ii, 4, Peter Laslett ed., 1960, 288-9) that all men were originally in a state of nature, "a state of perfect freedom to order their actions, and dispose of their possessions and persons as they see fit, within the bounds of the Law of Nature, without asking leave, or depending upon the will of any other man. A state also of equality, wherein all the people and jurisdictions are receptive, no one having more than another."

"The state of nature has a law of nature to govern it, which obliges everyone, and reason, which is that law, teaches all mankind, who will but consult it, that being all equal and independent, no one ought to harm another in his life, health, liberty or possessions." Impeccable conclusions, peccable logic – too many unsupported assumptions.

5†. The little-known Reverend William Wollaston came closest.

6†. The people of Enlightenment time had Enlightenment motivations. The American Revolution, for instance, was primarily a struggle for liberty and property rights and against unjust taxation (see Cord, "Love of Liberty, Not Profit Motive, Led American Colonists to Revolution," Indiana Evening Gazette, 11/10/75). It wasn't love of lucre that inspired *La Marseillaise*: "*Liberte, liberte cherie/Combats avec tes defenseurs/Contre nous/de la tyrannie,/L'etendard sanglant est leve*" ("Liberty, beloved Liberty, fight with your defenders, the bloody flag of tyranny has been raised against us").

7†. At least, he didn't say these rights were true "in my opinion." He wasn't mealymouthed.

8†. "I like the silent church before the service begins better than any preaching" (Ralph Waldo Emerson). And wrote Henry Wadsworth Longfellow: "Nature, the old nurse, took/The child upon her knee,/ Saying, Here is a story book/ Thy Father has written for thee./ "Come wander with me, she said,/ into regions yet untrod,/ And read what is still unread/ In the manuscripts of God."

9†. Wordsworth wrote, "Bliss was it in that dawn to be alive/ But to be young was very heaven."

10†. Friedrich Engels maintained, "In the eyes of dialectic phi-
      losophy, nothing is established for all time, nothing is ab-
      solute or sacred" (except for this statement?) – from Niko-
      lai Lenin, *The Teachings of Karl Marx* (1914) in Kapp &
      Kapp, *History of Economic Thought*, 1956, 269.
          To prove economic determinism, it is not enough to
      show that past events have had economic causes but also to
      show that these causes absolutely *determined* and not merely
      influenced events; history, however, can't prove this. Only
      the philosophy with which we approach history can.

11†. As historian George Mosse put it, "Social scientists were still
      to believe in the possibility of immutable scientific truth
      when scientists themselves no longer believed that there
      was any such thing" (*The Culture of Western Europe*, 208-9).
          Realism as a formal school of philosophy is in eclipse. In
      1975, I received this post card from Donald J. Zeyl, Associ-
      ate Professor of Philosophy at the University of Rhode Is-
      land: "The A.R.P. [Association of Realistic Philosophy] is
      currently in a state of suspended animation. The president
      elected several years ago has done nothing since his elec-
      tion. There is talk of reviving it soon. H.Q. are still in R.I."

12.   *ASPR Newsletter*, XX / 1 [1990s], 3.

13†. "Instead of mystic landscapes or romanticized heroes,
      painters turned to the [ashcan] reality of coal fields, rail-
      way stations, or factory workers" – George Mosse, *The
      Culture of Western Europe*, 208.

14†. "No man can struggle with advantage against the spirit of
      his age and country and however powerful a man might
      be, it is hard for him to make his contemporaries share
      feelings and ideas which run counter to the general run of
      their hopes and desires" (Alexis de Tocqueville, *Democracy
      in America*). No doubt it is hard, but I hope not impossible.

15.   Sigmund Freud, *Civilization and Its Discontents*, tr. J. Riv-
      iere (1930), 143.

16†. "A fire-mist on a planet / A crystal and a cell, / A jelly-fish
      and a saurian, / And caves where cave-men dwell; / Then a

sense of law and beauty / And a face turned from the clod / *Some call it Evolution, / And others call it God*" (William Herbert Carruth, italics added). Evolution and creationist debaters need first to clearly define evolution.

17†. Rarely has a theory been more misnamed; it might more accurately have been called a Theory of a Cosmic Absolute. Einstein himself suggested that his theory should have been called "the theory of invariance" (Stanley Jaki, in *Intercollegiate Review*, Spring-Summer 1985, 33). In any case, his theory was decidedly not relative: It stated that natural laws remain the same regardless of motion, and the speed of light is an absolute for all observers despite their frame of reference. Nevertheless, the name "relativity" incorrectly gave scientific sanction to the growing ethical relativism of his time (see David Greenberg, *Indiana Evening Gazette*, Spring 2000, A7).

18†. *Newsweek*, 10/4/71, 90. Nobel Prize-winning French biologist Jacques Monod asserted that everything about the living world could now be explained without recourse to purpose, significance, or larger powers: "Man knows at last that he is alone in the universe's unfeeling immensity, out of which he emerged only by chance" (*New Republic*, 10/12/98, 25). But how could Monod possibly know that the universe is unfeeling or that we emerged by chance? Maybe he should stick to biology. In any case, chance emergence or what the universe might feel has nothing to do with rationality or ethics.

Gregg Easterbrook recounts that he once asked an eminent astronomer what came before the Big Bang. The astronomer scrunched up his face and replied, "I can't stand that question!" (Ibid 26).

19. Barrett, *Irrational Man*, 181.
20. Ibid.
21. Ibid, 203-4.
22. *Reason* magazine, 10/96, 62.
23. *New York Times*, 6/1/99, 1.

24. *U.S. News & World Report*, 2/13/89, 21.

25†. Chambers, Harris & Bailey, *This Age of Conflict*, 390: "The civilization, the whole sociocultural complex of today [post-WWI]...reveals a deep-seated malaise. We have only to consider our chaotic arts and music, our styleless architecture, our literary aberrations, our empty churches, our overvocationalized and careerist education, our extravagant, unnatural urban life, our hectic pleasures, our declining birth rate, our uprooted homes and sundered families, our humorless cynicism, our falling standards of duty and collective obligation; it is against such a background that we can best see the why and wherefore of our political and economic trends, our regimes and constitutions, our Versailles and Locarnos, and all the other materials of this history."

26. Albert Shanker, 1980s, article in my possession.

27†. Wrote Browning: "Ah, but a man's reach should exceed his grasp/ Or what's a heaven for?" One way to avoid hypocrisy is to have very low (and therefore achievable) standards. Some people think that hypocrisy is worse than immorality.

28. William Halverson, *A Concise Introduction to Philosophy*, 430.

29. U.S. News & World Report, 10/25/93, 59.

30. Allen Otten, *Wall Street Journal*, 9/24/71, editorial page.

31. Tyler Cowen, economics professor at George Mason University, in *Reason*, 5/00, 30, 32. *The World Almanac* conducted the 1986 survey.

32†. *Reader's Digest*, 2/98, 5, quoting John Leo: "In 30 years of college teaching, Prof. Robert Simon has never met a student who denied that the Holocaust happened. What he sees increasingly, though, is worse: students who acknowledge the fact of the Holocaust but can't bring themselves to say that killing millions of people is wrong."

"Simon, who teaches philosophy at Hamilton College, says that ten to 20 percent of his students are reluctant to make moral judgments – in some cases, even about the

Holocaust. While these students may deplore what the Nazis did, their disapproval is expressed as a matter of taste or personal preference, not moral judgment. 'Of course I dislike the Nazis,' one student told him, 'but who is to say they are morally wrong?'"

Overdosing on nonjudgmentalism is a growing problem in our schools. Christina Hoff Sommers, author and professor of philosophy at Clark University, says that many students come to college "committed to a moral relativism that offers them no ground to think about cheating, stealing and other moral issues." (Ibid)

33. John Leo in *U.S. News & World Report*, 6/28/99, 16.
34. Robert Bork, *Slouching Towards Gomorrah*, 173.
35. *Wall Street Journal*, 2/7/95, A20.
36. Wm. Barrett, *Irrational Man*, 269-71.
37. Ibid, 167.
38†. Marc Trachtenberg, a professor of history at the University of Pennsylvania, wrote: "Just look at what goes on at the annual meetings of the main professional organizations, or what gets published in their journals. 'A Dual-Gendered Perspective on Eighteenth Century Advice and Behavior;' 'Constructing Menstruation;' 'Rationalizing the Body;' 'The Ambiguities of Embodiment in Early America' – these are the sorts of topics one sees all the time nowadays.

"Or look at the kinds of courses that now, increasingly, are being taught in major academic departments. One leading university lists a course called 'Introduction to Feminist Studies' as part of its history curriculum. Note the title: not women's history, not the history of gender relations, indeed not history at all, but 'feminist studies.' You don't have to be an expert in Foucault to deconstruct that.'" (*Wall Street Journal*, 7/17/98, W12)

39. Henry Bedford & Trevor Colbourn, *The Americans*, 1972, 497.
40. *Psychology Today*, 1970s, 55, copy in my files.

41†. "In his final years, R. D. Laing (1927-1989) was arriving at lectures addled with hashish and brandy" (Harvard University Press catalog, spring/summer 1998, 56).

42†. Robert Bork recounts an interesting episode at Yale University in 1969 in his book, *Slouching Towards Gomorrah* (Regan, 1997, 40): "The faculty sat in folding chairs that had been set out for them; the BLSU [Black Law Students Union] leaders stood before them like instructors – very angry instructors – before a class. Two large students stood at the door, seeming to prevent any faculty from leaving, and no professor chose to test that proposition. In violently obscene language, the BLSU leaders berated the faculty which sat submissively in their chairs and took it. When the dean, a man who had marched at Selma and had a long and distinguished record of fighting for racial equality, tried to speak, he was told that he must remain silent so long as any black had something to say. But for some reason, the BLSU leader did recognize the former dean, Eugene Rostow. He, however, refused to speak unless the present dean was given the floor. At that, the students swept angrily out of the room, much to the relief of a very frightened faculty [not all faculty members were in attendance]. Probably the students needed a pretext to leave since there was no reason for the gathering except to shout obscenities at the faculty, and, that having been fulsomely accomplished, continuation could only have been anticlimactic. When the BLSU was gone, a prominent member of the faculty turned to Alexander Bickel, from whom I had this account, and said, 'Wasn't that wonderful! They were so sincere!'"

43. *Newsweek*, 6/2/69, 69.

44. Bob Dylan lyrics.

45†. Ibid, 43. The suffering of crime victims was not given attention.

46. Arthur Schlesinger, *New York Times Magazine*, 5/26/68, 97, quoting from Marcuse's writings.

47†. PC has been strong enough, because it was in tune with the ethical relativism of the times, to even withstand the demise of the Soviet Union. Our view of reality and ethics is more important than superficial historical trends in determining the long-term course of history. Those views constitute the true motor of history.

48. *Washington Post*, 12/27/98, A18, citing its own poll for 1998 and the Gallup Organization for the 1965 data.

49. See *U.S. News & World Report*, 2/10/69, 44.

50†. Polls indicate the voters supported this war, though many college students facing the draft did not. When American troops were withdrawn from that troubled peninsula in 1973, South Vietnam still stood, and it stood for two more years until it lost the war against the North; in other words, when the U.S. left Vietnam, it had accomplished the goal of establishing an independent Vietnam. The Korean War had not achieved a similar result. When later the roof fell in and the expected communist-inspired bloodbath ensued, the protesters had gone on to other causes. It is worth noting that other countries had student protests even though they were unaffected by the war in Vietnam. It was growing existentialism and not the Vietnam War that caused the protests. The pre-existentialist Korean War did not produce student protests.

51. *Wall Street Journal*, 8/28/98, W11.

52. Robert Bork, *Slouching Towards Gomorrah*, 23, quoting Berger and John Neuhaus, *Movement and Revolution*, 1970, 60.

53. *Reason*, 5/99, 303.

54†. If you believe, clap your hands and let your nose light up.

55. Robert Bork, *Slouching Towards Gomorrah*, 139.

56†. See the C.B.S. poll reported by James Reston in the *New York Times News of the Week in Review*, 4/19/70, 16.

57†. misology = hatred of reasoning (as opposed to philosophy, love of knowledge).

Chapter 2

1†. The creationists take advantage of this relativist confusion among their Darwinist opponents by asserting that if, as many Darwinists assert, there is no objective truth, then Darwinism is no more provable than creationism; therefore creationism should be taught in public schools.

2. Etienne Rios, *Skeptical Inquirer*, 11-12/95, 42.

3. Ibid.

4†. In our zeal to defend rationalism, let us not wantonly attack parapsychological evidence, for which there is much evidence; see, for instance, Alexander Imich, *Incredible Tales of the Paranormal*, a fascinating and scientifically verified account of many paranormal events. Of course, we must always be on guard against quackery.

Paranormality can occur in everyday life. For instance, I have had an accurate psychometric reading – a psychometrician (we didn't know each other) held my watch at a party and revealed many specific things about my past which he could not normally know, and I have kept a record of my wife scoring 53% of the 25,394 doubles of the backgammon dice (I scored 47%); that's about 152,364 dice throws in all (I have kept all the records). Given the large number of throws, the result is statistically significant (beyond the laws of probability); my wife did even better on medalist count. These seeming contraventions of mad-dog materialism are more real when oneself is involved.

Perhaps the explanation for parapsychological events is no more than that some people have a parapsychological ability in the same way that others have a talent in their specialty (e.g., Mozart for music or Michael Jordan for basketball).

Also note this: "[Cardiologist Randolph] Byrd divided 393 heart patients in San Francisco General Hospital Medical Center into two groups. One was prayed for by Christians around the country; the other did not receive prayers from study participants. Patients did not know to which group they belonged. The group that was prayed for experienced fewer complications, fewer cases of pneumonia, fewer cardiac arrests, less congestive heart failure and needed fewer antibiotics." (*Reader's Digest*, 10/99, 153; also see Dr. Steven Lamm, "Mind Over Illness," in *New Choices*, 3/00, 21).

Parapsychology, though frightening to some, presents many well-verified facts in search of a relevant theory.

5. Robert Bork, *Slouching Towards Gomorrah,* 261.
6. *Social Text,* Spring/Summer 1996, 217.
7. Robert Bork, *Slouching Towards Gomorrah,* 296.
8. *American Heritage Dictionary* (Houghton Mifflin, 1992), 485.
9. See, for instance, Duncan Williams (Arlington, 1971), *Trousered Apes,* and Robert Bork (Harper-Collins, 1997), *Slouching Towards Gomorrah.*
10. *Time,* 3/8/71, 57.
11. quoted in Paul Johnson, *Modern Times,* 628.
12. Duncan Williams, *Trousered Apes,* 30.
13. Geoffrey Barraclough, *An Introduction to Contemporary History,* 239, quoting AndrÈ Gide, *Paludes,* 21.
14. Duncan Williams, *Trousered Apes,* 73.
15. *New York Times,* 6/8/67, 38.
16. *New York Times Sunday Magazine,* 1/29/67, 18.
17. Ibid.
18. *Wall Street Journal,* 3/18/98, A22.
19. He was reviewing Gertrude Himmelfarb's book, *On Looking Into the Abyss.*
20. Marya Mannes, *New York Times Book Review,* 2/9/64, 1.
21. Duncan Williams, *Trousered Apes,* 30.
22. Martin Esslen, *The Theatre of the Absurd* (1961), 17.
23. Ibid., 19.
24†. See Marilyn Stasio, *Cue* magazine, 2/8/69, 7 for evidence of the continuing influence of the Theatre of the Absurd. It tells us something about our society that the rationalist

Cue magazine has been replaced by the existentialist (now postmodern) *New York* magazine.

25. *New York Times,* copy in my possession.

26. Henry Grunwald, *Wall Street Journal* drama review, 5/2/96.

27. Judith Crist, *New York* magazine, 1972.

28. John Leo, *U.S. News & World Report,* 2/12/96, 18.

29. John Leo, *U.S. News & World Report,* 10/11/99, 20, also Steven Munson in *Commentary,* 1/00, 61.

30. Robert Bork, *Slouching Towards Gomorrah,* 129.

31. Gregg Easterbrook, *New Republic,* 10/12/98, 27, quoting Frederick Turner of the University of Texas.

32. Ibid.

33. Roger Kimball, *Wall Street Journal,* 2/15/94, A14.

34. *Time,* 1/8/79, 52.

35. Joan Peyser, *Columbia Forum,* Spring 1970, 12.

36. *Wall Street Journal,* 2/18/98, A22.

37†. Agnes de Mille, *New York Times Magazine,* 10/27/63. She writes as impressively as her grandfather.

38†. We could also mention skittish, slippery, squeamish, and screechy, also slimy and slithery, scrappy and screwy, not to mention deadening and desensitizing.

39. Classical music is maybe 2% of sales (*U.S. News & World Report,* 11/96).

40†. In some rail stations and airports, eighteenth- and nineteenth century classical music is played to calm the nerves of travelers.

41. Frederick Lewis Allen, *Only Yesterday,* 9.

42†. *U.S. News & World Report,* 10/25/93, 30; however, according to Rob Kyff (*Armstrong County [Pa.] Horse Trader,* 1/5/00, 21) the term "rock and roll" appeared in song lyrics as early as 1922.

43. *Wall Street Journal,* 9/9/94, A1.

44. Robert Bork, *Slouching Towards Gomorrah,* 134.

45†. Copyrighted by Paul Simon, Eclectic Music Co. (EMI). It is possible to reject ethical relativism and still like this song.

46†.   Michael Harrington, *Esquire* magazine, 8/72, 162-3). Harrington claimed Dylan's lyrics reflected the views of the earlier Students for a Democratic Society (SDS).

47†.   Forty-five of his songs topped the million-copy sales mark, and he was the biggest-selling recording artist in history, with more than 500 million discs sold worldwide – William A. Sievert, "The Elvis Generation," *The Chronicle of Higher Education*, 9/6/77.

48†.   For more on this, read *U.S. News & World Report*, 8/21/95, 6 about the death of rock star Jerry Garcia. Note that his band, "The Grateful Dead" (!) began in 1965, before the 1968 cultural rebellion; ethical relativism had been growing for a long time. Also read *Newsweek*, 4/18/94, 45.

49.   *New York Times*, 7/19/70, section 2, 5.

50.   *Reader's Digest*, 1/99, 54.

51.   Holmes (columnist, television commentator, and policy analyst), *USA Today*, 3/31/00, 17A.

52.   Duncan Williams, *Trousered Apes*, 29.

53.   *Reader's Digest*, 10/95, 156.

54.   Ibid.

55.   Ibid, 157.

56†.   *Reader's Digest*, 4/73, 73. The article's author is Dr. Jesse Steinfeld, professor of medicine at the University of Southern California and an official of the National Institutes of Health and U.S. Surgeon General from 12/1/69 to 1/20/73. Steinfeld summarized four professional studies showing that child aggressiveness is affected by aggression and violence on television.

57†.   *Wall Street Journal* (2/8/95, A1) says that Beavis & Butthead's commercial spin-offs have generated $100 million in sales.

58.   U.S. News & World Report, 1/3/94, 40.

59.   Ibid.

60.   *Wall Street Journal*, 2/9/01, W15, citing the Henry J. Kaiser Family Foundation.

61.   Ibid, 12/31/93, A6.

62. Charles Murray in *Wall Street Journal*, 2/6/01, editorial page.
63. *Wall Street Journal*, 6/18/99, W13.
64. Sissela Bok, in her 1998 book *Mayhem*, quoted in *U.S. News & World Report*, 5/3/99, 19.
65. Sales letter ANF EZQ06, received 1996.
66. *Reader's Digest*, 9/92, 24.
67. Charles Murray, *Wall Street Journal*, 2/2/99, A22.
68. Steve Rushin, *Sports Illustrated*, 6/21/99, 26. Rushin, tongue-in-cheek: "On our one-dollar bill George Washington ought to smirk like Mona Lisa."
69. *Reader's Digest*, copy in my possession.
70. *U.S. News & World Report*, 5/18/98, 38-42.
71. Ned Crabb in the *Wall Street Journal* (6/25/99), as quoted in the *Reader's Digest*, 12/99, 58, 60.
72. *Wall Street Journal*, 4/22/99, A22.
73. David Brooks in the *Wall Street Journal*, 6/8/99, A16.
74. *U.S. News & World Report*, 6/9/97, 38.
75. Philip Zimbardo, *Psychology Today*, 8/80, 71.
76. *Wall Street Journal*, 2/23/01, W15.

Chapter 3

1. *U.S. News & World Report*, 10/7/96, 14; also Citizen's Commission on Human Rights, *Psychiatry Destroying Morals*, 22, citing studies by the U.S. Department of Health and Human Services and U.S. Department of Commerce.
2. *U.S. News & World Report*, 10/27/75, 41.
3. *U.S. News & World Report*, 12/14/81, 40-1, also Ibid, 4/15/96, 16.
4. Quoted in *Time* magazine, 6/30/75, 17.
5. *Weekly Standard* (10/18/99, 34) citing Kay Hymowitz's book, *Ready or Not: Why Treating Children as Small Adults Endangers Their Future – and Ours*.
6. Stephen R. Covey, author and Ph.D, in *Reader's Digest*

8/99, 170, citing the Fordham University Institute for In-
novation in Social Policy.

7†.   This study was corroborated by an article in *The Wall
Street Journal*, 2/11/00, W1, which asserted that little
more than half the U.S. population is married compared
with 75% during the 1970s.

8.   *U.S. News & World Report*, 6/16/80, 48.

9.   Nick Gillespie, *Reason* magazine, 10/97, 63, citing Barbara
Whitehead, *The Divorce Culture*.

10.   Amherst Professor Hadley Arkes, *Wall Street Journal*,
4/16/96, A12.

11.   *U.S. News & World Report*, 2/27/95, 46.

12.   *U.S. News & World Report*, 3/20/00, 75.

13.   James Perry, *Wall Street Journal*, 3/5/98, A10.

14.   *U.S. News & World Report*, 10/7/96, 14; also Commission
on Human Rights, *Psychiatry Destroying Morals*, 22, citing
studies by the U.S. Department of Health and Human Services and U.S. Department of Commerce.

15.   *Wall Street Journal*, 4/16/96, A12.

16.   See John Leo, *U.S. News & World Report*, 10/2/00, for a list
of the bad effects on the children involved.

17†.   Dennis Prager presents an interesting alternative interpretation of divorce in his lecture titled *Marriage and Divorce*.

18.   *U.S. News & World Report*, 10/17/94, 41.

19.   *Reader's Digest*, 8/95 (citing Department of Health and
Human Services study), 117.

20.   Ibid, 3/5/98, A10; the 3.5% figure comes from Walter
Williams, *More Liberty Means Less Government*, 190.

21.   Ibid, 4/9/93, A11.

22.   *Investor's Business Daily*, 3/8/95, A1.

23.   *Wall Street Journal*, 6/7/95, A1.

24.   *Reader's Digest*, 3/94, 51, citing Charles Murray in *Wall
Street Journal*, 10/29/93.

25.   *Wall Street Journal*, 8/12/98, A14.

26.   Fund-raising letter postmarked 6/97.

27.   *Investor's Business Daily*, 10/16/95, A2.

28. Ibid, 9/26/96, A1.
29. *Wall Street Journal*, 10/11/98, A22.
30. *U.S. News & World Report*, 11/8/99, 22.
31. John Leo, *Two Steps Ahead of the Thought Police*, 34. eighteen thousand students were reportedly studied.
32. *Reason* magazine, 6/95, 53, quoting Gertrude Himmelfarb, *The De-Moralization of Society*.
33. *U.S. New & World Report*, 7/1/96, 57.
34. *Wall Street Journal*, 2/11/99, A26.
35. Amy Holmes, *USA Today*, 3/31/00, 17A.
36. Nick Gillespie, *Reason* magazine, 8-9/95, 52, referring to David Blankenhorn's *Fatherless America*.
37. *Wall Street Journal*, 12/11/98, A1.
38. *Reader's Digest*, 9/96, 51, citing a research study of the Child Trends organization.
39. *Reader's Digest*, 9/96, 51.
40. *Investor's Business Daily*, 11/12/97, A1.
41. Ibid.
42. Ibid, 36.
43. *Newsweek*, 5/10/99, 38.
44. Robert Bork, *Slouching Towards Gomorrah*, 173.
45. Michael Golay, *Where America Stands*, 1997, 78.
46. Robert Samuelson, "Do We Really Care About Truth?" *Newsweek*, 9/6/99, 76.
47. Ibid.
48. *U.S. News & World Report*, 12/7/98, 23.
49. *Wall Street Journal*, 6/2/98, A22.
50. Stephen R. Covey, prominent sociologist in *Reader's Digest*, 6/98, 208a (source not given).
51. *Thomas Jefferson Research Center Newsletter*, 1-2/84.
52. *U.S. News & World Report*, 10/7/96, 14.
53. *U.S. News & World Report*, 12/14/81, 42.
54. Ibid.
55. *U.S. News & World Report*, 10/27/95, 41.
56. *Newsweek*, 10/11/99, 71, citing Kay Jamison, author of two books on suicide.

57. Covey, *Reader's Digest*, 6/98, 208a (source not given).
58. CNN, 10/24/98, a.m.
59. *Wall Street Journal*, 7/29/99, A1.
60. Geoffrey Norman reviewing Kay Hymowitz's book *Ready or Not*, in *Wall Street Journal*, 10/20/99, A24.
61. *U.S. News & World Report*, 8/16-23/99, 74: "They [medieval peasants] would also mash up dried poppies, hemp, and darnel to produce a medieval hash brownie known as 'crazy bread.'"
62. Barbara Del Pizzo, *Wall Street Journal*, 11/13/98, A18.
63. *Reader's Digest*, 4/97, 150.
64. *Wall Street Journal*, 12/20/96, A1.
65. *Wall Street Journal*, 3/26/99, A22. Mr. Califano is president of the National Center on Addiction and Substance Abuse at Columbia University.
66. Mortimer Zuckerman editorial, *U.S. News & World Report*, 2/24/97, 68.
67. *U.S. News & World Report*, 12/26/94-1/2/95, 12.
68. *Wall Street Journal*, 9/26/96, B1, quoting Don Des Jarlais of Beth Israel Medical Center's Chemical Dependency Institute in New York.
69. *Reader's Digest*, 5/96, 132-3.
70. *U.S. News & World Report*, 6/17/96, 20, citing the Betty Ford Center for Drug and Alcohol Rehabilitation.
71. *The Economist*, 7/6/96, 48.
72. *USA Today*, 7/19/96, 20.
73. *Reader's Digest*, 7/98, 100.
74. *Newsweek*, 7/22/96, 69; USA Today, 7/19/96, 2D; *U.S. News & World Report*, 9/16/96, 60.
75. *U.S. News & World Report*, 10/25/93, 61.
76. Ibid.
77. *U.S. News & World Report*, 10/5/98, 62.
78. *Indiana Evening Gazette*, AP Dispatch, 9/26/99, 1.
79. Michael Golay, *Where America Stands*, 1997, 53.
80. *U.S. News & World Report*, 1/26/98, 65.
81. *Reader's Digest*, 11/98, 77.

82. *Indiana Evening Gazette*, AP dispatch, 7/2/99, 3.

83. *Bottom Line Personal*, 2/15/96, 7, citing *New York Times*.

84. *Newsweek*, 6/1/98, 27, and see Charles Colson, founder and chairman of the Prison Fellowship Ministries, in *Wall Street Journal*, 1/24/96, A12, also *Thomas Jefferson Research Center Newsletter*, 1/78.

85. *Reason* magazine, 12/94, 7.

86. *U.S. News & World Report*, 12/18/00, 56.

87. *Pittsburgh Post-Gazette*, 11/3/99, A4, citing the *Los Angeles Times*. 681 companies were surveyed.

88. Dennis Prager, *The Prager Perspective*, 10/1/99, 1.

89. *U.S. News & World Report*, 12/16/74, p. 30.

90†. *Wall Street Journal*, 2/12/98, A1. *Time* magazine (10/19/70, 60) also reported high insurance costs in 1970 and starting its article off thusly: "The U.S. is a riskier place than it was only a few years ago." It's riskier now.

91. *Wall Street Journal*, 2/27/95, B1.

92. *U.S. News & World Report*, 8/28-9/4//95, 83; also, see Ibid, 2/18/00, 56.

93. Michael Barone, *U.S. News & World Report*, 12/20/93, 34.

94. *Reason* magazine, 10/00, 11, citing ABS (government statistics).

95. *Los Angeles Times*, 8/20/99, A5.

96. *Washington Monthly*, 4/95, 57.

97. *Washington Monthly*, 5/98, 52.

98. *U.S. News & World Report*, 5/25/98, 40.

99. *Wall Street Journal*, 9/16/94, A12.

100. *Wall Street Journal*, 4/24/96, A15.

101. Paul J. McNulty (lawyer), *Wall Street Journal*, 11/9/94, A23.

102. George Gilder, *Wall Street Journal*, 10/30/95, A18.

103. Robert Bork, *Slouching Towards Gomorrah*, p. 155.

104. William Kells, son of a Chicago policeman, personal communication, 1998.

105†. Advertisement of Securilock (a Ford Motor Co. subsidiary) – *Newsweek*, 6/1/98, p. 30; also a flyer of the Maryland Vehicle Theft Prevention Council, which asserts that approximately 25%-40% of the cost of auto insurance is due to auto theft.

106. *Newsweek*, 4/19/99, p. 10.

107†. *Wall Street Journal*, 10/16/98, A14. Morgan Reynolds is an economics professor at Texas A&M University.

108. *Wall Street Journal*, 6/11/99, A1.

109. Citizens Commission on Human Rights, *Psychiatry Destroying Morals* (1995, no source given), 22. Also, see *Reason* magazine, 10/00, 11.

110. Ibid.

111. Charles Murray in *Commentary* magazine, 7/99, 80.

112†. *U.S. News & World Report*, 3/25/96, 68.

113. *Newsweek*, 5/3/99, 35.

114. Ibid.

115†. *Investor's Business Daily*, 12/25/95, editorial by Andrew Payton Thomas: "Over the past 25 years, local expenditures on police have risen more than 700% and the U.S. prison population has tripled. Yet crime rates have continued to rise."

116†. Gergen: "Since the juvenile population will grow considerably by the year 2000, there is serious danger that kids will soon be roaming urban neighborhoods like 'teenage wolf packs.'"

117. *Thomas Jefferson Research Center Newsletter*, 1-2/84.

118. *U.S. News & World Report*, 6/17/96, 64.

119. Leaflet of the *American Spectator*, received in the mail in early 1998.

120. *U.S. News & World Report*, 8/7/95, 10, citing the U.S. Justice Department.

121. Dennis Prager, *The Prager Perspective*, 10/1/99, 4.

122. *Wall Street Journal*, 8/19/96, A1, citing a U.S. Justice Department report. But there were 3.3 times as many Americans on probation or parole (*Where America Stands*, 1997, 148).

123. The *Reader's Digest* has run a series of article on this under

SOCIETY AT THE CRO§ROADS

the title of *Crime & Punishment, U.S.A.* ; see, for instance, the 2/99 issue, 51-55.

124. *Karin Fischer, Washington Monthly*, 1-2/98, 32.

125. *Reason* magazine, 6/00, 13.

126. *Washington Monthly*, 12/98, 20. *Wall Street Journal* (8/23/99 A1) says the total figure is 3%, not 2%.

127. *Washington Monthly*, 9/98, 19, 20.

128. *Wall Street Journal*, 12/19/96, 11.

129. *Reader's Digest*, 3/95, 169.

130. Trevor Armbrister in *Reader's Digest*, 9/98, 168.

131. Ibid.

132. Ibid.

133†. U.S. government at all levels (federal, state, local) took 47% of the national income in 1995, 28% in 1950, 14% in 1926, 7% in 1916, and probably less than 3% in 1790 – Harry Browne, *Why Government Doesn't Work*, 51.

134. Leaflet of the *American Spectator*, citing a Justice Department report; received in the mail in early 1998.

135. *U.S. News & World Report*, 5/9/98, 14.

136. *U.S. News & World Report*, 4/3/98, A1.

137†. Michael Golay, *Where America Stands*, 159, citing an op-ed article in the *Boston Globe* by David Nyhan, 7/12/96. Writes Nyhan: "Today we are giving the equivalent of a $33,000 scholarship to more than 1.5 million of the worst types of people. We cut back on teachers, welfare, medical care for the poor. We lay off doctors and nurses, social workers, and counselors. But we hire prison guards to beat the band." But ethical relativism gives us no other choice.

138. *New York Times*, 1/2/77.

139. *Investor's Business Daily*, 11/10/95, A2, citing *U.S. News & World Report*.

140†. *Investor's Business Daily*, 7/27/95, A2, citing Adam Walinsky's article in the 7/95 *Atlantic Monthly*). Robbery rates were three times higher in 1999 than in the 1960s (James Q. Wilson, *Wall Street Journal*, 8/17/99, A22).

141. Mortimer Zuckerman, *U.S. News & World Report*, 9/20/99, 76.

142. P. J. O'Rourke, *Eat the Rich*, 68.

143. *Wall Street Journal*, 11/22/99, A1.

144†. *Investor's Business Daily*, 10/26/93, 1. James L. Payne (in *Ideas on Liberty*, 6/00, 12) reports that sworn law-enforcement officials have increased 40% between 1980 and 1996 (not including President Clinton's promised 100,000 extra officers), and *U.S. News & World Report* (11/1/99, 99) reports that GIS systems are now used to combat criminality.

145. *Westchester [N.Y.] Journal News*, 5/30/99, 8A, 9A &1C has much on the new police techniques.

146. Professor Bruce Benson (Florida State University), *Ideas on Liberty*, 1/00, 23.

147. According to the *Washington Monthly* (4/99, 6) the U.S. rate of imprisonment has increased fourfold, 1975 to 1999.

148†. Don't overlook airport delays due to electronic baggage inspection, which, according to the *U.S. News & World Report*, 7/29/96, 3, adds $2-$3 to the cost of each ticket.

149†. U.S. News & World Report, 1-2/99, 5, citing *Washington Post* research. It is difficult to compare the crime statistics of different times; for instance, New York City police took a cavalier approach to crime-fighting in the 1960s but not more recently (see *Wall Street Journal*, 7/20/99, A20).

150. *Wall Street Journal*, 4/4/97, A28.

151. John J. DiIulio, Jr. (recognized Princeton University crime expert), *Wall Street Journal*, 9/6/95, A19.

152. John DiIulio, Jr., *Wall Street Journal*, 4/4/97, A28.

153†. Deconstructing ethical relativism isn't the only solution to the problem of crime. Convicted criminals could compensate their victims either monetarily (through wage garnishee with 10% interest) or service. Or they could be required to do community service. We could revive the stock and even the whip instead of the torturous prison. Drunk drivers could be required to display brightly colored "DUI" bumper stickers. Victims could be permitted to enter the homes of burglars and help themselves. Sex offenders could be required to post warning signs on their property. The Miranda requirement could be looked at again. Police can be allowed to stop a person for a twenty-minute interrogation sans lawyer. Bond for parolees could be required. Schizophrenics could be required to take their medicine at certain public stations. Juvenile crimes needn't be expunged from personal records. The juvenile crime limit could be lowered from age sixteen to fourteen. "Shall-issue" handgun laws seem to work. There could be more morality education in schools and jails. Lessening poverty (see Chapter 9) will lessen crime. These reforms would be more likely to work if there were no ethical relativism.

154†. In describing what he thought was the typical Puritan (*Harper's* magazine, 5/65, 65), Mencken referred to "…his unmatchable intolerance of opposition, his unbreakable belief in his own bleak and narrow views, his savage cruelty of attack, his lust for relentless and barbarous persecution." Wouldn't this apply equally as well to PC? If each person is regarded as the final arbiter of right and wrong, why be tolerant of differing views?

155. Dr. Hans Selze, *U.S. News & World Report*, 3/21/77.

156†. Marianne Jennings in *Wall Street Journal*, 5/3/99, A22, citing a survey conducted by the Lutheran Brotherhood, an insurance company. But note that fully 21% believe in an absolute ethical standard.

157. *U.S. News & World Report*, 10/1/84, 69.

158. *Thomas Jefferson Research Center Newsletter*, 9-10/90, 1.

159. *Wall Street Journal*, 7/10/95, editorial page.

160. Gregg Easterbrook, *New Republic*, 10/12/98, 29.

161. John Leo, *U.S. New & World Report*, 5/23/94, 2, citing a Mother Jones article.

162. *U.C.R.A. Measure*, 8-9/95, 1, citing an article in *Commentary* magazine, 8/95.

163. Susan Estrich, *USA Today*, 6/20/96, 15A.

164. Joseph Adelson (professor of psychology, University of

Michigan), *Wall Street Journal*, 10/20/95, A10, reviewing Charles J. Sykes' book, *Dumbing Down Our Kids*.

165. Ibid.

166. *Reader's Digest*, 10/95, 82.

167. *Wall Street Journal*, 4/8/96, A18.

168. *U.C.R.A. Measure*, 6/91, 2.

169. *Johnstown Tribune-Democrat*, 10/25/69, editorial page.

170. *Wall Street Journal*, 6/17/97, A18.

171. John Leo, *U.S. News & World Report*, 4/19/99, 19.

172. David Brooks & Frank Goble, *The Case for Character Education*, 28, citing Louis Rath, "What I Believe About Character Education," *Character Education Journal*, Fall 1972.

173. Quoted in David Brooks & Frank Goble, *The Case for Character Education*, 29.

174. John Leo, *U.S. News & World Report*, 10/18/93, 22.

175. Melanie Kirkpatrick, *Wall Street Journal*, 7/14/94, A8, reviewing the book *Who Stole Feminism?* by Christina Hoff Sommers.

176. *John Leo, U.S. News & World Report*, 5/31/99, 16.

177. *Investor's Business Daily*, 6/10/96, 1.

178. John Leo, *U.S. News & World Report*, 4/2/90, 16.

179. David Brooks and Frank Goble, *The Case for Character Education*, 23.

180. Townsend, *Washington Monthly*, 1/90, 30.

181. Ibid, 32.

182. Ibid.

183. Townsend, *Washington Monthly*, 12/92, 30.

184†. Marvin Stone, *U.S. News & World Report*, 12/8/80. Additional evidence that character education works is provided by David Brooks & Frank Goble in *The Case for Character Education*, 79, 80, 85, appendices A, B and C.

185. Gergen, *U.S. News & World Report*, 2/17/97, 76.

186. John Leo, *U.S. News & World Report*, 11/23/98, 16.

187. John Leo, *Two Steps Ahead of the Thought Police*, 172.

188. *Reason* magazine, 5/92, 31.

189. Article by Suzanne Alexander, *Wall Street Journal*, 4/27/93, B1.

190†. Citing a study by Linda Sax, director of the UCLA Higher Education Research Institute's 34th annual freshman survey. This study also found that doing homework was down but boredom was up, and that high school teachers didn't want to give out low grades because it might hurt the self-esteem of their students. In other words, students were doing worse but felt better about doing so.

191. *Allentown Morning Call* (AP dispatch), 4/19/98, A16.

192. *U.C.R.A. Measure*, 11/74, 3.

193. Ibid, quoting Professor Bradley Efron.

194. John Leo, "Damn I'm good!" *U.S. News & World Report*, 5/18/98, 21.

195. *I.U.P. Penn*, 9/30/98, 4 (Knight-Ridder dispatch).

196. *U.S. News & World Report*, 2/7/00, 50.

197. John Leo, *U.S. News & World Report*, 10/18/93, 22.

198. Ibid.

199. Peter Brownfield, *Campus* magazine, Sept. 1998, 15.

200. *Newsweek*, 5/17/99, Business Section.

201. John Leo, *U.S. News & World Report*, 11/15/93, 24. This happened at other universities. Also, see *Reason* magazine, 10/93, 63.

202. *Reader's Digest*, 10/95, 66.

203. *Wall Street Journal*, 8/18/94, A8.

204. *Time*, 8/20/68.

205. Robert Bork, *Slouching Towards Gomorrah*, 13.

206†. William Pritchard (*Wall Street Journal*, 11/17/95, A16) tells about a college president who in 1966 stood on an auditorium platform to applaud the visiting Robert McNamara but three years later signed an open letter in the *New York Times* defending an anti-war moratorium.

207. John Leo, *U.S. News & World Report*, 12/10/90, 22.

208. CNN, 4/13/98, 9 a.m.

209. *Investor's Business Daily*, 8/19/97, 1.

210. *Investor's Business Daily*, 5/5/98, p. 34.

211. *Reader's Digest*, 6/98, 208A.
212†. After the Columbine massacre, the cry went up "ban guns!" but the guns used by the killers were obtained illegally; they were motivated by hate and ethical relativism. Said our vice-president, "Every one of us is responsible for all of the children" (letter to the editor, *Wall Street Journal*, 5/3/99, A23).
213. Professor Marianne Jennings, *Wall Street Journal*, 5/3/99, A22.
214. Ibid, citing Marci Kanstoroom & Chester Finn, Jr., ed., *New Directions: Federal Education Policy in the Twenty-First Century* (Thomas B. Fordham Foundation, 3/99).
215. *U.S. News & World Report*, 11/8/93, 34, citing the Congressional Quarterly Researcher.
216. *Reader's Digest*, 8/99, 166.
217. *Washington Monthly*, 12/96, 5.
218. Lynne Cheney, *Wall Street Journal*, 5/12/99, editorial page.
219. John Leo, *U.S. News & World Report*, 11/1/99, 26.
220. *Reason*, 10/93, 63.
221. Walter Williams, *More Liberty Means Less Government*, 113 (from a 9/11/96 newspaper column).
222. *Investor's Business Daily*, 1/12/98, A36.
223. *Washington Monthly*, 5/99, 27.
224. American Legislative Exchange Council report, 4/27/98, 11.
225. Ibid, citing a 1996 National Center for Education Statistics survey.
226. *Wall Street Journal*, A15.
227. John Leo, *U.S. News & World Report*, 8/3/98, 15, quoting a reader for the list of teacher-education courses.
228. John Leo, *U.S. News & World Report*, 8/30/99, 20.
229. *Investor's Business Daily*, 1/15/97, A2. Many other examples are given.
230. *Investor's Business Daily*, 7/3/97, editorial, citing the *Los Angeles Times*.

231. Walter Williams, *More Liberty Means Less Government*, 123, (from a 4/14/97 article).

232. *Wall Street Journal*, 3/19/96, A18 and *Campus*, Spring 1997, 4.

233. Lynne Cheney, *Wall Street Journal*, 6/11/97, A22.

234. *Wall Street Journal*, 2/3/98, A22.

235. *Reader's Digest*, 11/97, 182, based on a *Wall Street Journal* article, 12/17/96, editorial page.

236. *Investor's Business Daily*, 11/14/97, A28, citing an *Education Week* study.

237. *U.S. News & World Report*, 3/23/98, 28.

238. Walter Williams, *More Liberty Means Less Government*, 101-2 (from a 10/4/95 article).

239. *Investor's Business Daily*, 5/12/98, A32.

240. *U.S. News & World Report*, 3/20/00, 20.

241. *Parade* magazine, 4/18/99, 4; for instance, only 58% of the students understood that when the demand for a product goes up but the supply remains the same, its price is likely to increase.

242. *Washington Post*, 10/3/83.

243. *Investor's Business Daily*, 3/23/98, A34.

244. *U.S. News & World Report*, 12/2/96, 16.

245. Walter Williams, *More Liberty Means Less Government*, 125 (from an article of 5/7/97).

246†. *Bottom Line*, 2/1/96, 9. National exams might help to raise standards, but each state can decide what to do with the results.

247. *Wall Street Journal*, 5/11/99, A1.

248. *U.S. News & World Report*, 5/16/94, 12

249. Irving Kristol, *Wall Street Journal*, 7/14/95, A12.

250. *U.C.R.A. Measure*, 4.

251. Robert Bork, *Slouching Towards Gomorrah*, 253.

252. John Leo in *U.S. News & World Report*, 11/14/94, 36.

253. *Wall Street Journal* (2/22/99, A16).

254. John Leo, *Two Steps Ahead of the Thought Police*, 151.

255. John Leo, *U.S. News & World Report*, 4/21/97, 14. I taught there.

256. *Indiana Evening Gazette* (AP dispatch), 9/28/99, 4.

257. William J. Bennett, *School Reform News*, 10/99, 15, citing *Digest of Education Statistics*, 1997.

258. William J. Bennett and David Breneman, *Remediation in Higher Education*,1998 (Brookings Institution).

259. *Los Angeles Times*, 11/28/99, M4.

260. Bennett, citing *Education and Training for America's Future* (National Assn. of Manufacturers).

261. John Leo, *U.S. News & World Report*, 3/9/98, 14.

262. Ibid.

263. *I.U.P. Penn*, 2/9/98, 6

264. Ibid.

265. *Investor's Business Daily*, 6/18/97, A30.

266. *Washington Monthly*, 4/98, 49, quoting Ross Perot.

267. David Gergen, *U.S. News & World Report*, 11/1/99, 104.

268†. For instance, students had 30 more minutes to answer questions, calculators were permitted, the difficult antonym section was deleted, the typical test-taker's results were boosted by as much as 100 points, students could get as many as four questions wrong yet still receive a perfect score – Bruno Manno, former Assistant Secretary of Education, *Wall Street Journal*, 9/13/95, A12.

269. *Indiana Evening Gazette* (AP Dispatch), 8/23/77, 7.

270. *Wall Street Journal*, 11/14/96, A22, relying on a study prepared for the Educational Testing Service.

271. Ibid.

272. Andrew Hazlett, *Wall Street Journal*, 2/22/99, A16.

273. Walter Williams, *More Liberty Means Less Government*, 110, quoting *Pocono Record*, 5/15/96.

274. *Wall Street Journal*, 11/17/98, A22.

275. *Commentary* magazine, 5/99, 79.

276. *Thomas Jefferson Research Center Newsletter*, 1-2/84.

277. George F. Will, *Newsweek*, 12/6/99, 98.

278. John Leo, *U.S. News & World Report*, 3/9/98, 14.

279. Ibid.

280. John Leo, *U.S. News & World Report*, 3/9/98, 14.

281.   Chester Finn, Jr., former U.S. Assistant Secretary of Education, *Wall Street Journal*, 2/25/98, A22.

282.   Heartland Institute, *Intellectual Ammunition*, 2/96, 15.

283.   Walter Williams, *More Liberty Means Less Government*, 101 (from a 10/4/95 article).

284.   Chester Finn & Herbert Walberg, *Wall Street Journal*, 6/22/98, op-ed. Finn is president of the Fordham Foundation (concerned with educational reform) and Walberg is a research professor of education and psychology at the University of Illinois, Chicago.

285.   *Investor's Business Daily*, 12/18/97, A2.

286.   *Newsweek*, 2/17/92, 57.

287.   *Investor's Business Daily*, 1/8/98, A28, citing the U.S. Department of Education.

288.   *Investor's Business Daily*, 1/12/98, A36, citing a Public Agenda 1998 poll.

289.   *Wall Street Journal*, 9/15/95, A14.

290.   *Investor's Business Daily*, 4/25/96, A1.

291.   *Washington Post*, 11/25/75.

292.   *Los Angeles Times*, 11/28/99, M4.

293.   *American Heritage*, 10/99, 53.

294.   Walter Williams, *More Liberty Means Less Government*, 122 (from an article of 4/14/97).

295.   *Time*, 2/24/97, 34.

296.   *Investor's Business Daily*, 9/18/97, A30.

297.   *American Legislative Exchange Council report*, 4/27/98, 11.

298.   *On Campus (AFT)* , 10/84, 14, citing Sommers' article in *The American Scholar*, Summer 1984.

299.   William Bennett, *School Reform News*, 10/99, 15, citing *Pursuing Excellence*, a U.S. Department of Education study, 2/98.

300.   *Investor's Business Daily*, 6/4/93, A1.

301.   *Wall Street Journal*, 6/22/93, A14.

302.   Heartland Institute publication, 1998 (copy in my possession), citing an article by Eric Hanushek, *Jobs & Capital*, Winter 1997.

303. Ibid, citing *Digest of Education Statistics* 1997, table 39.
304. Thomas Sowell, *A.I.E.R. Research Reports*, 4/19/93, 1, quoting from Thomas Sowell's *Inside American Education: The Decline, the Deception, the Dogmas* (1993).
305. *Reason* magazine, 4/00, 13, citing U.S. Department of Education. 1996 was the last year for which there was complete data.
306. *Investor's Business Daily*, 6/4/93, A1.
307. Ibid.
308. Wall Street Journal, 12/9/98, A22.
309. Bruce Fein letter, 8/93, citing a Washington, D.C. report.
310†. Do vouchers granted to church-operated schools violate religion-govt. separation? Not likely – first, such schools teach religion only part of the time (which might justify only a partial voucher reduction, at best). Second, when the First Amendment was passed, opposition to private schools was not intended. Third, the voucher grant is made to students, not to the school.
311. *Wall Street Journal*, 12/9/98, A22.
312. *U.S. News & World Report*, 8/30/99, 24, citing pollsters Geoff.

Chapter 4

1†. "Three-quarters of those polled who were not of the religious right said that the main cause of America's problems was 'moral decay'" – Gertrude Himmelfarb, *One Nation, Two Cultures*, 136 (citing the American Jewish Committee, *A Survey of the Religious Right*, 5/10-6/3 1996, 8).
2. Robert Bork, *Slouching Towards Gomorrah*, 5.
3†. *Wall Street Journal*, 10/1/99, B1. The Heritage Foundation's study titled *Income Inequality: How Census Data Misrepresent Income Distribution* convincingly criticized the Census Report as follows: the Census Bureau included 64.2 million people in the top quintile and only 39.2 million people in the bottom quintile, it failed to account for

taxes and noncash income, and it ignored the fact that those in the top quintile worked 34.6 hours per week versus 14.4 hours per week for those in the bottom quintile (*Tribune-Review*, Greensburg, Pa., 10/6/99, A6).

4. John Attarian, *Ideas on Liberty*, 1/00, 57, citing Michael Cox and Richard Alm, *Myths of Rich and Poor: Why We're Better Off Than We Think*, Table 1.2.

5. Lawrence Harrison (senior fellow at Harvard's Academy for Intl. & Area Studies) in *Wall Street Journal*, 7/13/99, editorial page.

6. *U.S. News & World Report*, 8/29/77, 12.

7†. It seems hardly necessary to substantiate the decline in poverty, but consider: in 1970, 6.9% of housing units lacked complete plumbing; in 1990, 1.1%. In 1970, it took 49 minutes of work time to buy gas for a 100-mile trip; in 1991, 31 minutes. In 1970, the index of pollution stood at 100.0; in 1990, 34.1. In 1970, life expectancy at birth was 70.8 years; in 1990, 75.4 (*Reason* Magazine, 12/95, 20-27).

8. Ibid, 2/73, 2.

9†. Ibid. For instance, in *El Barrio*, a dismal slum in New York, with prostitutes and drug dealers on every corner (also in between), 92% of juveniles were law-abiding; the children in the city at large did only 3% better (*New York Times News of the Week in Review*, 7/30/67, 1, also *New York Times Magazine*, 1/5/69, 71).

10. *The Freeman*, 10/99, 7, citing *Myths of Rich and Poor* by Michael Cox and Richard Alm.

11. *Ideas on Liberty*, 5/00, 64, citing a study by the Federal Reserve Board of Dallas.

12†. *Thomas Jefferson Research Center*, 11/79, 1 (citing FBI statistics); serious crimes committed by middle-class kids have increased 30% in the years prior to 1979.

13. Misology (from the Greek): *misos* = hatred, *logos* = discourse; hence, misology = hatred of reason, the opposite of philosophy.

14. Ibid, 2/4/99, A22. Ms. Himmelfarb is a professor-emeritus of history at the City University of New York.
15. *Wall Street Journal*, 10/14/98, A1, also Michael Barrone in *U.S. News & World Report*, 12/21/98, 33.

Chapter 5

1. Dewey, *An Introduction to American Philosophy*, 247-8.
2†. Some free enterprise advocates claim too much by asserting that economic welfare is the true measure of the ethical. There could be other factors producing prosperity, such as hard work, luck, ability, culture, natural resources, stealing, imperialism, etc. Free enterprise should be otherwisely justified.
3†. "Bridge of asses" (donkeys). Asses often have an irrational difficulty in crossing bridges, so the phrase has come to mean a test of rationality.
4†. David Hume writes that authors frequently make "observations concerning human affairs, when of a sudden I am surpriz'd to find that instead of the usual... *is* and *is not*, I meet with...*ought* and *ought not*...a reason should be given...how this new relation can be a deduction from the others, which are entirely different from it. But as authors do not commonly use this precaution, I shall presume to recommend it to the readers...." (*A Treatise of Human Nature*, Book 3, 1.1.27).
5†. Analytic philosophy mostly developed after 1900. It is a direct outgrowth of logical positivism.
6. John Rawls, *A Theory of Justice*, 137.

Chapter 7

1†. This book uses definitions that are in common use so as to avoid ambiguity (as when a word is officially defined one way but used another way). Let us use the word *things* rather than *reality*. We are not concerned here with

Absolute Underlying Reality. Let theologians wrestle with that.

3†.　"Each to his own taste." "Taste is not to be disputed."

4†.　For example, a chief columnist of *The Outlook* magazine (3/1/13, 467) said of Matisse that he was "not at all inspiring."

5.　Gregg Easterbrook, *New Republic*, 10/12/98, 25.

6†.　If evolution is defined as gradual physical change in species, then both sides could agree. Even Bryan said the Biblical days of creation were periods.

7†.　*Harvard Medical School Health Letter*, 2/98, 1, citing studies by Dartmouth and Duke medical researchers; see also *Reader's Digest*, 3/96; a Duke University study of some 4,000 elderly people found those who attend weekly religious services are 28% less likely to die in a seven-year period (*U.S. News & World Report*, 8/9/99, 67). Also *The Power of Prayer on Plants* (Franklin Loehr, 1959) contains photographs of plant seeds that were prayed for and sprouted healthily next to plant seeds that were not prayed for and died.

8.　Millard Burrows, *Outline of Biblical Theology*, 1946, 123.

9†.　For example, members of the thuggee caste in traditional Hinduism (in northern India) practiced murder and assassination, thereby denying the existence of equal rights; but because such religious beliefs were irrational, they were properly curbable. The Crusades were both defended and attacked on religious grounds; we don't stone adulteresses, execute apostates or punish the grandchildren of offenders, as the Bible urges.

10†.　Determinists would be more believable if they could predict the future (see the deprecatory article by Dr. C. K. Aldrich in the *American Journal of Psychiatry*, 1/86).

This free will versus determinism debate has moved good poets and bad to verse. For instance, here is Sir Richard Burton freely translated from *The Kasidah*, part v, st. i: "There is no good, there is no bad; these be the whims of mortal will;/ What works me weal that call I good, what harms and hurts I hold as ill./ They change with space, they shift with race, and in the veriest span of time,/ Each vice has worn a virtue's crown, all good been banned as sin or crime."

To which a free-willer replied, "What's thought right in Pandemonia/ May be frowned upon in Fredonia./ What's revered in Rome/ May be condemned at home./ What wins acclaim in Bonn/ May win a jail sentence on the Don,/ And so on, on and on./ But it does not follow as a sequel/ That all ethical standards are equal./ One standard may be truer than the rest,/ Though not everywhere recognized as best./ As two men may differ on the flatness of the earth,/ One being right and the other wrong,/ So might they differ on ethical worth,/ And to one, not the other, may the truth belong."

11†. The efficacy of unethical means can easily be overrated. They can create bad precedents. It is generally safer to abjure means which are per se unethical. For instance, spreading peace and democracy by the sword is a tricky business and quite apt to fail (although it succeeded with the defeated nations after World War II; even imperialism has had some good effects).

12. See any book on logic; e.g., Stephen F. Barker, *The Elements of Logic*, 151.

Chapter 8

1†. Definition: Freedom is the ability to act within one's physical and mental limitations, unconstrained by fate or necessity.

2†. *U.S. News & World Report*, 6/14/99, 28 estimates that 50 million people were killed in the wars of the twentieth century.

3†. When we die, empirical evidence indicates that a Light is likely to appear, which we should follow undistracted by other influences.

4. Edwin R. A. Seligman, *Essays on Taxation,* as reprinted in Edna Bullock, *Selected Articles on the Single Tax,* 141.

5. *U.S. Statistical Abstract 1997,* tables 477 (source: U.S. Bureau of the Census, Government Finances, No. 2) and 698 (source: U.S. Bureau of Economic Analysis, *National Income & Product Accts. of the United States.*

6†. "London's Financial Times recently reported that after Great Britain privatized its rail system, delays were reduced by 30 percent...and numbers of passengers are increasing on most routes" *U.S. News & World Report,* 3/31/97, 56.

7. Yale Brozen, early 1970s article, x.

8. Harberger, *American Economic Review,* 6/66, 393.

9. See *Incentive Taxation,* Spring 1978. The entire issue is devoted to the effects of monopoly.

10. See Louis Philips, *Effects of Industrial Concentration: A Cross Section Analysis for the Common Market,* Amsterdam 1971.

11. *Incentive Taxation,* Spring 1978, 3.

12. Ibid, 3, citing the *U.S. Statistical Abstract 1973,* 706-9.

13. Ibid, 3, citing Alvin Toffler, *Future Shock,* 70-1.

14. *Wall Street Journal,* 2/10/00, A1, citing a study by Peter Golder, a marketing professor at New York University.

15. Neil Jacoby, *Conference Board Record,* 6/71, 48.

16. MIT study, *The Job Generation Process.*

17†. Adam Smith (in his 1776 *Wealth of Nations*): "It is not from the benevolence of the butcher, the brewer, or the baker, that we expect our dinner, but from their regard to their own interest.... [The seller] intends only his own gain and he is in this...led by an invisible hand to promote an end which was no part of his intention."

18. See especially *Incentive Taxation,* 5/83, 6-7/85, 7-8/85, also a letter dated 11/6/74 of Thomas E. Kauper, Asst. Attny.-General, Antitrust Division to the author (a copy is available).

19†. There is a strong correlation between freedom and prosperity throughout the world – see *Wall Street Journal*, 12/1/98, A22.

20. *Washington Monthly*, 9/99, 40-44.

21. *Reason* magazine, 7/93, 42.

22. *Wall Street Journal*, 2/14/97, A14. Also see 1/27/99 (book review) and 4/6/99, A26.

23. See recent U.S. Statistical Abstracts.

24. As Locke asks, "When do they [potatoes] begin to be his? When he digests? Or when he eats? Or when he boils? Or when he brings them home?" – Herbert Spencer, *Social Statics* (1850 edition), 120.

25†. By gradually increasing the tax rate on slave values, slavery could have been ended sooner in America without a terrible war.

26†. *American Journal of Economics and Sociology*, 1/99, 84, citing Harvey Jacobs, *Who Owns America?* (Univ. of Wisc. Press), 1998, 229.

27†. Gene Wunderlich, U.S.D.A. 1978 landownership survey. *The Wall Street Journal* reported (11/25/83, 37) that the Great Northern Paper Co. alone owned 2.1 million acres of Maine timberland, or 11% of that state. God's gift to us all doesn't seem to have been equally distributed.

28. 1979 report of the Royal Commission on the distribution of income and wealth.

29†. Herbert Spencer, *Social Statics* (1850 edition), 104: "The original deeds were written with the sword, rather than with the pen: not lawyers, but soldiers, were the conveyancers: blows were the current coin in payment; and for seals, blood was used in preference to wax. Could valid claims be thus constituted? Hardly."

30†. See the study in *Incentive Taxation*, 7/85, 1-2, also the 6/88 issue (either are available from C.S.E. for $10 each) and John Young, *The Natural Economy*, 90-2. Ronald Banks in his book titled *Costing the Earth* (1989) carefully estimated the true annual rental of Great Britain's land and natural re-

sources to be 22.4% of national income in 1985, a reasonably representative year. Kenichi Omae, the manager of
McKinsey & Co.'s Tokyo office, estimated that all U.S. land
was worth 1.4 times all U.S. then-publicly traded stock
(Wall Street Journal, 11/30/88, A30). In the United States
today, the annual Federal Reserve Board Flow of Funds
statements typically list land values (usually on p. 24 or 25)
at one-quarter of U.S. domestic net worth, even though an
FRB researcher admitted to me by phone (Betsy Fogler,
1985) that was an underestimate because natural resource
land was not included at full value; "we used the best estimates available to us." In addition to LVT, the government
could legitimately collect bona fide user fees.

31†. Did you think that if our primary adjustment to nature –
our land tenure system – is out of joint, it would have no
disjointing effect on our economy? We can disregard
equal rights and the taxation of land values, but we will
suffer from the ill effects nevertheless.

32†. "Since the beginning of this century, governments have
murdered 170 million people, mostly their own citizens" –
Professor Walter Williams (economics, George Mason
University), *More Liberty Means Less Government*, 68, citing
Death by Government by Professor R. J. Rummel (Political
Science, University of Hawaii). This crime is so enormous
as to have escaped the attention of many analysts.

33†. A Mobil ad in *The Wall Street Journal* (8/12/99, A12), states
that "the concentration of CO_2 in the atmosphere is 30
percent higher than it was in the days before industrialization." Atmospheric CO_2 is deleterious and has a long life;
its concentration is likely to steadily increase in the future.
There is no private profit to be made in CO_2 control. But
not everything committed in behalf of the environment is
sensible – for instance, reverting to organic methods of
farming would require plowing far more acres of wilder-
ness to feed the world. It would result in an increase in
cancer (Ibid, A22).

34†. Taxable land value includes natural resource land as well as locational value land. Spectrum and airport landing rights could be taxed on the same principle as land values.

35†. For a good exposition about regulations needed to alleviate or prevent black lung in coal mining, see *Washington Monthly*, 1-2/99, pp. 42-4.

36†. The percentage of voter turnout has steadily declined in America, no doubt elsewhere. Ethical relativism could account for this. Citizens in a democracy should vote out of ethical duty, not because their vote will decide the election, which is most unlikely.

37†. The Japanese surrendered soon after I registered for the draft on July 22, 1945, but I don't claim cause and effect. I lost the chance to storm the beaches of Kyushu like the Mongols did in 1274 and 1281; the Japanese didn't have the reputation of throwing snowballs at invaders. (One has an ethical duty not to present misleading half-truths, as in "Tiger Woods has not beaten me in golf for the last three years.")

38†. At least some fetuses are aware of what's happening in the world (see Carol Bowman, *Children's Past Lives*, 65; 269 cites research by Thomas Verny and John Kelly, *The Secret Life of the Unborn Child* and B.R.H. Van den Bergh in *Pre- and Peri-Natal Psychology*, Winter 1990, 119-29; 288 quotes research by Dr. Winafred Lucas, *Regression Therapy: A Handbook for Professionals*, v. 2, 270). This is to be expected, given the many verified cases of reincarnation from past lives.

39. George Will, *Newsweek*, 9/27/99, 76.

40†. Are the women who pose for nude pictures as culpable as the mostly male customers?

41. *Reason* magazine, 4/98, 20, citing an article in the *American Economic Review* (5/98) by Stephen Bonars (University of Texas economist) and John Lott (Univ. of Chicago law professor), using data from 1977 to 1992.

42. *Reason* magazine, 6/00, 40.

43†. Some 40% of all U.S. homes have guns (*U.S. News & World Report*, 5/31/99, 25). There are 240 million guns in America (Ibid, 30). Can total gun control be enforced?

44†. A letter (5/00, 2) from Congressman Ron Paul asserts that 500,000 times a year, away-from-home gun carriers defend themselves; almost half are women defending themselves against sexual abuse. Many more defend themselves with guns at home. The number of gun accidents is much less than this.

45. *Wall Street Journal*, 11/27/98, A1, quoting the National Audobon Society.

46†. The following extract from an article in *Reason* magazine (10/00, 26) is instructive: "The great kidney transplant pioneer Dr. Thomas E. Starzl was once asked why he used dogs in his work. He explained that, in his first series of operations, he had transplanted kidneys into a number of subjects, and that the majority of them died. After figuring out what had enabled a few to survive, he revised his techniques and operated on a similar group of subjects; a majority of them survived. In his third group of subjects, only one or two died, and in his fourth group all survived. The important point, said Starzl, was that the first three groups of subjects were dogs; the fourth group consisted of human babies. Had Starzl begun his series of experimental operation on people, he would have killed at least 15 people. Yet there are activists who believe, in the name of animal rights, that that is what Starzl should have done."

47†. A good article describing differences between the sexes can be found in the *Reader's Digest* (4/99, 108-12).

48†. Once, when I was in France for a year, I was involved in protecting a young girl from having her mind forcibly altered by her parents; they kidnapped her and employed an evil psychiatrist to use mind-altering drugs to change her philosophical orientation. They didn't like her ideas. With the help of the press, we eventually won, although she nearly died. Her rights were clearly being violated.

49†.   Mark Skousen, *Ideas on Liberty*, (1/00, 49) lists the details of 170 million killed by governments in the twentieth century plus 37 million killed in wars. Also, read Aaron Friedberg's review (*Commentary*, 2/00, 59) of Robert Conquest's recent book *Reflections on a Ravaged Century*, if you still think no ethical proof is necessary because everyone shares your equal-rights views. Just imagine if George Washington had decided to seize the crown offered to him in 1783, or if Hitler hadn't overreached himself by declaring war on the United States; wouldn't there be less equal rights in the world today? Suppose the Afghans, no lovers of equal rights they, hadn't clobbered the Soviet army in the 1980s.... History is one damn thing after another. So far, the United States has been lucky, but we may not always be. Equal rights must be constantly fought for and should never be taken for granted.

50.   This view was expressed by William Barrett, *Irrational Man*, 115.

Chapter 9

1.   See the study of Professor Nicholas Tideman and Florenz Passman (Va. Tech U.) titled *The Impact of Two-Rate Property Taxes on Construction in Pennsylvania*, 10/31/95, available for $10 ppd. (2001) from the Center for the Study of Economics (CSE, 1422 Chestnut Street (#414), Philadelphia, PA 19102). Also, see Godfrey Dunkley's study (based on South African government statistics from its 1985 Municipal Yearbook) in *The Evidence for Land Value Taxation*, 24 (also available from CSE for $10, 2001).

2†.   1984 study by CSE using city and national figures. Residential construction and maintenance also increased. Congressman Bill Coyne reported that building permits issued in Pittsburgh for new housing rose 15%, 1979 to 1983, while for the same time period they dropped 19% in the surrounding areas (*Incentive Taxation*, 4/83, 3).

University of Maryland professors, Wallace Oates and Robert Schwab compared 1960-79 building activity to 1980-89. Oates & Schwab concluded that two-rate Pittsburgh far out-constructed and out-renovated 14 other large one-rate northeastern cities; they praised two-rate LVT. *The Pennsylvania League of Cities Reporter* (1989), a magazine, reprinted the Oates-Schwab study.

3.   1985 study, 16. Afterward, the PEL urged other cities in Pennsylvania to go two-rate.

4.   1989 CSE study.

5.   1983 CSE study.

6.   Ibid.

7†.   1991 CSE study. A summary of the land value tax story, with a listing of the empirical studies, is available to any reader from CSE for $10 ppd. (2001). Unfortunately, CSE is in serious financial straits and desperately needs contributions.

8.   *Incentive Taxation*, 1999 issue.

9.   Professor Ray Northam, *Land Economics*, 11/71.

10†.   Assessment accuracy can be increased and costs lowered if land only and not buildings are assessed. In Chicago, 18 appraisers are needed for land assessing but 133 are needed for building assessing, according to the *Illinois Georgist*, Summer 1998, 3, citing the 1998 Cook County assessment budget.

11.   See CSE for proof of this.

12.   See numerous back issues of CSE's publication, *Incentive Taxation*.

13†.   1968 report of the President's Committee on Urban Housing, 351, tables 47, 48, as well as many issues of CSE's *Incentive Taxation*. In fact, it's even *better* than this for poor people: Just about every economist asserts that the tax on land values *cannot* be passed on to tenants (because the supply of land is fixed), in which case *all* and not *most* poor tenants pay less rent.

14†.   If in times of depression the land value tax would be insufficient to pay for government costs, the government could always borrow to supplement it.

15. *USA Today*, 1/2/01, A1.

16†. The sales tax is imposed only once at time of sale, but the property tax on buildings is annually imposed.

17†. Much farmland is already rented out (41% in Ohio, according to *The Ohio Farmer*, 8/80) and mortgaged; also, many farmers are really farm employees, not landowners.

18†. In New South Wales (Australia) in 1966, thirteen rural municipal or county councils and various farmer associations endorsed their existing LVT. The U.S. Farm Foundation, in a joint report with the National Public Policy Education Committee, endorsed LVT. So did F. W. Stover, president of the U.S. Farmers Association (*U.S. Farm News*, 6/74 – see *Incentive Taxation*, 3-4/79, 4). Many other instances of farmer support could be cited.

19. *U.S. Statistical Abstract 1998*, table 675 (citing U.S. Bureau of Labor Statistics, *Employment & Earnings*, and unpublished data).

20. Ed Ayres, educational director of the Worldwatch Institute, in *Time*, 11/8/99, 107.

21†. "Full-time farmers ages 35 to 44 averaged $61,344 net cash return last year, well above the overall average of $40,280" – *Forbes* magazine, 5/17/99, 60. A USDA study in 1997 found that farm household income averaged $52,347 (including pay from off-farm jobs) compared with $49,692 for the average U.S. household (*Wall Street Journal*, 8/12/99, A6).

22†. North Dakota, a farming state, exempts farmland improvements (*U.S. News & World Report*, 4/3/78, 54).

23†. Richard Dennis in *Reason* magazine, 4/93, 29 writes that "the average full-time farmer is 10 times wealthier than the average householder, with roughly $700,000 in assets.... only $1 [of farm subsidies] out of every $10 goes to needy farmers."

24†. Says Edward Thompson of the American Farmland

Trust: Exurbanites want " suburban comforts, but they don't understand why a farmer needs to start his tractor before dawn" (*U.S. News & World Report*, 4/12/99, 31). Also, a 278-page federal government report (*The Cost of Sprawl*) found urban sprawl costs to be enormous (reported in *Christian Science Monitor*, 10/8/75).

25†. A 67-page study by William Fischel (Economics, Dartmouth) provides evidence that in the long run, most growth controls simply don't control growth but do increase commuting time, traffic, and automobile pollution. Growth is forced onto less efficient sites elsewhere. Growth controls discriminate against potential future residents. They increase the cost of housing. And at the slightest whiff of recession or local unemployment, they tend to disappear or are circumvented. Also, see the study of Thomas F. Hady (of the USDA's Economic Research Service) as reported in *Incentive Taxation*, 1-2/82, 4. Also see the 9/75 study of the *Nation's Cities* magazine (N.L.C.) titled *Costs of Sprawl*; it endorses LVT.

26†. "Over half of Brazil's arable land, much of it uncultivated, is owned by only 2 percent of the population. In March [1998], hundreds of squatters occupied government buildings in 10 state capitals to press their demands for reform" (*U.S. News & World Report*, 4/6/98). We hope they were demanding LVT instead of communal or equal landownership, but we doubt it.

27. See *Tax Features*, 3/97, 8 (source: Tax Foundation, Census Bureau).

28. Henry George, *The Standard*, 1/29/87, 1.

29†. This study is available for $9 (plus $3.50 for pph) from the Lincoln Institute of Land Policy, 113 Brattle Street, Cambridge MA 02138, or call 1-800-LAND-USE.

30. William Drayton (MacArthur Fellow) in *Barron's Weekly*, 2/24/97, 1.

31†. Quickly stated: During a period of prosperity, land speculation grows faster than the gross national product, thereby lowering wages and return on capital. Production then becomes unprofitable, leading to recession or depression. There certainly are other factors causing inflation.

32. Bruce Bartlett has written a good article on this – see *Wall Street Journal*, 10/7/99, A30.

33†. I have managed to get twenty of these jurisdictions, as of this writing, to collect about $72 million a year in LVT (as of this writing) above what they would have collected if I had not visited them. (My associate, Joshua Vincent, is primarily responsible for getting two more jurisdictions to go two-rate.) This was not done through extraordinary salesmanship but by using the previously mentioned *sine qua non* formulas and procedures. No other LVT is being induced in the United States by anyone beyond what the current local property tax happens to collect. (How this $72 million per year in extra LVT is figured is described in *Equal Rights*, 2/99, 1, available at $10/copy ppd. [as of 2001] from CSE.)

34. In 1981, more than one in four will cheat on their income tax (*NBC Evening News*, 4/8/81, quoting Prof. Robert Mason of Oregon University).

35. *People & Taxes*, 12/80. The situation doesn't seem to have improved – in 1999, among the items recorded in the IRS books but not found were a Chevy Blazer and a $300,000 laser printer (*Wall Street Journal*, 3/3/99, A1). Well, no one's perfect.

36. *Investor's Business Daily*, 4/17/98, A1.

37†. *Wall Street Journal*, 3/13/99, A1 and 3/17/99, A26. Stefan Tucker, head of the American Bar Association Tax Section, wrote to then-U.S. Treasury Secretary Rubin, "On behalf of the American Bar Association and its Section of Taxation, I'm writing to express disappointment that the Administration has proposed to add a multitude of new credits to the federal income tax system." Tucker's suggestion hasn't been adopted, nor did he mention LVT as the alternative.

38. *Tax Features*, 10/97, 4.

39. *Wall Street Journal*, 2/18/88, B1, but maybe they've improved recently.

40†. But not to worry too much: "Less than one in 300 tax returns will be audited for the tax year 1999, compared to one in 67 in 1981 (*Reason*, 5/00,8) – an indication of income tax complication.

41. *Investor's Business Daily*, 4/17/98, A1, and *Wall Street Journal*, 3/3/99, A1.

42. *Newsweek*, 3/3/00, A1.

43. Ibid, 3/23/88.

44. *Investor's Business Daily*, 7/1/97, A24.

45†. Surprisingly, the LVT is more of an ability-to-pay tax than the income tax because the poor generally have an income but own very little land value. For instance, Anthony Pileggi's study showed that in Indiana, Pennsylvania (population 15,000), 1.5% of the richest landowners paid 53.5% of a land value tax compared to the 30.6% of the U.S. income tax paid by the richest 3% (*Incentive Taxation*, 4/80, 1). In bigger cities, the disparity would be even greater.

46†. These pamphlets are available from CSE ($10 in 2001).

47†. Localities contemplating two-rate LVT adoption should first get a random-sample "who-pays-more-who-less" study, which only CSE does efficiently and inexpensively. Contact CSE – (215) 988-9998.

48†. There is another equally valid formula for figuring the land value tax rate in a building-to-land tax shift: PLTR = Revenue – (BA × CBTR) divided by LA, but it is difficult to get accurate figures for next year's property tax revenue. Revenue needs often change during the budget-adoption process; it is not a publicly available figure (so you may be given this year's figure); next year's revenue figure might be affected by exemptions, classifications, and abatements (which should be disregarded). When it becomes possible to replace a nonbuilding tax by an LVT, use this formula: LTR = Revenue needed divided by LA.

49†. *Incentive Taxation*, 11/91 (William Vickrey, then the president-elect of the American Economics Association, later won a Nobel Prize in economics), plus about *600* urban experts, listed in Issue 4 of each volume of *Incentive Taxation*.

50. I learned this rhyme in childhood (I altered it somewhat); I suspect Ogden Nash was the original author.

51†. In 2018, nearly 20% of the U.S. population will be over 65, the same as in retirement-haven Florida today. The rest of the world is aging, too.

52†. Louis F. Post relates that James Maguire, a congressman-friend of Henry George, was attracted to a crowd gawking at a picture in a store window in San Francisco. He stopped, looked and said to an onlooker that he saw nothing special about the picture; it seemed to depict an ordinary landscape. "Look carefully," said the onlooker, "Do you see the cat?" "What cat?" said Maguire, and then all at once he saw it. It was a double picture not only of the obvious landscape but also of a huge superimposed (but artfully obscured) cat. He could then hardly see the landscape for the cat. "Do you see the cat?" soon became an in-phrase with single taxers, meaning, "Do you see the full import of the single tax amidst the welter of economic details?" Perhaps many single taxers can't see the whole economy for the single tax.

Chapter 10

1†. When President Clinton said he didn't know what "is" was, one can presume he would also have trouble with "should." Let us hope he wasn't buying into the postmodernist notion that neither "is-ness" (reality) nor "should-ness" (rationality) are knowable.

2. P. J. O'Rourke, *The Enemies List*, 135, citing Michael Kelly's

interview with Ms. Clinton, *Time* magazine (date and page number not given).

3†. If someone, usually a very young child, makes statements remembering a previous life, Stevenson empirically verifies each statement whenever possible, taking extreme scientific precautions against being misled.

The best book on reincarnation is Carol Bowman's *Children's Past Lives*. She writes beautifully and clearly, ably summarizing the extensive reincarnation literature. She compares the proof for reincarnation to the proof for a duck (126): "If it walks like a duck, looks like a duck, quacks like a duck, then it's a duck."

But what about two people who claim to come from the same past-life soul? Well, one or both may be wrong; memory in both past and present lives is sometimes faulty. (Fantasy can enter reincarnation memory, as when one subject reported that in a previous life he saw some soldiers coming to kill him so he climbed a tree to escape them, and it turned into a stairway to someplace else [Roger Woolger, *Other Lives, Other Selves*, 90]. But fantasy can't account for all past-life recalls, many of which have been empirically verified). Furthermore, it is possible that two or more souls can spring from one past life.

4†. At death the body crumbles physically – what vivified it when it was alive? Obviously, a soul (or spirit or essence, whatever). Reincarnation and verified out-of-body experiences corroborate this.

5†. Moral balancing cannot logically be part of reincarnation, writes Rabbi Dennis Prager, because then "the Nazis who killed six million innocent Jews will themselves suffer in their next lives. "But they can only endure such suffering if other human beings in the next life inflict it on them. Therefore this understanding of karma and reincarnation ensures perpetual evil.... For if there is any diminution in the suffering of innocents, the souls of the evil people of the past will not have suffered their just deserts." (*Prager*

INDEX

Perspective, 8/00, 8). With this interpretation of karma, no social improvement would ever be possible!

6†. Stevenson provides no evidence that *everyone* reincarnates (nor can we be sure that the sun will rise tomorrow). But we can be *rationally* sure it will rise tomorrow. Also, some people have better memories than others. (Because industrialization favors verbal rather than image memories, pre-industrial people have more reincarnation experiences).

7†. Just today, a crook stole the license plates on my car. I have spent four days getting it replaced while driving without license plates; I can understand the travail of those who have become victims of more serious crimes.

8†. The dictionary clearly defines *to be* (from which *is* is taken) as "coinciding in identity with; *existing* or having reality; living, maintaining a certain position" (italics added).

9. *Reason*, 6/99, 62, citing *A House Built on Sand: Exposing Postmodern Myths About Science*, by Noretta Koertge.

10. John Leo, *Two Steps Ahead of the Thought Police*, 241.

11. Roger Kimball, *Wall Street Journal*, 5/29/96, A18.

12. One postmodernist asks, "Is e = mc² a sexed equation? He answers, "Perhaps it is" – *Free Inquiry*, Fall 1998, 24, citing Luce Irigaray, *Sens et place des connaissances dans la sociète*, 110.

13. *Free Inquiry*, Fall 1998, 28.

14. John Caputo, *Against Ethics*, 17.

15. Jacques Derrida in Elizabeth Weber, ed., *Points... (Interviews with Derrida, 1974-1994)*, 201.

16. Charles Reese, columnist, *Indiana Evening Gazette*, 2/25/00, 2, citing *Free Arab Voice*, www.fav.net.

17† If there is no ethical proof, Hitler wasn't wrong. He would be entitled to his opinion.

18†. *Free Inquiry*, Fall 1998. Says Caesar in George Bernard Shaw's *Caesar and Cleopatra*, Act. II: "Pardon him, Theodotus: he is a barbarian, and thinks that the customs of his tribe and island are the laws of nature."

Page numbers enclosed in square brackets indicate pages that have no printed number on them.

This book presents the antidote to the cultural crisis posed by *ethical relativism*. It puts forward the most important statement ever made.

If a society tells criminals that no one has any provable rights to life, liberty, or property and that ethics is a matter of personal opinion only, then it will have a high crime rate, also other social dysfunctions.

Merely labeling an ethical belief as cultural or religious does not make it true. If these beliefs contradict reason, reason takes precedence.